Understanding
FRIEDRICH DÜRRENMATT

Understanding Modern
European and Latin American
Literature

James Hardin, *Series Editor*

volumes on

Ingeborg Bachmann
Samuel Beckett
Thomas Bernhard
Johannes Bobrowski
Heinrich Böll
Italo Calvino
Albert Camus
Elias Canetti
Camilo José Cela
Céline
José Donoso
Friedrich Dürrenmatt
Rainer Werner Fassbinder
Max Frisch
Federico García Lorca
Gabriel García Márquez

Juan Goytisolo
Günter Grass
Gerhart Hauptmann
Christoph Hein
Eugène Ionesco
Milan Kundera
Primo Levi
Boris Pasternak
Luigi Pirandello
Graciliano Ramos
Erich Maria Remarque
Jean-Paul Sartre
Claude Simon
Mario Vargas Llosa
Peter Weiss
Franz Werfel

Christa Wolf

UNDERSTANDING

FRIEDRICH
DÜRRENMATT

ROGER A. CROCKETT

UNIVERSITY OF SOUTH CAROLINA PRESS

Published in Columbia, South Carolina, by the
University of South Carolina Press

Manufactured in the United States of America

02 01 00 99 98   5 4 3 2 1

Library of Congress Cataloging-in-Publication Data

Crockett, Roger A. (Roger Alan), 1947–
   Understanding Friedrich Durrenmatt / Roger A. Crockett.
      p.   cm. — (Understanding modern European and Latin American
   literature)
   ISBN 1-57003-213-0
   1. Durrenmatt, Friedrich—Criticism and interpretation.
I. Title. II. Series.
PT2607.U493Z59 1998
832'.914—dc21   97-33889

Contents

Editor's Preface

Understanding Modern European and Latin American Literature has been planned as a series of guides for undergraduate and graduate students and non-academic readers. Like the volumes in its companion series *Understanding Contemporary American Literature,* these books provide introductions to the lives and writings of prominent modern authors and explicate their most important works.

Modern literature makes special demands, and this is particularly true of foreign literature, in which the reader must contend not only with unfamiliar, often arcane artistic conventions and philosophical concepts, but also with the handicap of reading the literature in translation. It is a truism that the nuances of one language can be rendered in another only imperfectly (and this problem is especially acute in fiction), but the fact that the works of European and Latin American writers are situated in a historical and cultural setting quite different from our own can be as great a hindrance to the understanding of these works as the linguistic barrier. For this reason the UMELL series emphasizes the sociological and historical background of the writers treated. The peculiar philosophical and cultural traditions of a given culture may be particularly important for an understanding of certain authors, and these are taken up in the introductory chapter and also in the discussion of those works to which this information is relevant. Beyond this, the books treat the specifically literary aspects of the author under discussion and attempt to explain the complexities of contemporary literature lucidly. The books are conceived as introductions to the authors covered, not as comprehensive analyses. They do not provide detailed summaries of plot because they are meant to be used in conjunction with the books they treat, not as a substitute for study of the original works. The purpose of the books is to provide information and judicious literary assessment of the major works in the most compact, readable form. It is our hope that the UMELL series will help increase knowledge and understanding of European and Latin American cultures and will serve to make the literature of those cultures more accessible.

Preface

Friedrich Dürrenmatt's characters are most often involved in some form of game, and understanding how and why they play is a big part of understanding the author. An old lady manipulates a town from the balcony of her hotel like a puppeteer playing with marionettes. One detective uses live bait to go fishing for a child killer, while another plays with a murderer like a cat with a mouse. Cat and mouse is also the game a photographer choreographs and films between a deranged killer and the women he attacks. A general plays blind man's buff with a captive duke. Four retired jurists play a courtroom game with a hapless houseguest. A beggar and a king engage in a begging contest with a rare and wonderful prize at stake. War becomes a game for soldiers who have lost their purpose after the nuclear holocaust. A prime minister plays factions off against each other in a political chess game; a billiards master eliminates his opponents *a la bande;* and a couple fights a twelve-round marital boxing match. Often the playing takes the form of play-acting: A self-appointed judge plays at being Roman Emperor; three physicists play at being insane; a frustrated actor/director stages a religious uprising; Theseus puts on the mask of the Minotaur in order to slay him; and inmates of a mental institution perform modern history as role therapy. Even the labyrinth, a central motif particularly in the later works, is an elaborate game: monster in the maze.

That so many of his characters play games and act roles—the latter itself a type of deception and control game—is a logical manifestation of the way the author views reality. The predictability of human nature gives a false sense of security to just and unjust alike, for it only masks the underlying chaos of the cosmos. In a chaotic, unpredictable world, any game of skill turns into a game of chance. Precisely those game strategies that are best conceived, that seem to take the most variables into account, are most vulnerable to the whims of chaos. Heisenberg, not Leibniz, designed Dürrenmatt's universe. What kind of God, if any, sits behind this chaos? Is justice possible? Is corruption inevitable? Are free choice and human responsibility only illusions? Can the world be changed, and if so, how? Through ideology, as Brecht believed, or perhaps by courageous individuals of conviction?

Around such weighty questions revolve Dürrenmatt's games, as well as his whole dramatic and narrative oeuvre. If the games often turn deadly, it is because the stakes are so high. These questions are the themes that run through the works—lifelong concerns of a writer who stopped short of a planned doctoral dissertation in philosophy but never stopped being a philosopher, and who never lost his love of a good game.

Acknowledgments

I wish to thank Washington and Lee University for supporting this project with a grant from the Glenn Fund. My sincere gratitude goes to Diogenes Verlag AG, Zürich, for permission to quote from the collected works of Dürrenmatt (*Das Gesamtwerk,* copyright 1986 by Diogenes Verlag AG, Zürich) and to James Hardin, University of South Carolina Press, for his patience with a slow writer. Thanks to my wife, Anna, for invaluable assistance in proofreading the manuscript, and apologies to Adam and Erika, who had to put up with my absence so often in the late stages of the project.

Note on Translations

The bibliography lists the published English translations used. Translations of quotations from all other works by Dürrenmatt are my own. Titles of works when first introduced appear in German, followed in parenthesis by the English title. The English is italicized if it is a published translation and not italicized if the translation is mine. Subsequent references to long titles are often abbreviated.

Chronology

1921	Born in Konolfingen, Canton Bern, son of Pastor Reinhold Dürrenmatt and Hulda Zimmermann Dürrenmatt.
1935	Family moves to Bern. Struggled in school, and failed in 1939 to be promoted.
1941	Received his High School Certificate in Older Languages. Wanted to become a painter. The Jury at the Art Academy urged his parents to let him study literature instead. Enrolled at the University of Bern.
1942	Brief stint of military service in summer—discharged because of poor eyesight. Transferred to the University of Zürich at the start of Winter Semester. On Christmas Eve he wrote his first short narrative, "Weinacht" ("Christmas").
1943	Officially registered as a student in Zürich. In the circle of expressionist painter Walter Jonas, Dürrenmatt led a Bohemian lifestyle and continued to write narratives. A long illness forced his return to Bern in late fall.
1943–1946	Studied philosophy at the University of Bern. First published narrative: "Der Alte" ("The Old Man") in *Der Bund*, 1945. Continued writing narratives.
1946	Instead of a planned dissertation on Kierkegaard, D. wrote play *It Is Written*. Radio play *Der Doppelgänger* refused by radio Bern. Married actress Lotti Geißler, October 11, and moved to Basel.
1947	*It Is Written* premieres in Zürich, April 19, under direction of Kurt Horwitz. Play created a scandal (which D. welcomed) and won the Prize of the Welti Foundation. Wrote narratives Pilatus" and "Die Stadt." Birth of son Peter on August 6.
1948	Premiere of second play, *The Blind Man*, in Basel, January 10. Family moves to Schernelz on Lake Biel. D. fails to complete planned play about the Tower of Babel. Writes cabaret sketches to feed his family.

1949	Premiere of *Romulus the Great*, D.'s first comedy, in Basel, April 23. Daughter Barbara born September 19. Diabetes diagnosed 1950. *The Judge and His Hangman* appeares in serialization in *Schweizerischer Beobachter* from December 1950 to March 1951.
1951	Serialized sequel to *Judge*, entitled *The Quarry*. Family moves to a house above Ligerz on Lake Biel. Daughter Ruth born October 6. Radio plays *The Trial of the Donkey's Shadow* and *Midnight Conversation with a Despised Person*.
1952	D.'s "blasphemous" comedy *The Marriage of Mr. Mississippi* premieres in Munich. Radio play *Stranitzky and the National Hero*. Writes the narrative "The Tunnel" and publishes his early narratives under the title *The City*. Beginning of relationship with Peter Schifferli's "Verlag der Arche," that would publish D.'s works until 1978. Purchases house above Lake Neuchâtel.
1953	*An Angel Comes to Babylon* premieres in Munich.
1954	Radio plays *Hercules and the Augean Stable* and *Operation Vega*. Two literature prizes for *Angel*. Essay "Problems of the Theater."
1955	Prose comedy *Once a Greek.* . . . Work on both radio play and narrative version of *Die Panne* (*Traps*).
1956	Premiere of *The Visit* in Zürich, January 29. Both versions of *Die Panne* published. Radio play *Episode on an Autumn Evening*.
1957	Wrote filmscript for *It Happened in Broad Daylight*. Prize of the Blind War Veterans for radio play *Die Panne*.
1958	Broadway version of *The Visit* with Alfred Lunt and Lynn Fontanne. Prix d'Italia and Prize of the Tribune de Lausanne for radio plays. Rewrote *It Happened in Broad Daylight* as the novel *The Pledge*.
1959	*Frank the Fifth: Opera of a Private Bank* with music by Paul Burkhard premieres in Zürich, March 19. Mannheim Schiller Award. New York Drama Critics' Award for *The Visit*.
1960	Trip to London. Grand Prize of the Swiss Schiller Foundation. Writes script for film version of *Mississippi*.
1962	*The Physicists* premieres in Zürich, February 21–23.
1963	*Hercules and the Augean Stables*, adapted from the radio play, premieres in Zürich, March 20. Volume of satirical caricatures *Heimat im Plakat* (Homeland in Posters) published.
1964	First trip to Soviet Union, for ceremony honoring Shevchenko. Filming of *The Visit* (with altered ending) starring Anthony Quinn and Ingrid Bergman.

1966	Premiere of *The Meteor* in Zürich, January 20. *Once a Greek(...)* is filmed. *Writings and Speeches about the Theater* published.
1967	Premiere of *The Anabaptists* in Zürich, March 16. Second trip to USSR, for Fourth Soviet Writers Conference. Speech entitled "Israels Lebensrecht" (Israel's Right to Exist) in Zürich in wake of Six-Day War.
1968	"Monster Lecture on Justice and the Law" at the University of Mainz. Collaboration with Werner Düggelin in the Basel Theater Collective. Production in Basel of the Shakespeare adaptation *König Johann*. Grillparzer Prize from the Austrian Academy of Sciences.
1969	*Play Strindberg* premieres in Basel, February 8. Heart attack and subsequent departure from Basel. Receives Literary Prize of the Canton of Bern and divides it up among three Swiss political dissidents. Trip to USA in the fall and Honorary Doctorate from Temple University.
1970	Stages Goethe's *Urfaust* in Zürich. *Portrait of a Planet* premieres November 10, and the Shakespeare adaptation *Titus Andronicus* on December 12, both in Düsseldorf. Publishes *Sätze aus Amerika* (Sentences from America).
1971	Publishes narrative *Der Sturz* (The Fall). Vienna premiere of Gottfried von Einem's opera based on *The Visit*.
1972	Stages Büchner's *Woyzeck* in Zürich.
1973	*Der Mitmacher* (The Collaborator) premieres March 8 (and fails) in Zürich. D.'s son Peter receives jail sentence for refusing military service.
1974	Trip to Israel. Made Honorary Fellow of the Ben Gurion University in Beersheba. Produces Lessing's *Emilia Galotti* in Zürich.
1976	*Der Mitmacher—Ein Komplex* published. *The Judge and His Hangman* filmed. Welsh Arts Council International Writers Prize.
1977	*Die Frist (The Grace Period)* premieres in Zürich, October 6. D. receives Buber-Rosenzweig Medallion for Christian-Jewish cooperation, and two honorary doctorates: from Nice and the Hebrew University in Jerusalem.
1978	Publication of a volume of Dürrenmatt's paintings and sketches.
1979	Stage version of *Die Panne* goes on tour with Dürrenmatt directing. Literature Prize of the City of Bern. Lecture on Albert Einstein in Zürich.

1980	Publishes thirty-volume *Werkausgabe* (Complete Works Edition) with his new publisher, Diogenes Verlag in Zürich.
1981	Swiss Writer in Residence at the University of Southern California. Honorary Doctorate from University of Neuchâtel. Publishes *Stoffe I–III* (Subject Matter I–III), retitled *Labyrinth* in 1990.
1983	Death of wife Lotte. Premiere of *Achterloo* in Zürich. Meets Charlotte Kerr. Visits to Greece (with Charlotte and Maximilian Schell) and South America. Honorary Doctorate from the University of Zürich.
1984	Marries Charlotte Kerr on May 8. Her film portrait of D., *Portrait of a Planet,* shown on German television December 26. Carl Zuckmayer Medal of Rheinland-Pfalz and Austrian State Prize for European Literature 1983.
1985	Two prose works published: *Minotaurus: A Ballad* and *The Execution of Justice*. Bavarian Jean-Paul Prize. Trip to Egypt.
1986	*The Assignment* published. Prizes: Sicilian *Premio Letterario Internationale Mondello, Georg Büchner Preis, Ehrenpreis des Schiller Gedächtnis-Preises*.
1988	Directs his farewell to the theater, *Achterloo IV* in Schwetzingen. Prix Alexander Tolstoy in Lausanne.
1989	Novel *Durcheinandertal* published. Receives Robert Curtius Prize for essays.
1990	*Turmbau: Stoffe IV–IX* published. Dies December 14 of a heart attack at his home in Neuchâtel, three weeks before he was to have celebrated his 70th birthday at the Czech premiere of *Achterloo* in Prague.
1992	Publication of *Gedankenfuge* (Thought Fugue), a collection of essays.
1993	Publication of *Das Mögliche ist ungeheuer* (The Possible Is Monstrous), a collection of poems.

Abbreviations

Works by Dürrenmatt cited in the text are abbreviated as follows:

A	*The Assignment*
D	*Durcheinandertal*
EJ	*The Execution of Justice*
FF	*Frank der Fünfte: Oper einer Privatbank*
FP	*Four Plays by Friedrich Dürrenmatt* (quoted from this collection are: *Romulus the Great, The Marriage of Mr. Mississippi,* and *An Angel Comes to Babylon*)
GH	*Gesammelte Hörspiele*
GW	*Gesammelte Werke in sieben Bänden*
M	*The Meteor*
MU	*Das Mögliche ist ungeheuer*
OG	*Once a Greek . . .*
P	*The Physicists*
P&E	*Friedrich Dürrenmatt: Plays and Essays* (quoted from this collection are: *The Judge and His Hangman,* "Problems of the Theater," and "A Monster Lecture on Justice and the Law")
PS	*Play Strindberg*
TB	*Turmbau: Stoffe IV–IX*
TP	*The Pledge*
Q	*The Quarry*
T	*Traps*
V	*The Visit*

For other works I have cited the *Werkausgabe in dreißig Bänden,* abbreviated in the notes as WA, but in the text these entries are by volume and page number only.

Understanding
FRIEDRICH DÜRRENMATT

CHAPTER 1

Biography

When Dürrenmatt's children were small, a woman passed them on the street where they were playing and asked them what their father did for a living. Whether she was merely making small talk or whether she was genuinely suspicious of the neighbor who stayed home most of the day, kept unusual hours, and did not seem to have a visible means of income, she was even more shocked at the children's answer: "He tells stories." In this regard, Dürrenmatt did not differ all that much from his father, Pastor Reinhold Dürrenmatt, who entertained his congregation every Sunday with stories from the Bible, and who fired the imagination of his son at an early age with biblical as well as worldly tales. In particular his father introduced him to the mythical heros of classical antiquity: Hercules, Prometheus, Daedalus, Theseus and the Minotaur. What his father did not tell him he could read on his own from the school library or from his father's copious collection: John Bunyan, Karl May, Jules Verne, Jeremias Gotthelf.

The village Konolfingen, where Friedrich was born on January 5, 1921, is located southeast of Bern, in the Emmental. The parsonage in which he spent his first fourteen years was a stately three-story house which, while not opulent, was comfortable and roomy enough to permit boarders and houseguests. As his parents were by nature generous, there was always an extra place or two at supper for whoever wanted or needed the hospitality. Growing up as the son of the village minister was not easy. The adults expected much more of him than of the other children, and the other children mistrusted him. He felt himself somewhat of an outcast. Christianity was all-pervasive in Friedrich's upbringing. He wrote: "I grew up in a Christian world, which even later did not relinquish its grasp on me. My son became a minister."[1] A minister is what Friedrich, too, would have become, if he had followed his father's advice. But Friedrich did not inherit his father's conventional piety. Instead he would become, indeed was already becoming, a free-thinker like his paternal grandfather, who had been a fiery, anti-establishment journalist in Bern. He never questioned his father's sincerity—his devotion to God or to his congregation. Yet the stumbling block to communication between father and son was this strict religiosity, and it was against this, and not against the person of his father, that Friedrich rebelled. He would later regret, as he described seeing his father's casket lowered into the ground, that he had never really known him (GW 6:196).

Friedrich's mother, Hulda, born Zimmermann, more than his father was the authority figure in the home. She kept order and served as academic taskmaster over Friedrich and his sister, Vroni. Hulda, too, was a pious Protestant from a mountain village, who narrated to the children from the Bible, taught Sunday school, and organized charitable groups in the village. To her mind, all the blessings the family enjoyed came as a direct answer to her prayers, and she did not miss an opportunity to boast of this fact. As well-intentioned and sincere as this belief was on her part, it enraged Friedrich, who found it indecent and unacceptable (GW 6:202). It certainly contributed to his rebellion against the simplistic Christian world in which he was raised.

As a pupil at the "prison for children we call school" (GW 6:41), Dürrenmatt did not distinguish himself. There a "foreign language," Standard German, was imposed upon him, competing with the medieval-sounding Bern dialect of his village. Already an avid reader, he resented having to read "that material, which adults like to see children read, because they wish the child's reality were the same as that which the writers of children's books present" (GW 6:41). Yet there were teachers who did inspire him. From a teacher named Fluri, who lived for a time in the Dürrenmatt house, he acquired at an early age his fascination with astronomy. It was one of the passions that never left him, and he later gained respect in scientific circles as an outstanding lay astronomer.[2] His early interest in painting also dates from the Konolfingen years, aroused by illustrated books about Dürer, Rubens, Rembrandt, Michelangelo, and Böcklin, but also by local artists, acquaintances of his father who frequented the parsonage.

Konolfingen may well have been the "ugly accumulation of buildings in petit-bourgeois style" (GW 6:19) Dürrenmatt described, but it was likewise a mysterious world in which an active imagination could create infinite realities. The fields of grain, the fir forests, bales of hay in the neighbors' barns, and the cluttered windowless loft of the parsonage were labyrinths, through which Theseus could pursue the Minotaur or soldiers chase each other as though through subterranean passages. Dürrenmatt was fourteen when his father accepted a position in Bern in 1935. The city with its narrow winding streets provided a new set of mazes but also new challenges. The beginning was not auspicious. His woes in school continued. The Christian preparatory school he attended was the same one in which both his parents had been outstanding pupils. After less than a year there, he was relegated to a private school "for failures and hard working loners" (GW 6:52). Dürrenmatt lost interest, feigned illness, and became a truant. He spent his days in the cafes reading Lessing, Nietzsche, Wieland, and Hebbel. The city introduced Dürrenmatt to the theater—his uncle had a loge at the Stadttheater—although at the time it interested him little. In general

2

he hated this phase of his youth, and continued in his adulthood to remember it disdainfully as "a time . . . in which I received the first wounds which never healed, regardless of whether I gave them to myself or others gave them to me" (GW 6:55). He was no longer Theseus in this scenario, and the maze was no game anymore. "I never got along with the city, we repulsed each other. I groped around in it like the Minotaur in his first years in the labyrinth—it must have taken a long time for him to grasp that he was in a hopeless situation, if he comprehended it at all—" (GW 6:55). Except for his years at the university, Dürrenmatt never lived in a city again, but in his narratives the city often reappears as an expressionistic hell or the scene of a surreal nightmare.

The decision to study art and become a painter was not the decision his father had hoped he would make, but it was a sensible one given Friedrich's poor, sometimes failing, grades in school. After a short period of intense preparation, during which physics, a subject he had particularly neglected, began to fascinate him, Dürrenmatt took and passed the *Maturität* (qualifying exams). Later he would regret not having studied physics and mathematics more diligently, whereas he would consider his study of Latin and Greek "superfluous" (GW 6:232). "In reality I only passed them," he wrote of his exams, "because I listed my professional goal as painting. Who would wish to fail a painter, who would never be seriously considered for university study?" (GW 6:232).

The art academy, however, would remain an unfulfilled dream. A nonconformist like his grandfather, Dürrenmatt was swimming against the current. He was loathe to submit to the prevailing artistic trend in Bern, which was impressionism. His paintings were expressionistic, wildly imaginative. They did not impress the artists charged with judging his work. The verdict: He should go back and learn to sketch apples.[3] The artists convinced Dürrenmatt's parents to let him study literature instead, and in October 1941 he matriculated at the University of Bern, where he stayed for two semesters studying German literature. The summer of 1942 saw his brief military career end during basic training. His poor eyesight earned him a dispensation to *Hilfsdienst* (auxiliary service), where he made soldiers' dog tags to be worn in combat, in the event Hitler should invade. In this brief encounter with compulsory service, the seeds of his pacifism and his cynical outlook on the Swiss military were sown. "The training was nonsense: drill, yelling and eternal shoe polishing before roll-call" (GW 6:67). Later, when his own son Peter was given a jail sentence for refusing induction, Dürrenmatt supported his decision.

A two-semester-long interlude at the University of Zürich followed. There he admits he did not study much. He was continually short of money and spent many weekends at home in Bern so that he could eat well at least two days out of the week. It was a Bohemian lifestyle for the frustrated artist, and he sought artistic contacts. The most important one Dürrenmatt made was the expressionist painter Walter Jonas, to whose inner circle he was admitted. Formal university study was neglected in favor of dusk-to-dawn sessions with Jonas and his cronies, who included "journalists, musicians, men of letters (today well-known), students and eccentrics" (GW 6:309). Through the Jonas clique, Dürrenmatt not only grew as an artist, he expanded his literary horizons as well. He tried his hand, and failed, at writing a comedy. Only years later would he finish a greatly altered version of it. On Christmas Eve, 1942, he penned in a cafe the very short, staccato narrative "Weihnacht" (Christmas), which he would eventually publish along with eight other stories in the collection entitled *Die Stadt* (The City, 1952). Under his name on his room door in Zürich he gave himself the designation "Nihilist Author" (GW 6:312).

A prolonged illness that forced Dürrenmatt home to Bern ended a year in Zürich, during which he had discovered the German expressionists Heym, Kafka, and Brecht; the works of the Austrian cultural philosopher Rudolf Kaßner; and a tremendous potential literary talent within himself. Three more years of study in Bern followed. "I fled back into a city out of which I had fled barely a year before: as senseless an undertaking then as my return was now. Both were the equivalent of the false steps a rat takes in the artificial maze of a laboratory. It does not comprehend that it is in a maze, let alone that the maze is in a laboratory."[4] What seemed at the time to be leading in one direction was in fact leading in quite another. In part because of a personality conflict with the most influential Germanist in Bern, Fritz Strich, and largely as a rebellion against his father's uncompromising religiosity, Dürrenmatt changed his course of study to philosophy and continued to write narratives. By winter of 1946 a dissertation should have been forthcoming. But Dürrenmatt was in the throes of a crisis. Three years studying philosophy—Hegel, Kant, Kierkegaard, and Heidegger—had led him to the same realization he had had in Zürich: he wanted to be a writer. He admitted in retrospect: "I was afraid to fail as a writer as I had failed as a painter" (TB 127). Yet to cling to philosophy as a security blanket was to fail as a thinker, for if everything he had learned could not give him the courage to dare this leap of faith, then the little epistemological niche he had carved for himself would become his intellectual grave. Instead of a dissertation, Dürrenmatt wrote *Es steht geschrieben* (*It Is Written*), his first completed drama, in 1946. He withdrew from the university, but he never abandoned philosophy, just as he never abandoned painting.

Dürrenmatt met actress Lotti Geißler in the summer of 1946, and the couple was married in a civil ceremony on October 11. The following day his father

4

performed the religious rites. The couple moved to Basel, where Lotti was performing at the Stadttheater. They lived in spartan quarters, described thus by a visitor: "I was invited into a poorly furnished, gigantic room, a table, a few chairs, a double bed, a crate in which a child slept, a double-burner gas stove, pots, cups, a faucet, typical lodging for a young, unemployed writer."[5] Incidentally, the child sleeping in the crate was purest fiction. Their first child, Peter, was not born until months later. The visitor was Peter Lotar of Kurt Reiß AG, theatrical publisher in Basel. Lotar had stumbled by accident on Dürrenmatt's manuscript of *Es steht geschrieben* (*It Is Written*) on the desk of actor/director Kurt Horwitz in the Stadttheater. So stunned was Lotar by the brilliance of what he read there that he sought to find the author and to get the play produced. Reiß paid an advance of 200 francs, and Dürrenmatt accepted first right of refusal terms by the publisher for all future dramatic works.[6] Lotar's vigilance was the break the young author needed. After Basel initially refused, the Schauspielhaus Zürich accepted the play, and the premiere was set for April 19, 1947, under Horwitz's direction.

While *It Is Written* did not achieve overwhelming success at its premiere, Dürrenmatt got the next best thing: a scandal. He had chosen a historical/religious theme for his first play, the Anabaptist revolt in Münster. The riot broke out as the revered Wilhelm Tell actor Heinrich Gretler in the role of Knipperdolinck stood nearly naked on stage and addressed an erotic poem to the moon. Many people, however, were favorably impressed. The play won the Drama Prize of the Welti Foundation. Dürrenmatt had found a publisher, made several key friends within the profession, and, above all, had defeated his own fears of failure.

January 10 of the following year saw the production of his second play, *Der Blinde* (The Blind Man), this time in Basel, starring Horwitz, and directed by Ernst Ginsberg. There was neither scandal nor success, only indifference. Disillusioned, Dürrenmatt withdrew *Der Blinde* from further production. He wrote a few sketches for the well-known *Cabaret Cornichon* in Zürich, but by summer he, Lotti, and their infant son, feeling the financial pinch once again, moved from Basel to Schernelz on Lake Biel. There they lived with Lotti's mother, taking what handouts they could get from friends. Lotti had for all practical purposes given up her acting career. Their financial problems were acute—Dürrenmatt would simply have to write his way out of them.

During the following decade Dürrenmatt changed his emphasis from serious drama to comedy. He also wrote several successful prose works, a half-dozen radio plays, and a movie script. His first radio play had been rejected by Radio Bern in 1946, but Dürrenmatt had not given up on the genre. In 1951

Studio Bern broadcast *Der Prozeß um des Esels Schatten* (The Case of the Donkey's Shadow), based on the Wieland tale. For a short time he even became that which he would grow to despise in later years: a theater critic. The initial breakthrough came with his first comedy: *Romulus der Große* (*Romulus the Great*). Under Ginsberg's direction, the play had its premiere on April 23, 1949, in Basel. It was successful; how successful is a disputed matter. Egon Karter of Reiß publishers called it simply a "very great success."[7] Critics tended to be cooler in their reception. Nevertheless, the play was produced the same year in Zürich and Göttingen. Dürrenmatt considered the play one of the three best he ever wrote. Yet he never seemed completely satisfied with it: by 1980 he had put Romulus through five revisions.

This one play, however, would not solve the family's financial woes. In late summer of 1949, both Friedrich and Lotti needed medical treatment. She was about to give birth to their second child, and he was suffering from an illness later to be diagnosed as diabetes. Dürrenmatt told Heinz Ludwig Arnold in an interview how he creatively financed the problem. "I called up every publisher I knew and told him a story, which I would write as a novel or novella. I must honestly say that I told each a different story. And by evening I was financially out of the woods."[8] He never wrote any of the stories, and only one of the publishers ever demanded his money back. A month later their daughter Barbara was born, and the family felt compelled to move into larger quarters. They rented a house above Ligerz on Lake Biel, that Dürrenmatt called the "Festi" from the German word *Festung* (fortress). The following year he did earn an advance honestly. The weekly magazine *Schweizerischer Beobachter* advanced him 500 francs for a serialized detective novel. *Der Richter und sein Henker* (*The Judge and His Hangman*) appeared from December 1950 through March 1951 in eight installments. Dürrenmatt later claimed that while he was writing the first chapter he did not know how he was going to end the tale. The novel's success demanded a sequel. The same detective, Police Commissioner Bärlach, returned to solve another crime the following year in *Der Verdacht* (*The Quarry*), also published in installments in the *Beobachter. The Judge and His Hangman* remains to this day Dürrenmatt's best-known and best-selling prose work. In 1976 it was filmed under the direction of Maximilian Schell, with Dürrenmatt himself playing a small but significant role. Dürrenmatt's daughter Ruth was born in October 1951, and five months later the family finally acquired their own house, located in the Vallon de l'Ermitage above Lake Neuchâtel. Dürrenmatt lived the rest of his life there, expanding the property with later acquisitions and adding two more houses to the estate.

Getting his next play on the stage proved problematic. He had been working on *Die Ehe des Herrn Mississippi* (*The Marriage of Mr. Mississippi*) since 1949. The cynical play deals with such themes as religious and judicial fanaticism, adultery, and revolution. Mississippi was rejected by all the major Swiss theaters, and Reiß refused to publish it. The play was rescued when Hans Schweikart, director of the *Münchner Kammerspiele,* staged it on March 26, 1952, in Munich. It was Dürrenmatt's first play to premiere outside of Switzerland, and despite all Swiss reservations, it was a major success. A grateful Dürrenmatt entrusted his next play, *Ein Engel kommt nach Babylon* (*An Angel comes to Babylon*), the following year to Schweikart, this time with only lukewarm audience reaction. Disillusioned and depressed, he decided to write no more plays, but rather to stick to prose. One day, years later, Dürrenmatt would make the same decision and stand by it. For now, however, he still had his greatest theatrical triumphs ahead of him. *Angel* was not without its rewards— two literature prizes, from the Canton Bern and the City of Bern respectively, were forthcoming in the following year. He returned to prose in 1955 with the romantic fairy-tale *Grieche sucht Griechin* (*Once a Greek . . .*). Dürrenmatt wrote the narrative in a very few days and with a sense of urgency and foreboding. Lotti needed surgery, and the prognosis was alarming. Once again, he desperately needed money. Lotti's prognosis turned out to be a false alarm, but the literary product it spawned maintains a unique position among Dürrenmatt's prose works. In 1966 *Once a Greek . . .* was filmed, with famous German actor Heinz Rühmann in the lead role.

Dürrenmatt continued to write radio plays. *Die Panne,* translated variously as *Traps* and *A Dangerous Game,* was written in 1955 and broadcast the following year on German Radio. Almost immediately, Dürrenmatt adapted *Die Panne* as a novella. Soon, however, his resolve to quit the theater proved to be short-lived. On January 29, 1956, Dürrenmatt returned to the Schauspielhaus Zürich, nine years after his first drama had scandalized the audience there. His new play, *Der Besuch der alten Dame* (*The Visit*), did more to propel Dürrenmatt to international recognition than had all his previous plays and novels combined. Within two years it was a hit on Broadway under the direction of Peter Brook, with actors Lynn Fontanne and Alfred Lunt. This American performance earned the author the New York Drama Critics' Award for 1958. The Twentieth Century Fox film version from 1964 starred Ingrid Bergman and Anthony Quinn. The play was eventually translated into twenty-five languages, and an operatic version by Gottfried von Einem premiered to enthusiastic applause in 1971 in Vienna. The wolf would never be at the Dürrenmatts' door again.

Recognition in the form of literary prizes began to pour in, and not just for *The Visit*. *Die Panne* won the Blind War Veterans' Prize as the best radio play of the year 1956, as well as the literary prize Tribune de Lausanne. For another radio play from the same year, *Abendstunde im Spätherbst* (*Episode on an Autumn Evening*), he won the Prix d'Italia. He was awarded the Schiller Prize of the City of Mannheim in 1959 and the Grand Prize of the Swiss Schiller Foundation in 1960.

A film for which Dürrenmatt wrote the script in 1957, *Es geschah am hellichten Tag* (*It Happened in Broad Daylight*), dealt with the subject of sexual crimes against children. It was a detective film with a didactic theme which was eventually shown in seventy countries. A year later Dürrenmatt rewrote the film script as his third detective novel, *Das Versprechen* (*The Pledge*), with the subtitle "Requiem for the Criminal Novel." The unique success of *The Visit,* for all its career-enhancing benefits, had created one notable difficulty for its author. Expectations were high for his next play—unfortunately much too high. *Frank der Fünfte: Oper einer Privatbank* (Frank the Fifth: Opera about a Private Bank) was a dismal failure. Dürrenmatt again took a break from the theater, as he had after the disappointment with *Engel.*

Trips to New York, London, and Berlin and work on a novel highlighted the three years between premieres. When the next premiere came, however, in February 1962, it lasted three days and was an international media event. *Die Physiker* (*The Physicists*) became Dürrenmatt's second highly acclaimed theatrical triumph. Like his first, it starred Therese Giehse. Kurt Horwitz directed and Teo Otto designed the set. Nearly sixteen hundred performances at fifty-nine theaters made it the most performed play of the 1962–63 theater season in German-speaking Europe.[9] What was true for *The Visit* was to prove equally true for *The Physicists*—the play that followed it was doomed. Perhaps instinctively, certainly providentially, Dürrenmatt offered a weak play as the obligatory sacrificial lamb. *Herkules und der Stall des Augias* (Hercules and the Augean Stables) was a stage adaptation of a radio play with the same title from 1954. Audiences and critics reacted negatively.

Dürrenmatt traveled to the Soviet Union twice in the decade of the sixties. The first time, in 1964, he and Lotti were guests of UNESCO for a month. They travelled extensively and enjoyed celebrity status, primarily as a result of *The Visit.* That play had been particularly popular with Soviet audiences because it was interpreted as exposing the evils of capitalist society. The Moscow Gorki Institute gave a reception in Dürrenmatt's honor. Three years later he returned to attend the Fourth Congress of Soviet Writers in Moscow. This visit was more controversial, since many other Western authors refused the invitation in protest against government mistreatment of Soviet dissidents. Dürrenmatt chose to protest in his own way. His impressions at the congress, where authors droned on in boring, politically correct language, while the politburo sat stone-faced behind them, found satirical expression in the narrative *Der Sturz* (The Fall), published in 1971.

After the *Herkules* debacle, Dürrenmatt was due for another dramatic success. While he did not approach his two masterpieces, he succeeded in 1966 with *Der Meteor* (*The Meteor*) both in regaining the respect of audiences and critics and in insulting the church. A reluctant modern Lazarus, who cannot die, directly or indirectly causes the death of most everyone with whom he comes in contact. Charges of blasphemy were predictable and immediate. The comedy kindled a public debate in which the clergy took an aggressive part.

The next six years were active ones for Dürrenmatt, yet during this time he brought only one original play to the stage. Instead he turned his creativity toward adapting existing dramas. He began with his own first fruit, *It Is Written*. Twenty years after the premiere and short run of the expressionistic Anabaptist play, he adapted it in 1967 as the comedy *Die Wiedertäufer* (The Anabaptists). This was followed in 1968 with Shakespeare's *King John* and in 1969 with August Strindberg's tragedy *Dance of Death,* which in Dürrenmatt's adaptation became the grotesque comedy in twelve rounds *Play Strindberg*. Nineteen-seventy saw two adaptations: Goethe's *Urfaust* and Shakespeare's *Titus Andronicus*. Finally, in 1972, he adapted Büchner's *Woyzeck*. The one original creation during this span was *Porträt eines Planeten* (Portrait of a Planet) in 1970.

This was also a time of increased political involvement for the author. Egypt's six-day war against Israel, the occupation of Prague, the escalation of the Vietnam War and the student revolution of 1968, from which not even Zürich was spared, moved Dürrenmatt to polemic in the form of essays and speeches. Just days after his return from the Soviet Writers' Congress, the Six-Day War broke out. He sided immediately and unequivocally with Israel. The address "Israels Lebensrecht" (Israel's Right to Exist), given on June 17, 1967, in the Schauspielhaus Zürich, was sensitive to both sides of the Palestinian issue, but unwavering in its pronouncement that Israel is a political necessity. Reacting to the invasion of Czechoslovakia in 1968, he urged a constructive reevaluation of both political power blocs, which are by nature in constant danger of falling victim to the reactionary rigor mortis of dogma. He expanded this criticism in the "Monstervortrag über Gerechtigkeit und Recht" ("Monster Lecture on Justice and the Law"), given first in a shorter version to students at the Johannes Gutenberg University in Mainz in 1968, and published in the expanded version the following year. Dürrenmatt takes capitalism and communism to task for the hypocrisy inherent in both systems. Yet his harshest criticism is reserved for

Switzerland and its intolerance of dissention under the guise of "Intellectual National Defense."

Dürrenmatt briefly joined a newly formed theater collective in Basel under the direction of his friend Werner Düggelin, director of the Stadttheater. His work with the collective lasted less than a year, from summer of 1968 to spring of 1969. Differences of opinion with other members, both in the political and the artistic realm, coupled with a serious heart attack the author suffered in April, ended the collaboration. The failure of the project upon which he had embarked with so much optimism left him again disillusioned about the state of the theater in Switzerland. However, 1969 would end better than it had begun for him. After an extended recuperation in the hospital, Dürrenmatt received the Cultural Prize of Canton Bern for literature. He divided the lucrative prize among three political dissidents: a journalist, a historian, and a conscientious objector. Highly visible in the audience at both the award ceremony and the banquet which followed were members of the counterculture, hippies and rockers, for whom Dürrenmatt professed a deep personal admiration. As expected, the event caused a scandal that Dürrenmatt seemed to welcome. His acceptance speech was highly critical of the Swiss artistic establishment.

Accompanied by Lotti, Dürrenmatt flew to the United States at the end of 1969 to receive from Temple University the first of his honorary doctorates. Their subsequent trip to Florida, Mexico's Yucatan, the Caribbean, and New York City is chronicled in *Sätze aus Amerika* (Sentences from America), a desultory string of cultural and political observations. In the final analysis he concludes that, while the American dream may be tarnished, America is still a land of opportunity. In the Soviet Union there are few opportunities left except for the ruling elite.

Controversy had been dogging Dürrenmatt's footsteps in recent years: his participation in the Moscow conference, the failure of the Basel experiment, a scandal over *Titus Andronicus* in Düsseldorf, the hippies at the prize ceremony in Bern, his conferring of his own prize money on dissidents, the sharp criticism of the Swiss government's policies toward the theater, and most recently a slander suit brought by Hungarian novelist Hans Habe. Dürrenmatt had called Habe a fascist in reaction to Habe's criticism of Harry Buckwitz, Dürrenmatt's friend and director of the Schauspielhaus Zürich. Dürrenmatt had become for the Swiss state an international literary figure too important to denounce, a cause célèbre with the people, but the same time somewhat of a political embarrassment. On January 5, 1971, Dürrenmatt celebrated his fiftieth birthday. German Chancellor Willi Brandt sent his congratulations. The Swiss government was silent.[10]

In 1972 Dürrenmatt was to have taken over the direction of the Schauspielhaus Zürich as Harry Buckwitz's successor. He refused, claiming that in reality he was not wanted. Was this unwarranted paranoia or a justifiable assumption after the backstabbing and infighting he had experienced in Basel? In either case it was symptomatic of his frame of mind as he prepared his latest play, *Der Mitmacher* (The Collaborator), for production in 1973. It is a tale of corruption so deep-seated and all-pervasive that no act of heroism is possible. Its failure left him hurt but philosophical. The theater, where he had once counted for something, had passed him by. For this he had to share the blame. Three years later he wrote the longest epilogue he had ever written, *Der Mitmacher: ein Komplex,* not, he assures the reader, in defense of a failed play, but rather to record the thought processes that led him to write the play.[11]

When the Yom Kippur War broke out on October 6, 1973, Dürrenmatt once again stood behind Israel. The following year he visited for the first time, at the invitation of the Israeli government, the country he had twice defended. His lectures at several universities were enthusiastically received. The Ben Gurion University in Beersheva made him a fellow. In 1975 he dedicated a long essay entitled *Zusammenhänge: Essay über Israel* (Connections: Essay about Israel) to the university that had honored him. The same year he gathered signatures against the "Zionism equals Racism" resolution of the United Nations.

There were more honors for the author in 1977. The Society for Christian-Jewish Cooperation awarded him the Buber-Rosenzweig Medallion in Frankfurt. The University of Nice and the Hebrew University in Jerusalem awarded him honorary doctorates. However, there was also another theatrical failure. Although *Die Frist* (The Grace Period) probably deserved a better fate, the critics, even more than the audience, reviled it. A second version did little to improve its popularity. Dürrenmatt did not attend the premiere. He later wrote that the comedy had been "an attempt to test how far he had distanced himself from conventional theater. The distance can only be indicated in light years" (25:161).

Determined not to write for the theater any more, Dürrenmatt turned his full attention to prose. A project on which he had been working intermittently for some years was the quasi-autobiographical *Stoffe* (Subject Matter), a search through his past experiences to find the origins of his literary themes and to trace them forward in time as they developed into published as well as unpublished or still unwritten works. When an acquaintance in France asked Dürrenmatt for permission to adapt the radio play/novella *Die Panne* into a stage play, the request was readily granted. Dürrenmatt simply had no more interest in writing for the stage. His publisher Egon Karter had other ideas, and made him an interesting offer: Dürrenmatt should immediately adapt the novella himself. Karter, who directed his own travelling theater company, promised a first-class ensemble, two hundred performances, and complete control of the author over the production. Dürrenmatt put *Stoffe* on hold and took the gamble. The premiere in the German town of Wilhelmsbad, near Hanau, on September 13, 1979, was well received. As a whole the play was neither an overwhelming success nor a stunning failure. Karter gave the play glowing accolades, but he was far from impartial. Other significant events of the year 1979 included a lecture given in Zürich on the occasion of the one-hundredth anniversary of Albert Einstein's birth, and the Grand Prize for Literature awarded by the city of Bern.

The monumental task to which Dürrenmatt devoted the entire year 1980 was the thirty-volume *Werkausgabe* (Complete Works Edition) for Diogenes Publishing House. To this end the author composed newer versions of several works and included some previously unpublished pieces, chief among them a reworking of the play he had begun while a student in Zürich but never finished. He spent the spring of the following year as Swiss Writer in Residence at the University of Southern California, participating also in an International Dürrenmatt Symposium in Los Angeles—this after celebrating his sixtieth birthday with an honorary doctorate from the Université de Neuchâtel. (Two years later he was to receive another from the University of Zürich.) Later that year he finally published the first volume of autobiographical reminiscences, *Stoffe I–III,* containing three previously unpublished narratives with the history of their inspiration and development.

A political comedy in an insane asylum would be Dürrenmatt's next dramatic project. Begun in 1982 under the working title *Napoleon will ins Bett* (Napoleon Wants to Go to Bed), the work was staged the following year as *Achterloo.* During the work on *Achterloo,* Dürrenmatt's wife Lotti died suddenly. She had had a fever, and a recent problem with blood pressure, but there was no warning of imminent danger. Dürrenmatt described her death and its effect on him in a moving passage in *Turmbau: Stoffe IV–IX* (Construction of the Tower of Babel: Subject Matter IV–IX) (TB 15–18). He dedicated *Achterloo* to Lotti and threw himself intensely into the therapeutic work involved in readying it for the stage. On October 6, 1983, *Achterloo* was performed in the Schauspielhaus Zürich. Attending the premiere was a German actress and documentary filmmaker, Charlotte Kerr. She had met Dürrenmatt a month earlier in Maximilian Schell's flat in Munich, where they had talked most of the night. Charlotte was fascinated by Dürrenmatt and was determined to make a documentary about him. In Zürich, Kerr sensed that the audience had not understood the play, had laughed in the wrong places, and she told him so.[12] It was the beginning of their collaboration on *Achterloo*. Their marriage, the ultimate collaboration, took place several months later on May 8, 1984, hours after the filming ended on Charlotte's Dürrenmatt documentary, *Portrait of a Planet*. In December the four-hour-long film was shown on German television. In the next five years, *Achterloo* underwent three revisions. In its final form it is known as *Achterloo IV*. Like every play since *The Meteor,* the adaptations excepted, *Achterloo* failed to excite either the audience or the critics, the most famous of whom did not even attend. "*Achterloo IV* is my farewell to the stage, to the theater" Dürrenmatt wrote in the epilogue to the play. "Not that I see no future for the medium. Theater will always be performed. But it is no longer my medium."[13]

With the exception of *Achterloo,* the years with Charlotte Kerr can be described as a creative explosion of prose: *Minotaurus: Eine Ballade* (Minotaur: A Ballad) (1985) illustrated by the author; Justiz (*The Execution of Justice*), a novel; *Der Auftrag* (*The Assignment*), a novella; and *Durcheinandertal* (Valley of Confusion), a novel. Dürrenmatt would see one more project through to completion: the sequel to the first volume of "Subject Matter," entitled *Turmbau: Stoffe IV–IX*. His last posthumous publications to date are a collection of essays entitled *Gedankenfuge* (Thought Fugue), a fragment of a criminal novel entitled *Der Pensionierte* (The Retired Man) and a speech given in 1990 in honor of Václav Havel: "Die Schweiz ein Gefängnis" (Switzerland—a Prison). The years with Charlotte Kerr were also filled with awards and recognitions. Between 1984 and 1989 he received the Carl Zuckmayer Medal of the State of Rheinland-Pfalz, the Austrian National Prize for European Literature, the Bavarian Jean-Paul-Prize for Literature, the Premio Letterario Internationale Mondello, the Georg Büchner Prize, the Schiller Memorial Award, the Prix Alexi Tolstoi, and the Ernst-Robert Curtius Prize for Essay Writing.

Dürrenmatt's fatal heart attack on December 14, 1990, came only three weeks before he would have turned seventy. He died at home in Neuchâtel. On January 5, 1991, the city of Prague staged a celebration of what would have been Dürrenmatt's seventieth birthday with a most enthusiastically received performance of *Achterloo IV* in the newly reopened Nove Mesto. Dürrenmatt, who was to have been the guest of honor at the performance, would have appreciated the irony.

CHAPTER 2

Earliest Prose and Dramatic Works

Dürrenmatt's decision to become a writer instead of pursuing a doctorate in philosophy was not completely the result of a leap of faith. He had, after all, been writing and publishing short stories since the winter semester of 1942–43. He continued working on them until 1952, although three stage plays, several radio plays, and the Bärlach novels intervened. A volume of the early prose containing most of the early narratives was published in 1952 under the title *Die Stadt* (The City).[1] The first five of these narratives are to a greater or lesser extent indictments of God.

"Weihnacht" (Christmas) is a nihilistic anecdote in a staccato, expressionistic style. Only 122 words long, the narrative contains 28 sentences, many of them fragments. A winter landscape is equated with death. The narrator finds the Christ Child frozen in the snow. He eats the halo, which tastes like stale bread. He bites off the head: old marzipan. He walks on. The tone is matter-of-fact, the narrative devoid of interpretation, but the theme is clearly "the death of hope, of all human emotions."[2] The second narrative, "Der Folterknecht," is the most compact, expressionistic form of a motif which recurs in the early prose as well as in later narratives and dramas: God as unjust judge and torturer. This theme continues through three more short, insignificant narratives: "Die Wurst" (The Sausage), "Der Sohn" (The Son), and "Der Alte" (The Old Man).

The rest of the early narratives are longer. In "Das Bild des Sisyphos" (The Picture of Sisyphus) Dürrenmatt, through the narrator, considers the question of whether it is possible to create something out of nothing. In "Der Theaterdirektor" (The Theater Director), written in 1945, he explores the mechanism of political scapegoating by means of a parable set in the theater. The theater represents the world; the director, Hitler or Stalin or a demagogue yet to be born. Aesthetic norms are interchangeable with religious beliefs, social standing, national origin, or moral codes. "Die Falle" (The Trap) is a nihilistic tale about a man who is obsessed with death. The entire narrative takes place against a background of desolation: winter landscapes, bloody corpses, and flocks of black birds. The most powerful scene in this tale is a nightmare which the nihilist experiences: all of humanity is racing headlong into the fires of hell. The protagonist turns and fights his way back upstairs against the crowd, but as the red glow fades behind him, only murky darkness and increasing coldness lie ahead of him. There is no God, only hell. Screaming "where is the grace," he throws himself headlong back down the stairs toward hell and the humanity from which he had separated himself. "Die Stadt" (The City) and a companion narrative written five years later, "Aus den Papieren eines Wärters" (From the Papers of a Jailer), make extensive use of the labyrinth. "Papers" remained a fragment, but was conceived as an expansion of the labyrinth theme from the second part of "The City." Whereas the labyrinth in "The City" is a subterranean prison, it is transformed in "Papers" into a theater of war, in which everyone is everyone else's enemy. "The City" will be discussed at length in the chapter on *The Visit*. The premise as well as the setting of "From the Papers of a Jailer" will reemerge in expanded form as *Der Winterkrieg in Tibet* (The Winter War in Tibet), published in 1981.

Out of this collection of generally lightweight early narratives, three in particular deserve a closer look. In "Pilatus" Dürrenmatt narrates Christ's trial, mockery, and execution from the perspective of the judge. Whereas the biblical Pilate merely saw Christ as innocent, Dürrenmatt's Pilate knows from the moment he lays eyes on the prisoner that he is a god. What he cannot comprehend, and what becomes his nemesis, is the god's humanity, particularly his humility. Pilate assumes that the god has come to kill him. "He saw that this form of the god was the cruelest one, which could deceive the people, and only in an incomprehensible hatred could it have occurred to the god to appear in this lowly mask" (18:102). Any kind of sign from the god, and Pilate would have fallen on his knees and worshipped him in front of the crowd. Yet Pilate realizes that he is the only one who recognizes the deity in the man, and this realization increases his paranoia. "So he was forced to commit one cruelty after another on the god, because he knew the truth without understanding it, and he buried his face in the hands which still dripped with water from the bowl" (18:112). He is convinced that the god will come down from the cross in triumph, even more so when darkness falls and the earth begins to quake, but his hopes are dashed. Three days later, as he stands before the empty tomb, Pilate's eyes are cold, his face "immeasurable as a landscape of death" (18:115).

"He knew the truth without understanding." This phrase lies at the heart of the problem. It may seem surprising, after all the indictments of God as torturer or arbitrary tyrant, that Dürrenmatt appears to show his Protestant colors with a narrative of the crucifixion and resurrection. Such a presumption would be premature, for this is only tangentially a narrative about Christ. Dürrenmatt identifies with Pontius Pilate, whom he characterizes as a God-seeker and thus, typical for Dürrenmatt's early works, a doomed figure. The chasm between God and humanity has been breached, and Pilate is the only human being in the story,

Jew or Roman, to sense this fact. But an equally gaping chasm exists between his sensing the truth and his truly understanding it. Like the water which reached up to Tantalus's chin and no farther, grace is just out of Pilate's reach.

"Der Hund" (The Dog) is the most abstruse work from the early prose, and one of the more intriguing. That the dog embodies evil is evident from his sulfurous eyes and teeth and his shiny black fur, as well as from his size and ferocity. Otherwise the story is open to interpretation, indeed begs interpretation, particularly the ambiguous ending. The labyrinth is present; it is the winding streets of the city in which the narrator continually loses track of his quarry, an itinerant preacher and the dog. The narrator is fascinated by the incongruity between the preacher's lucid exegesis of the Gospel of John and the devil-dog which accompanies him through the streets. The preacher has followed the biblical dictates to the letter, sold all he owned, left his wife, and gone out to preach the gospel—and still the evil has come. It is an evil which exerts more and more control over the life of the preacher, until he is reduced to cowering in the corner in fear, unable to pray. The preacher's daughter, on the other hand, who lives with her father and the dog in the spartan basement, believes the narrator to be her salvation from the evil. By seducing the narrator, under the watchful sulfurous eyes of the hell-hound, the girl rids herself of all fear concerning her safety. Three days after the dog attacks and kills the preacher, the girl, who has been the subject of a citywide search, appears in the middle of the night in front of the narrator's house. At her side walks the dog, gentle as a lamb.

Written in 1951, this narrative certainly has roots in the author's student days.[3] An anecdote from the Zürich year lends credence to this contention. In the first volume of *Stoffe* (Subject Matter), published in 1981, Dürrenmatt wrote about a liaison he had with a French girl, a painter, in the winter of 1942–43: "The first night of love. We both lived carefree, unconcerned about the world around us" (GW 6:313). He admitted being in rebellion against his parents at the time. In "Der Hund," the narrator's first night of love with the preacher's daughter has precisely this liberating effect on both of them. Dürrenmatt's analysis of his own creative processes in *Stoffe* allows us to appreciate better in retrospect what is happening in "Der Hund." The young author's rebellion against his father's religiosity, his own liberating love affair while in college, and the childhood experience of having been attacked by a dog, have fused and resurfaced in an allegorical form. The girl replaces Dürrenmatt as the victim of the religious fanatic father, and Dürrenmatt in turn becomes the catalyst for the girl's salvation. This role reversal allows the author the freedom to write the story, which would have been too transparent otherwise. The beast mangles the father—a final repudiation of his counterproductive withdrawal from the world into a religious cocoon—while Dürrenmatt's own passionate embrace of life in the world, as represented by erotic love, is vindicated.

"Der Tunnel," written in 1952, is the best-known and most anthologized of the early prose works. About twenty minutes out from Bern on the rail line to Zürich, which Dürrenmatt took almost every weekend during his year at the University of Zürich, lies a short tunnel. This one time, however, inexplicably, the tunnel does not end. Instead the train full of passengers is sent careening toward the center of the earth. On a beautiful day when the passengers are mindlessly complacent, horror invades their world. Science fails, logic fails, and the reader's primal fears become reality for the duration of the ride.[4] Dürrenmatt is no longer the narrator but the protagonist: a student on his way to Zürich for a Monday seminar he has already decided to cut. A somewhat corpulent young man, he wears dark glasses, smokes cigars, and stuffs cotton balls in his ears; that is, he covers or fills the orifices in his body to keep out the horrors of the world. By the end of the narrative he has lost the cigar, broken his glasses, had the cotton popped out of his ears by the air pressure, and been forced to face those horrors head-on. Mesmerized by that which had so recently horrified him, the student stares from the locomotive down into the onrushing abyss, "the goal of all things," with fascination. He is the only one on the train who can accept and face the full implications of the truth. To the conductor's anguished question "What can we do?" the student answers: "Nothing. God has dropped us, and so we fall towards him."[5] Scholars have suggested that this is a parable of salvation, because the train is falling toward God, and whoever can accept this, like the student, already lives in God's grace.[6] In this case, "The Tunnel" may be seen as the answer to the anguished cry of the nihilist in "The Trap": "Where is the grace?" Such an interpretation is consistent with Dürrenmatt's extreme theological position in the early dramas. The only alternative to despair is a Kierkegaardian *credo quia absurdum* (I believe by virtue of the absurd) in a universe in which God is remote, where humans are "abandoned by God . . . to a senseless existence, plunging through a dark tunnel to death."[7] In the revision of the narrative for the *Werkausgabe* in 1978, Dürrenmatt removed this final theological reference, allowing the student only to say "Nothing." This deletion demonstrated the philosophical change that had taken place in the interim. Dürrenmatt was still wrestling with God in 1952. By 1978 he had given him up as irrelevant.[8]

Dürrenmatt has noted that the stories were all conceived between 1942 and 1946, that is, before the dramas, for which the narratives represent a necessary preliminary step. A reader who attempts to read a single common theme into all the narratives—whether the philosophy be nihilism or Calvinism; whether God

17

be torturer, *deus absconditus* (hidden God), Old Testament tyrant, or New Testament savior—soon encounters pieces of the puzzle which do not fit. Certain only is that Dürrenmatt was wrestling with the problems that necessarily arise when a strict religious upbringing clashes with a study of Kant, Kierkegaard, and Kafka. He was also plagued with self-doubts and faced questions about his own future: Should he paint, write the philosophical dissertation, or pursue fiction writing full-time? Dürrenmatt's often cited assertion in the afterword to *Die Stadt* places the narratives in their proper perspective: "This prose is not to be seen as an attempt to narrate any particular stories, rather as a necessary attempt to fight something out with oneself, or, as I perhaps put it better after the fact, to fight a battle that can only make sense, if one has lost it" (18:197). The early prose works are not ones for which Dürrenmatt will be particularly remembered, but we should not dismiss them as a dead end. They serve rather as an incubator for themes. There exists in Dürrenmatt's oeuvre something akin to conservation of matter. Themes are recycled and recombined; metaphors reappear often enough to be considered leitmotifs. It should, then, be apparent that we will see essential elements from the early prose again and again.

Es steht geschrieben (It Is Written)

Dürrenmatt's first play is his longest. It is as though the author had waited so long to begin his career as a playwright while he languished in indecision as a philosophy student, that he could not contain his imagination when he finally gave it free reign. Form and content are complementary, both chaotic. The tremendous creative energy which gave birth in 1946 to Dürrenmatt's dramatic career hurled a large number of partially developed ideas in all directions. Later, gravity would catch the debris and organize it into tighter literary constellations that would obey the laws of theatrical convention. For the present, however— in the immediate wake of the big bang—the raw power of the spoken word, a scattershot of grotesque and humorous inspirations, deep philosophical thoughts, and an as yet undisciplined but razor-sharp satirical wit combined to baffle and dismay critics and audiences alike. *Es steht geschrieben* opens itself to a number of interpretations, precisely because the author has packed so many disparate elements into it. It has been correctly labeled "both unconventional and a typical first play, including the sum total of its writer's ideas."[9] Due to the play's length (three hours) and its basically undramatic form, characterized more by monologue than by dialogue, the drama is perhaps more suited for reading than for staging.[10]

Central to the plot, as can be deduced from the title, is religion. That Dürrenmatt wrestled with his religious upbringing during his philosophy study is apparent, not only through the prose fiction, but also from his writings and statements in interviews about this period. At the end of his study was to have been a philosophy dissertation. *Es steht geschrieben* did not replace this dissertation; for all practical purposes it is his dissertation. Søren Kierkegaard—the dissertation was to have been entitled "Kierkegaard and the Tragic"—presents faith as the last and greatest of a series of movements, which one can only make after renouncing all that one holds dear in the finite realm. "The infinite resignation is the last stage prior to faith, so that one who has not made this movement has not faith; for only in the infinite resignation do I become clear to myself with respect to my eternal validity, and only then can there be any question of grasping existence by virtue of faith." The full extent of human knowledge and experience dictates that all hope must be abandoned, that the cause is lost. Yet the "Knight of Faith" says with confidence: "I believe nevertheless that I shall get [it], in virtue, that is, of the absurd, in virtue of the fact that with God all things are possible."[11]

Enter Karl Barth, the well-known Protestant Swiss theologian, whom Dürrenmatt would later come to know personally, and in whose commentary on the "Epistle to the Romans" Dürrenmatt was immersing himself simultaneously with his philosophy studies.[12] The young Karl Barth of the *Romans* commentary was influenced by Kierkegaard, whom he cites repeatedly throughout the copious volume. Barth presents a concept of God quite different from that to which Dürrenmatt had been exposed in his youth, and thus intriguing. Unlike the imminent good shepherd deity with whom Hulda Dürrenmatt carried on dialogues and who answered her every prayer, Barth's God is unapproachable. The qualitative gulf between God and humanity is a chasm that can only be crossed in one direction: from above. Always beyond human comprehension, the "divine incognito" can only be apprehended with faith. Referring to Luther, Barth affirms: "Faith directs itself toward the things that are invisible. Indeed, only when that which is believed on is hidden, can it provide an opportunity for faith. And moreover, those things are most deeply hidden which most clearly contradict the obvious experience of the senses."[13] Grace (*Gnade*) comes down from God in the same way. It cannot be earned or deserved, but rather represents Christ's incomprehensible way of momentarily bridging the gulf between himself and humanity. Religion is guilty of "criminal arrogance" when it tries to comprehend the world in relation to God. This perception of final truth proceeds only "from God outward." One need not stretch imagination to see Kierkegaard and Barth lurking behind *Es steht geschrieben*.

Three static characters and a developing one form the nucleus around which revolves a constellation of minor, mostly comic characters. Most of the minor characters remain only episodically involved. They are types: avaricious, simple-minded, opportunistic, militaristic, or simply milieu characters like those found abundantly in Schiller's *Wallenstein's Camp*. Of the leaders of the Anabaptists, Jan Matthison, the baker's apprentice from Leyden turned prophet in Münster, is the least problematic. Rising statue-like out of the orchestra pit, Matthison is a caricature of an Old Testament patriarch. Tall, lean, and bearded, with a sword as long as his body, he begins by chiding the director and author for presenting the Anabaptists in such an undignified manner, as though they were all fools. Soon he proves himself to be the greatest fool of all. A scriptural literalist, Matthison attempts to live his life, and force his followers to live theirs, by strict adherence to the Bible. That he is an egomaniac is apparent from his opening monologue. He really has only a handful of biblical passages, out of context, that govern his actions: chief among them "Consider the lilies of the field," with which he justifies the order not to defend the city. Matthison's ludicrous assumption that he can conjure up a miracle at will gets him slaughtered the moment he steps outside the gates alone. Matthison's faith is a lie, founded in egocentrism. He has made none of the movements of faith, does not understand its complexities, and, worst of all, has made the false assumption that he can manipulate God through his own will—call down a large order of grace to go.

Equally lacking in complexity is Johann Bockelson. In contrast to Matthison, whose hubris is so great that he is convinced of his calling, Bockelson is never anything but a cynical con artist. He arrives in Münster with a hedonistic agenda and exploits the naivete and moral weaknesses of its citizens, who have suffered under Matthison's oppressive regimen. His technique is the elevation of immoral behavior to the status of religious rite, thereby legitimizing it in the eyes of a pleasure-starved populace all too eager to accept it as divine revelation. With his power thus consolidated, he does not need to pander to the common people any more. It is enough that they believe in him. As Bockelson and his palace entourage debauch, the city starves.

However, it is not Bockelson on whom the spotlight falls at the end of the play and not his words that bring down the curtain. That honor falls to Bernhard Knipperdolinck, the only relentless seeker of truth among the play's principals. It cannot be said that Knipperdolinck is a hero in the positive sense of the word, for in the grotesque carnival which the Anabaptist revolt has become there are no heros. Like Matthison, Knipperdolinck takes a biblical dictum literally to heart and pursues its realization to a disastrous conclusion.

In ridding himself of his wealth, which according to the admonition in Luke 18:25 is standing in his way of attaining the kingdom of God, Knipperdolinck misunderstands the meaning of poverty. By throwing his wealth indiscriminately among the people, he merely fans the greed of those who fight each other for the coins rather than doing the maximum good for those in greatest need. By divesting himself of all his worldly authority, he forfeits any chance to administer justice tempered with mercy, and by abandoning his family to Bockelson he places his daughter, who loves him, in a dilemma that results in her death at the hands of the bishop. The act of following the one biblical dictum to the letter has led him to the very edge of existence from which he is unable to follow any of Christ's other exhortations, such as the charge to feed the hungry. He has become Bockelson's fool. His extremism in a holy cause has been as fruitless as Matthison's.

Those critics who stress the hopelessness in the play's ending are right, as far as justification in this world is concerned.[14] Bockelson and Knipperdolinck, the con man and the God-seeker, die on the wheel side by side. Their fates, as controlled by earthly justice, are identical, a fact prefigured in the macabre, wildly expressionistic dance on the roof which the two men share just before their execution. No reward comes to the God-seeker for the fact that he has actively sought at great sacrifice, but Kierkegaard and Barth have already said as much. God approaches Knipperdolinck at that moment when all his striving has ceased, as he is dying on the wheel, passive and resigned. Only then does God's grace fill him, and he sees a vision of impending salvation. Through faith born of infinite resignation he is given, as a divine gift, that for which no human works were sufficient. This is indeed extreme protestantism.

Unable to partake in this grace, because he is too much caught up in the world, is the Bishop Franz von Waldeck. The bishop, with his ninety-nine years of experiencing the horror of the world, knows God's remoteness, and thus he has retreated into nihilism. He sees the world as unchangeable, the human condition as unredeemable. Thus he struggles only to maintain the status quo, an unjust condition nevertheless better than chaos. For this reason he has Knipperdolinck killed, even though he admits to admiring him and envying him for the strength of conviction that he himself lacks. Knipperdolinck, dying on his wheel, has found God, or more correctly been found by him. The bishop in his wheelchair must live on without grace. He bears most closely the features of the author, who is characterized by Matthison in his introductory monologue as: "in the broadest sense of the word an uprooted Protestant, afflicted with the tumor of doubt, distrustful of that faith which he admires, because he has lost it, . . ." (1:58).[15] Thus, like Kierkegaard, who can venerate Abraham for his depth of faith although he cannot share in it, the bishop (and through him the author) admires his adversary Knipperdolinck for that faith which he himself has lost.

Why, then, did Dürrenmatt couch this serious religious plot element in comedy? The explanation lies in Kierkegaard's understanding of the tragic, the subtext of this dissertation in dramatic form. When the individual transgresses against the universal, which is the ethical, he accrues guilt. Through his death he purges this guilt and restores the universal. This is tragedy. The religious person is, for Kierkegaard, the isolated individual, whose position of conflict is with himself rather than against any universal ethic. His position becomes paradoxical, and thus dramatic, but not tragic. Through religious belief the individual is removed from the universal, and rendered incapable of participating in the tragic. In the realm of the religious, Dürrenmatt concludes, there can be no tragedy, only comedy (TB 124–25).

Surrounding, or better, swirling around this religious plot is a plethora of distractions: scenes that have little or no bearing on the religious drama and that only make sense if the play is seen as a huge cabaret performance with all of society as the object of its satire. Several of the scenes and individual gags in this world-cabaret seem to be there for no reason other than their comic effect. Other scenes seem to have little bearing on the plot until one looks below the surface. That the world is in chaos, and why, is evident from the bishop's audience with Emperor Charles the Fifth. The emperor cannot remember that he is in Germany, or why he is in Germany, or why he has granted the bishop an audience at all. A forgetful old man? An unfit ruler? Why take a whole scene to satirize an emperor who has no other role to play in the drama? In his introductory monologue Charles tells the audience exactly why: "I have much to rule over, but I love the monotony which alone befits my heart, which beats deep under this cloak, neither recognized nor known by any man, for God in his wisdom has erected a wall between me and the people and the world. . . . In me the Lord planted the monument to his distance and his obscurity" (1:84). Charles is not only conscious of his role as God's deputy, he has also taken on God's characteristics. His aloofness and disinterest in the affairs in Münster are but an allegory of the divine remoteness. History is no more being controlled by earthly authority than it is from above. It is out of control, subject to the whims of chance. All this is underscored in the scene with the emperor.

Another character whose relevance to the plot is not immediately obvious is the monk Maximilian Bleibeganz. Following the three grotesque Anabaptists of the prologue onto the stage, only to apologize to the audience for their terrifying howling, the monk immediately changes the tone of the play from serious to humorous. The monk himself confesses to his own fictitiousness. He is nothing more than filler, whom a director, pressed for time or short an actor, can easily leave out. His is a Hanswurst role, and like the Hanswurst of Viennese folk comedy, he is blessed with a quick tongue, survival skills, and good luck in the midst of calamity, whether in escaping execution at the hands of the Anabaptists or beating the Protestants at dice in the camp of the bishop's army.

Beginning with the monk's monologue, the play remains self-referential throughout. Characters step out of their roles to address the audience directly. Scenes function as self-contained units much like sketches in a revue. Pervading the play is a pessimistic view of the world that immediately brought Dürrenmatt in opposition to a German dramatist with whom he often had to endure comparison, Bertolt Brecht. For the Communist Brecht the world could be changed for the better by indoctrinating the people with the proper ideology and altering the distribution of wealth. Dürrenmatt, who rejected Marxist philosophy as metaphysical, did not perceive the world as changeable through ideology. He demonstrates this belief at the outset of his dramatic career through the failed Anabaptist commune at Münster, which he portrays as corrupt, exploitive, and founded on religious fanaticism. History has not been changed, and it will inevitably repeat itself. The status quo returns and nothing has been learned. Münster, like Jonestown and Waco, remains an episode.

Der Blinde (The Blind Man)

"*Der Blinde* portrays faith as an elemental force, independent of its 'content.' The story takes place during the Thirty Years' War and is invented—even if influenced by the Biblical Job" (25:142). While superficial parallels to Job are obvious, Dürrenmatt leaves very little of the biblical message intact. Dürrenmatt tells his Job story without God. In archaic-sounding language he takes a biblical plot, removes the theological frame, and anchors it firmly in the secular realm. Only the blind duke still believes in God. Those who can see know that life is meaningless. God, if he exists, is so remote as to be a nonentity for the victims of the senseless religious war that has ravaged not only this dukedom, but most of Europe. While the biblical Job curses God, then repents, the duke never waivers from his absolute faith, taking every blow as it comes with calm acceptance. However, while Job is ultimately rewarded for this faith many times over, the duke is left homeless, penniless, and friendless by the tempter amid the ruins of his war-ravaged dukedom. The duke has only his faith at the end, and it is an absurd faith.

An illness, that rendered the duke comatose during the destruction of his army, land, and palace by Wallenstein's troops, has left him blind. Through the deception of his son, Palamedes, and his court poet, Gnadenbrot Suppe, the duke believes he is living in his former splendor with all his power intact. The tempter, in the person of an Italian nobleman in Wallenstein's service, Negro da

Ponte, happens by the ruins, whereby the duke entrusts him with everything he believes he still owns. He makes da Ponte, whom he does not know, his governor. This irresponsible act appears unmotivated; however, the cause lies in the duke's all-or-nothing attitude toward faith. His blindness has created only two choices for him: he can either trust everyone or no one. To trust no one would be to render his isolation total. Yet only a complete fool could trust everyone. It is an absurd premise but one which, once accepted, enables the duke to trust Negro da Ponte as easily as he could anyone else.

The "elemental force" of faith, of which Dürrenmatt wrote, comes into play when faith is "blind." Jesus says to Thomas in John 20:29: "Have you believed because you have seen me? Blessed are those who have not seen and yet believe." Dürrenmatt turns this admonition upside down by demonstrating through the character of the duke that faith is only possible for those who cannot see. Palamedes can see, and he has given himself completely over to despair. Octavia can see, and she has become a hedonistic existentialist. Negro da Ponte can see, and his is the greatest cynicism of all. The duke interprets his affliction as a blessing, as grace: "You fool, only the blind man sees!" (1:230) he shouts, as he strangles the poet Gnadenbrot Suppe, who wants to tell him the truth about his situation. Is the duke "blessed" because he has not seen and yet believed? Job believed, and the Lord blessed his latter days more than his beginning. Abraham believed, and Isaac was restored to him. The duke, too, believes and is left with nothing but his naked, existential faith.

The duke is the Kierkegaardian loner. He readily accepts the paradox of his faith. Contradictions in logic no longer pose a threat to him. The extent to which his dogged adherence to the principles of his faith have obliterated any vestiges of reason becomes apparent when da Ponte denounces Palamedes as a traitor to the duke. If Palamedes would deny the charge, the duke declares himself ready to believe that both parties are telling the truth, although logic would dictate this to be impossible. Logic demands that either Palamedes or da Ponte must be lying. The duke's position is absurd, but Kierkegaard declared faith to be anchored in the absurd. The duke's faith cannot be broken. Why, then, was it necessary for him to kill Gnadenbrot Suppe? A faith that strong should not be threatened by the words of a bad poet. Negro da Ponte's miscalculation of the duke's motivation can easily become the audience's or reader's misinterpretation as well, because da Ponte summarizes the murder in these words immediately after it happens: "The blind man strangled him . . . in order not to hear the truth, my friend. But that will be of no use to him, he will not escape it" (1:230). In fact, the duke has long since rejected any "truth" that comes from the world of the sighted. He and Suppe could not have had any meaningful dialogue about truth, because they reject a priori each other's definition of the term.

For the duke, possession of the truth, that can only come from God through faith, is a prerequisite of sight. Sight without faith is a lie. To Suppe, on the other hand, only that which is perceivable through the senses is believable. So the emissary from the world of the sighted, the world of human beings without faith, enters the world of the faithful blind man and is renounced there as a traitor. It is out of righteous anger, not out of fear, that the duke strangles Suppe. He does not kill him in self-defense, rather he executes him for the crime of treason, just as he had ordered his son's execution for the crime of betrayal, of which he was wrongly accused. The duke's derisive words chide a misguided fool, whose intention was to bring despair to a blind man but who has recklessly ventured into a realm which he does not comprehend: "You fool, whose body I surround with my arms, what is the truth, that you bring me? It is more fleeting than water, more changeable than wind and less substantial than the song of a drunkard. Why do you want me to care about that world from which you come? How can you believe you know about light, because you have two eyes? You fool! Only the blind man sees" (1:229–30). From this misinterpreted gesture, Negro da Ponte draws the erroneous conclusion that the duke is frightened, that his armor of confidence is cracking, and that the victory over him is assured. In fact, it is da Ponte's defeat which is already sealed.

In the character of Negro da Ponte, Dürrenmatt prefigures a character type he will later explore in depth in two detective novels: the amoral villain for whom heinous acts are merely expressions of absolute nihilistic freedom. Like Gastmann and Emmenberger against Bärlach, Negro da Ponte wages an ideological war against the duke, in order to prove that his own nihilism is stronger than the duke's faith in God, justice, and the inherent goodness of the human race. The cards are clearly stacked against the believer. The rule of the game for da Ponte is that there are no rules. The identity of da Ponte as a general under Wallenstein, and thus the duke's enemy, is carefully concealed from his quarry. The villain has a whole entourage of actors who play their roles adequately enough to fool a blind man—actors who share his contempt for the duke and the optimism to which he clings. In his corner the duke has only a son who suffers too much from melancholy to be of any comfort to his father, and a daughter who has long since abandoned him to become da Ponte's lover.

Negro da Ponte's erroneous belief that he has chosen a weak opponent and that victory is at hand not only causes him to underestimate the duke's depth of faith, but also renders him susceptible to the factor which, from this play on, will become Dürrenmatt's dominant dramatic principle: the worst possible turn of events (*die schlimmstmögliche Wendung*). Coincidence (*Zufall*) replaces God as the prime mover in Dürrenmatt's dramatic universe. Coincidence strikes to thwart human beings—protagonists and antagonists are equally vulnerable since morality is irrelevant—when they are most confident they have a foolproof plan. In da Ponte's case, the worst possible turn of events manifests itself in the suicide of Octavia. She is to be his trump card in breaking down the duke's illusory world. Placing the body of Gnadenbrot Suppe dressed in woman's clothes under a shroud, da Ponte announces the death of the duke's daughter. Having convinced the duke that she has died by her own hand, he intends to bring out the live Octavia and thereby ridicule his adversary into comprehending that his absolute faith in his fellow man has been a sham. Yet Octavia really does lie under the shroud. She has died just as da Ponte has proclaimed. In his diatribe against the duke he has only made a fool of himself.

The "Angel of Death" can only depart from the duke and move on to his own lands. "I retreat from you, groping about like a blind man. You have not resisted me and you have defeated me. I have been destroyed by the one who did not defend himself. I leave you now, like Satan left Job, a black shadow" (1:242). If this has been an allegorical struggle between faith and nihilism, who has come out the winner? With Dürrenmatt one must always be careful not to draw the obvious conclusion too quickly. Da Ponte has not been able to break the duke's faith, but Dürrenmatt has shown at every point the destructiveness inherent in that faith. Palamedes, Octavia and Suppe all fell victim to it. What is left after the tempter departs is not the happy ending of Job, but a scene of absolute isolation. The duke's only consolation in his dark loneliness is the sense of lying "shattered in the countenance of God" and living "in His truth" (1:242). This is not truth, but illusion. Faith has not won a great victory, and the duke remains nothing more than an old, blind fool.

In *Der Blinde,* as in *Es steht geschrieben,* Dürrenmatt was exploring the extreme manifestations of radical Kierkegaardian faith. His fascination with faith at the time was partly a result of his philosophy study, but there was a more compelling historical motivation. From his perspective in a country that evaded the war, Dürrenmatt was intrigued by the question of "how Hitler, and the belief in him had become possible" (25:142). In what must be seen as thematic companion plays, despite their dissimilar structure, the author explores first, the misuse of faith as political power, and second, blind faith as an elemental force capable of negating reason and logic.

Der Blinde was written to be performed at the Stadttheater in Basel, which had more limited resources than the Schauspielhaus Zürich. One stage set suffices, on which the duke in his imagination journeys to the borders of his dukedom and back. It is a play rich in philosophical debates and long monologues with little action, for unlike the Anabaptists in Münster who lived by the written text, the blind duke is a slave to the spoken word. Dürrenmatt retracted the play after nine performances in Basel and two short runs in Germany. Karl Barth saw the play and participated in a discussion about it. "I don't think that he particularly liked *Der Blinde,*" Dürrenmatt later wrote of Barth. That faith has its foundation in blindness, was something he could not accept within the constellation of the play. . . . For Barth, faith is a blessing, independent of the situation in which the person finds himself" (TB 192). The blessing for Dürrenmatt's career was that the play failed so miserably. Had he enjoyed a modicum of success, he might have continued a while longer in this same vein, penning serious dramas of epistemological significance. Instead he abandoned the stilted archaic language and turned to comedy as his medium.

CHAPTER 3

The Turn to Comedy

Romulus der Große (Romulus the Great)

When Dürrenmatt was preparing his texts for the critical *Werkausgabe,* published in 1980 by Diogenes, he revised his first comedy, 1949's *Romulus der Große (Romulus the Great),* for the sixth time. Although officially the 1980 version was known as version five, there were in fact two variants of the text performed in 1949. When a work undergoes so many revisions, it is obviously indicative of that work's importance to the author.

Out of the historical last emperor of Rome, the mere teenager Romulus Augustulus, Dürrenmatt makes a middle-aged ruler who hardly seems to deserve the designation "the Great." For twenty years the passionate chicken farmer isolated in his villa outside Rome has done nothing to prevent the Germanic advance that threatens his empire's existence. However, Romulus has only been playing the fool. It has long been his secret purpose to liquidate the empire, a decadent state that has lost its moral right to exist. He intends to sacrifice himself in order to bring down Rome, for the Teutons will surely kill him when they come. The knowledge of this sacrifice appeases his conscience, for many more will also fall along the way. Though he has the best-conceived plans, Romulus is to become the first in a long line of Dürrenmatt's comic heros to be thwarted in their expectations and to be forced to accept the opposite of their stated goals. Romulus's adversary Odoaker proves to be a humanist (and a fellow passionate chicken farmer). Odoaker pardons Romulus and assures him a pension and a life of comfort. But nothing has been accomplished, for lurking in the wings is Odoaker's belligerent nephew, Theoderich, to whom the future belongs. He will surely replace Rome with something much more brutal. This sobering conclusion from the 1957 variant—a plot that remained basically unchanged through two subsequent revisions—replaced a comic happy ending from 1949, in which all ends well and Romulus enjoys his retirement with a clear conscience.

The questions raised in *Es steht geschrieben*—whether society can be changed for the better, whether history can be redirected through the intervention of individuals—are revisited in Romulus. The play is carefully constructed so as not to reveal the emperor's agenda too early. The audience should be able to agree with Spurius Titus Mamma's exclamation at the conclusion of act 1: "Emperor, you're a disgrace to Rome!"[1] and with Ämilian's resolute: "Down with the Emperor!" (FP 84), which ends act 2.[2] Until this point the title begs an ironic interpretation. How could this ineffective clown in a toga playing head-in-the-sand politics while the Teutons advance on Rome have any claim to greatness? The emperor's actions suggest early senility or a type of genetic madness produced by inbreeding. While Dürrenmatt saves the plot reversal for act 4, the beginning of the great revelation for the audience as well as for the other characters in the play begins at the end of act 2 and continues in act 3. When he first rejects Cäsar Rupf's offer to save Rome in return for Rea's hand in marriage, the emperor's motive seems to be his daughter's happiness—understandable in human terms if somewhat unrealistic in the political arena. In act 1 Romulus proclaims to his wife, Julia, that he has no intention of bargaining away his daughter. By the end of the second act, however, the rhetoric escalates. Romulus has a method to his madness, though its essence will remain a mystery for a while longer. Ämilian joins Rea in trying to convince Romulus of the necessity of Rea's marriage to Cäsar Rupf, to no avail: "My daughter will submit to the Emperor's will. The Emperor knows what he is doing when he throws his empire to the flames, when he lets fall what must break and when he grinds under foot what is doomed" (FP 84). It is not until the midnight conversations with his wife and daughter in act 3 that Romulus reveals the whole secret, which he has been keeping from his family for twenty years. The son of a bankrupt patrician, he only married Julia in order to become emperor, and he only wanted the throne in order to bring the empire to an end: not as Rome's traitor but as Rome's judge.

Comedy dominates the first two acts, a comedy based upon anachronism, political and social satire, and incongruity between the spoken word and the apparent situation. The monumental exhaustion of imperial messenger Spurius Titus Mamma quickly becomes a running gag, a leitmotif for the meaninglessness of exaggeratedly heroic deeds in an unheroic time. Both the trouser manufacturer Cäsar Rupf, whose name combines imperial power with the verb meaning to pluck chickens or to fleece a customer, and the antiquaries dealer Apollyon stand above the fray. Whichever side wins, they stand to make a large profit. Culture is merely a commodity: buy low and sell high.

War Minister Mares and Minister of State Tullius Rotundus have all the cliches of Nazi Germany at their disposal as they talk a fierce battle against the approaching Teutons. Mares, who is given the title "Reichsmarschall" in the first act, speaks of "Total mobilization" when there is no one left to mobilize. Propaganda slogans worthy of Joseph Goebbels ring familiar and hollow in the face of total desertion by all the Roman troops who have not been captured or killed: " Our strategic position grows more favourable hour by hour. It improves from defeat to defeat" (FP 71). Yet these *milites gloriosi* run away at the first (false) alarm that the Teutons are coming. Zeno, the third member of this triumvirate, believes in the power of positive thinking. Rome would rise to its former splendor and military might if everyone could just believe in the final victory. He, too, echos Hitlerean concepts: "unsere geschichtliche Sendung" (our historic mission) (FP 58); "Weltgefahr des Germanismus" (Teutonic threat to the world) (FP 58); "Glauben an den Endsieg des Guten" (belief in the final triumph of right) (FP 69). This last slogan loses much in the translation, for the word *Endsieg* has an unmistakable connotation to a German speaker immediately after the war that the translation "triumph" simply does not convey. Zeno is fleeing when he first appears onstage, and he is still fleeing at the end. The audience learns that he was the only one from the court who successfully made it to safety in Alexandria, from which point he has boasted he will continue his "indefatigable fight against the Teutonic menace" (FP 59). "Teutonic menace" echoes not only Hitler's use of communism as a rallying cry (although not as well as the original text's *Germanismus* echoes *Kommunismus*), but also the entire "red menace" mentality of the decade following the war.

Although Dürrenmatt denied that he was targeting his homeland with his satire in Romulus, he plays the role of Switzerland's bad conscience through this play as well as through numerous other later works. Among his targets are the profiteers from "dubious transactions with the Nazi economy during the war" and "the Old Guard in Switzerland who refused to give up the heroic attitudes of the past."[3] Then, too, as one scholar has noted, the whole atmosphere of Romulus's villa resembles more that of a farm house in Canton Bern than a Roman Imperial summer residence, and the emperor reveals more the sluggishness of a Bernese farmer than the mentality of Gandhi.[4]

Two characters who are treated seriously in the first three acts are the lovers Rea and Ämilian. Rea becomes a metaphor for that which deserves love and devotion, in stark contrast to Rome, the fatherland, which does not. She studies Greek tragedy, as befits a young woman whose betrothed has languished for three years in German captivity. That the lovers are willing to renounce their happiness to save their country creates a potentially tragic moment. That they are denied the opportunity to make this sacrifice is consistent with Dürrenmatt's belief that tragedy is no longer possible. Romulus asks Rea in act 1: "Why study that tragic old text? Why not comedy? It's more fitting for our time" (FP 51). He counters Julia's objections with: "Calm yourself, my dear wife; people whose number is up, like us, can only understand comedy" (FP 52). In his essay "Problems of the Theater" (1954), Dürrenmatt would elaborate upon this position: "Tragedy presupposes guilt, despair, moderation, lucidity, vision, a sense of responsibility. In the Punch-and-Judy show of our century, in this backsliding of the white race, there are neither guilty nor responsible individuals any more. No one could do anything about it and no one wanted to. . . . We are all collectively guilty, collectively bogged down in the sins of our fathers and of our forefathers. We are the children of our forebears. That is our misfortune, but not our guilt: guilt today can exist only as a personal achievement, as a religious act. Comedy is the only thing that can still reach us" (P&E 254–55).[5]

When, in their most heroic moment, their sacrifice is rejected by imperial decree and they have no choice but to flee together, Rea and Ämilian are denied the status of tragic hero and heroine. They are true patriots, in stark contrast to the pretentious patriotism of Zeno, Mares, and Tullius, but their patriotism is anachronistic, because it is no longer rational. Their allegiance is to an ideal long since destroyed by collective guilt, for which no further personal sacrifice is possible. Their death at sea in the unheroic act of fleeing is ironic; it is horrible, but not tragic. Their fate has taken the worst possible turn, in that a meaningless drowning accident has replaced their intended sacrifice to save Rome. As Romulus rejected the lovers' sacrifice and denied them tragic status, so too will a second worst possible turn render Romulus's great tragic moment comic.

The coincidence that brings about the worst possible turn is always a variable with which the protagonist does not reckon, could not possibly reckon, because it lies so far outside the range of probability. For Romulus this stumbling block is the fact that Odoaker, out of all the Teutonic warriors who have risen to new heights of barbarism on their campaign against Rome, is a humanist and a passionate chicken breeder like himself. The unforeseen element for Odoaker, conversely, is Romulus. Had Romulus been justified in expecting to be killed by his adversary, so could Odoaker logically expect his own surrender to be accepted. While Romulus has been inactive for twenty years in order to bring about Rome's downfall because he despised Rome's past, Odoaker now wishes to liquidate the Germanic Empire out of a fear of its future. Both men are fools for failing to realize that the only thing either leader has any control over is the present, and neither has given the present any thought. As dialectical antipodes each thwarts the other's ambitions. Each brings the other to an uncomfortable middle ground which nevertheless represents reality.[6] The synthesis will not be a great movement of history, but a short period that Romulus predicts history will hardly record. Historians are more impressed by the "bloody greatness of Theoderich" against which Odoaker begs Romulus to protect the world. Yet Theoderich's tyranny must come to pass. It cannot be stopped, only delayed for a few years, which will be counted among "the happiest this confused world has ever lived through" (FP 115).

The answer to the question of whether individuals can change the course of history remains negative. Rome may have deserved to fall, but peace and prosperity are everybody's business. Dürrenmatt will have more to say about this later in his "21 Points to *The Physicists.*" Romulus's error was also Odoaker's error. Both tried to act alone to change history, an attempt that demands the utmost courage but which is doomed to failure. All that is left is two "failed politicians" playing comedy one more time, as though history had been changed, humanity restored. The mood is not joyous; it is subjunctive.

That Romulus is brave cannot be questioned. *Mutige Menschen* (courageous people) is Dürrenmatt's term for the character type: "The lost world order is restored within them" (P&E 255). But courageous is not infallible. In over-emphasizing Romulus's courage it is possible to engage in unjustified hagiography. Errors of judgment aside, Romulus is no candidate for sainthood. Dürrenmatt himself described him as "in the final analysis a person who acts with extreme severity and lack of consideration for others and who does not shrink from demanding the utmost from others as well" (2:120). Like Knipperdolinck and the duke, Romulus is ready and willing to sacrifice his loved ones for the sake of an idea.[7] One question remains then: Why does Dürrenmatt call him "The Great?"

The inspiration for turning the historical Romulus Augustulus, barely seventeen years old when he was dethroned by Odoaker, into the mature and purely fictional Romulus the Great, who rules Rome for twenty years, came from a political debate into which the author was eager to plunge. Dürrenmatt writes: "The absurd discussion, which arose in Germany, whether the would-be assassins of July 20, 1944, had been traitors to their country or not" had given him the idea to transform the child emperor into a "national traitor on the throne, who betrayed his empire to the Teutons, because he no longer believed in the right of the Roman Empire to defend itself" (25:144). This theme of justification of the traitor was of primary concern to Dürrenmatt, not only in *Romulus* but also later, in *The Physicists.* He clearly wanted this question opened to serious public debate, and was annoyed when its importance was not recognized. By calling Romulus "The Great," then, Dürrenmatt was not only commenting on the emperor's stoicism in accepting his unalterable fate or the wisdom of turning a huge loss into a small but meaningful gain—he was attempting nothing less than a revaluation of values.[8] History will acknowledge Theoderich as "The Great" for his military prowess and loyalty to his Teutonic heritage. History should, Dürrenmatt believed, recognize instead the courageous but technically traitorous acts of men like the June 20, 1944, conspirators, the cold war–era scientists who suffered persecution for resisting the nuclear policies of their governments, or pacifists from any nation who refuse military service.

The flaw in *Romulus the Great,* despite—or more accurately as a result of—all the revisions it has undergone, is that the fourth act is packed with so many conflicting intellectual agendas. Romulus acting alone in a matter of universal concern dooms that action to failure. The presence of coincidence as nemesis, negating the most perfectly laid plans, is by now a firm tenet of Dürrenmatt's dramatic theory. Superimposed upon an existing comic plot, however, they effectively neutralize the intent behind that comedy. For the righteous traitor theme to have its intended effect, that is, to be taken seriously by the audience, there were two possibilities: Justification through a comic happy ending, as the author had done in the play's first version in 1949, or justification through tragedy, which he rejected. Romulus could either win the day with his wit or die Antigone-like, betraying earthly tyranny to serve the will of the gods; however, he does neither. In the tragicomic conclusion reality "corrects" him. His actions for the past twenty years, including his perfectly planned betrayal of Rome, are shown to have been meaningless. Neutralized by conflicting intentions, this theme gets lost in the philosophical ether of the fourth act.[9] This is why the play has not been an effective catalyst to the ethical debate on treason, and perhaps, too, why the play never achieved more than mild success, despite being one of the author's personal favorites.

CHAPTER 4

Three Detective Stories

The Bärlach Novels

In 1950 Dürrenmatt needed money. Lotti required medical treatment and the author himself had just been diagnosed with diabetes. Two detective novels—instant successes with the reading public—alleviated his financial crisis. Both works appeared in eight semimonthly installments in the popular journal *Schweizerischer Beobachter,* the first running from December 1950 to March 1951, the second following a year later. The first novel, *Der Richter und sein Henker* (*The Judge and His Hangman*) is the more conventional detective story. When the policeman Ulrich Schmied is found murdered in his car above Lake Biel, the case is referred to Bern Police Commissioner Hans Bärlach. Suffering from stomach cancer and about to retire, Bärlach appoints a young criminalist named Tschanz to head the investigation. Suspicion immediately falls on a shady millionaire named Gastmann, a facilitator of illegal international arms deals, whose soiree Schmied had been attending under an assumed name the night he was murdered. Commissioner Bärlach's relationship to Gastmann, not revealed until the second half of the novel, goes back forty years to a night in a Turkish bar when the two had made a wager over the feasibility of the perfect crime. That wager had set the former friends off onto opposing careers: Bärlach as a successful criminalist, Gastmann (not his real name) as a brilliant criminal who had stayed a constant step ahead of his antagonist ever since. It was Bärlach who had sent Schmied to gather evidence against Gastmann, and Schmied's murder appears to have robbed Bärlach of his last opportunity to prove his nemesis guilty of a crime. When Tschanz kills Gastmann in a gun battle in apparent self-defense, the police close the book on the case of Schmied. Yet Bärlach has known all along that Tschanz killed Schmied out of jealousy, and has appropriated him as his hangman to bring Gastmann to his belated justice. Confronted with Bärlach's knowledge, Tschanz commits suicide. The scene in which Bärlach exposes Tschanz is a grotesque eating orgy, in which the terminally ill commissioner suddenly summons the strength to consume a sumptuous feast. But this last explosion of the life force leaves Bärlach near death.

An emergency operation buys an extra year of life for the now retired commissioner, who cannot resist taking on one more case, this time privately. It is 1951, and in *Der Verdacht* (*The Quarry*), Bärlach is convalescing in a Bern hospital under the care of Dr. Hungertobel. There he sees a photo in *Life* magazine of the "butcher" of Stutthof concentration camp, Dr. Nehle. Hungertobel's uneasiness about the picture catches Bärlach's attention. Although Nehle is supposed to be dead, his body having been identified, the picture bears a striking resemblance to Dr. Fritz Emmenberger, head of the Clinic Sonnenstein in Zürich. Hungertobel was in medical school with Emmenberger and believes him capable of the Stutthof atrocities. Before acting on the suspicion, Bärlach sends for his old Jewish friend Gulliver, a shadowy figure who always seems to know more than the police. In their midnight visit, Gulliver tells a gruesome tale of being the only survivor of Nehle's knife and of having taken the picture published in *Life* himself. Bärlach pays an eccentric journalist, Fortschig, to break the story that Nehle has been found alive and will soon be caught. He then has Hungertobel deliver him to Sonnenstein under an assumed name, where he hopes to prove that Emmenberger was the Stutthof doctor and that after the war he killed his double, whose name he has been appropriating.

As the first half of the novel ends, so does the actual detective work. The second half is given over to long philosophical discussions and considerable suspense. Bärlach has greatly underestimated his opponent. Sonnenstein is a trap, from which no one has ever come back alive. Instead of frightening Emmenberger, Fortschig's story gets the incautious journalist murdered. Hungertobel is to be next, and for the commissioner is planned Emmenberger's specialty: an operation without anesthetic. Emmenberger gives Bärlach one chance to escape death and obtain his freedom. He needs only to convince the Nazi doctor that he possesses a belief in anything strong enough to stand up to the latter's nihilistic credo. Bärlach remains silent. The hours pass, and Bärlach awaits death. His rescuer, Gulliver, appears as a deus ex machina to kill Emmenberger just as he is about to operate.

Switzerland has spawned the villains of both novels, and, more important, has facilitated their criminal careers. Gastmann, merely the final alias of a man whose real name is never revealed, returns as an old man to establish the base of his illegal empire in the village of his birth, Lamboing. In reality it is less nostalgia that draws Gastmann to the hills above Lake Biel than the anonymity and privacy his native land affords him. Swiss bureaucrats ask no questions, especially when the answers threaten to be embarrassing. Von Schwendi, member of the National Assembly and Gastmann's attorney, is such a bureaucrat. He knows what Gastmann is doing, but keeps silent for three reasons. First, the deals are lucrative to his client, and thus indirectly to him; second, this is nothing unusual in Switzerland, where the right to privacy is so greatly revered; and finally, to expose Gastmann at this point would embarrass not only the Swiss government, but also some very powerful foreign governments whose diplomats are exploiting their immunity to consummate the illicit deals. Von Schwendi's permissiveness taken to extremes results in a perversity of logic, by which Gastmann is justified and those trying to stop him are portrayed as anti-Swiss. Yet Von Schwendi's plethora of titles so daunts Bärlach's superior Lutz that he forbids further interrogation of Gastmann. The message is clear.

In Emmenberger we have a villain of a different magnitude, and through him Dürrenmatt explores a considerably more complex and taboo subject. As a Nazi death camp doctor, Emmenberger represents a national shame the German people bore. However, Dürrenmatt is so bold as to question whether his own people would have resisted the demons any better had they not been spared Hitler's influence by that wall of neutrality. He illustrates universal human vulnerability to evil by bringing a miniature death camp into metropolitan Zürich. One can already hear the protestations of unfairness. Sonnenstein is, after all, a fictional place, posited into downtown Zürich by an ungrateful Swiss author whose patriotism could be questioned. How dare he claim to know how the people of his country would have acted in a hypothetical situation? Bärlach answers that question for the author in his first face-to-face meeting with Emmenberger: "What happened in Germany, happens in every country if certain conditions occur. These conditions may differ. No person, no nation, is an exception."[1] Of course, Emmenberger and Gastmann are extreme *fictional* manifestations of evil. Dürrenmatt was not implying that Switzerland is full of Gastmanns and Emmenbergers. Rather, he was concerned with possibilities created as a result of real conditions in society; and he was convinced that, on a smaller scale, there were many such anonymous villains enjoying freedom, privacy, and economic advantages in a land conditioned by centuries of neutrality to see no evil.[2]

If perceived corruption in Dürrenmatt's homeland was a motivation in the Bärlach novels, so too was the state of detective fiction. Dürrenmatt has certainly not written conventional detective stories. While all the famous fictional detectives have their signature idiosyncrasies, nearly all play more or less by the rules, just as writers of detective fiction are expected to follow certain rules out of fairness to the reader.[3] That the system works, justice is rational, and crime does not pay are universal lessons of the detective novel. It is actually a conservative, baroque form of literature. Through it a rupture in the pre-ordained order of society, created by the commission of a crime, is healed; the moral status quo is restored through the solving of the mystery and the apprehension of the antisocial perpetrator.[4] For the detective to restore the social order in the mind of the reader, however, he or she must employ the legitimate methods sanctioned by that order. Were the detective to stoop to the criminal's level and employ blatantly illegal methods to entrap him, the result would be an affirmation of anarchy rather than of order.

Dürrenmatt had serious reservations about the reality distortion inherent in these rules of traditional detective fiction. Seven years after the completion of the Bärlach novels, in his third detective novel entitled *Das Versprechen* (*The Pledge*), the author states these objections in systematic detail. His spokesman is the fictional Dr. H., retired commandant of the Zürich Cantonal Police. Dr. H. accuses the detective novel of perpetrating a fraud, whereby he is willing to overlook the lie that the criminal is always punished: "Such pretty fairy tales are morally necessary, I suppose. They are in the same class with the other lies that help preserve the state, like that pious phrase that crime does not pay. . . ."[5] Dr. H. rails rather against the other, bigger lie, namely, that police work is always statistical and logical—a neat and tidy procedure that denies the supremacy of the unpredictable. The truth is, he explains, that a crime can never be solved like a mathematical equation because we never know all the necessary factors—usually only a few secondary ones—and because coincidence, the unforeseeable, plays too great a role. So the criminologist constructs statistical models, which work only in general terms, whereas the individual crime stands outside the scope of the calculable.

That Dürrenmatt was already thinking these thoughts in 1950 is apparent, for Dr. H's objections are precisely the point on which Bärlach's wager with Gastmann turns. Both the young detective and the potential criminal accept as premises human imperfection, the unpredictability of the individual, and the pervasiveness of coincidence. The difference is in their interpretations of the consequences. For Bärlach, these uncertainties render the perfect crime impossible and spell defeat for the criminal. Gastmann wagers that precisely this unpredictability gives the advantage to the malefactor. The young Bärlach's credo is consistent with that of the traditional detective in literature; Gastmann's is essentially that of the stereotypical fictional criminal. Ironically, the virtuous detective represents that reactionary, status quo–confirming philosophy to which the author takes exception, while the villain speaks for the author in objecting to the "big lie" of detective fiction.

Dürrenmatt's modus operandi in carrying out his deconstruction of detective fiction is similar to that of his emperor Romulus in bringing down Rome. Through legitimate means—the discovery of a body, introduction of the detective, the gathering of clues—the author gains the reader's confidence and raises the expectations associated with the traditional detective novel. Once in possession of the reader's confidence, Dürrenmatt does what his fictional Dr. H. would later say he must do, he discards the rules. The search for Schmied's murderer, that seems to dominate the first half of the novel, is revealed to have been a red herring. Bärlach has long since solved that crime, albeit without telling the reader. The focus suddenly shifts to Bärlach's forty-year-long cat and mouse game with Gastmann and his desperation to bring his nemesis to justice in the short time he has left. Tschanz's murder of Schmied has only been the latest in a series of incalculable coincidences that have thwarted the detective's many attempts to win the wager fairly. The justice ultimately meted out to Gastmann is flawed, because Bärlach has had to resort to extralegal means, to vigilante justice. His inability to win fairly proves the validity of Gastmann's claim and discredits his own fanatical belief in the justice system, the same belief that underlies traditional detective fiction. Dürrenmatt's trap, however, is a subtle one. It is quite possible, even probable, that the casual reader will miss the point, for Bärlach remains a brilliant detective throughout, exercising sovereign control over his investigation. He is clever enough to trick one murderer into eliminating another. Admittedly he places himself in mortal danger at one point, but even that is a calculated risk, in which the advantages of darkness and familiarity of the surroundings are on the side of the detective.

Considerably less subtle are the tactics Dürrenmatt employs in *The Quarry.* There Bärlach is not only defeated by the villain, being rendered physically and morally defenseless, but he brings the dilemma on himself by exercising appalling judgment. The same detective who had wrapped his arm in a towel in anticipation of Gastmann's dog now enters a killer's lair without any backup and without so much as an emergency plan. Failure to realize that his retirement picture was in the newspaper allows him a false sense of anonymity. He causes Fortschig's death by failing to anticipate how the alcoholic journalist would surely act if suddenly in possession of money. His most conspicuous error, however, is grossly misjudging his adversary. Bärlach seriously expects that a Nazi death camp torturer, having murdered his double after the war in order to assume his identity, and having established himself as a wealthy clinic director in Zürich, would suddenly confess his past and surrender to an unarmed, defenseless, and terminally ill retired police commissioner. While the novel is quite suspenseful, more so than *The Judge and His Hangman,* the reader is much less likely to overlook the criticism of the genre in *The Quarry.*

Both Bärlach novels were intensely popular with the reading public. *The Judge and His Hangman,* the more popular of the two, has sold several million copies in paperback worldwide. This fact, of course, does not qualify a novel as great literature; however, the two works do possess unique qualities which set them apart from the standard murder mystery potboiler. One such quality is their genre-critical standpoint. Another is the abundance of philosophical monologues and discussions. The philosophy does not arise situationally from the plot, but rather it drives the plot, especially in the second novel. The combatants for their part take on allegorical properties as personifications of good and evil. Here, an honorable, principled man who has dedicated his life to bringing criminals to justice through legal means; there, two villains for whom life is a game without a rule book—biologically human, but seemingly soulless, or at least lacking any semblance of a conscience. One villain commits crimes on a whim, the other tortures as an expression of nihilistic freedom. Such a fight cannot possibly be fair; neither fight can be won by the book. In *The Judge and His Hangman* Bärlach compromises his philosophical position in order to win the physical struggle. In *The Quarry,* with the physical struggle long since lost, attention is focused on the clash of ideologies.

Most intriguing is Dürrenmatt's injection of his own persona into *The Judge and His Hangman* as "the writer." Disguised from the casual reader—only the initiated would recognize the author's humble house in Ligerz, the little white family dog, and the cries of baby Barbara in the next room—and obscured from Bärlach's and Tschanz's view by the insidious glare from the window, Dürrenmatt himself grants the detectives an interview. Whatever else is said and done in the novel to throw the reader or the detectives off the scent, none of that is happening in chapter 13,[6] where every one of the author's pronouncements is honest and infallible.[7] Framed in the blinding light of the window, that places a corona around his head but renders his face impossible to look upon, the creator holds forth to Bärlach and Tschanz about his prize creation. Gastmann is capable of any foul deed, but he is not the murderer of Schmied. He is evil, but out of whim, not out of conviction. "Gastmann represents the negative pole of evil. For him evil is not the expression of a philosophy or an instinct, but of his freedom, the freedom of the nihilist."[8] Speaking *ex cathedra,* the creator foretells the coming of one more demonic than Gastmann, a chilling prophecy that sets the stage for the next novel. Evil has two poles. Gastmann's opposite pole must be a person who commits crimes "simply because evil represents his moral system, his philosophy," and who "would pursue his calling just as fanatically as another would pursue the good" (P&E 207). The author is certain that such a man exists. Perhaps, he tells Bärlach, you will meet him someday. "If you meet the one, you will meet the other" (P&E 207).

When Bärlach does finally encounter Gastmann's opposite pole, he is not at all equipped to fight him. Emmenberger believes in two things: matter, and his existence as part of that matter. There can be no justice, since material cannot be just or unjust. There is only freedom, and this cannot be earned, it must simply be taken. This appropriation of freedom amounts to criminality: "Freedom is the courage to commit crime, for freedom itself is a crime" (Q 147). What does Bärlach believe that can counter this? The debate over Bärlach's enigmatic silence has had many participants, and the diversity of their conclusions underscores the complexity of the question. It is certainly prudent to leave the fiction of the novel and look to Dürrenmatt himself for the solution. There were numerous answers Bärlach could have given to save his life, answers that would have included God and reaffirmed the natural order. His silence, though, is motivated by a factor exterior to the plot. Bärlach does not speak, because if he did, he would extricate himself from Emmenberger's clutches, carry the day, and win the moral victory. Dürrenmatt could not let his protagonist even seem to win the philosophical battle. To do so would be to vindicate Bärlach's methods and reestablish the legitimacy of the fiction that truth always triumphs over falsehood, justice over injustice. In short, it would have overturned all he had been seeking to accomplish through the Bärlach novels. Dürrenmatt did have an answer to Emmenberger, and very soon it would be delivered in person, silently and swiftly, somewhere in the halls of Sonnenstein. Dürrenmatt's answer to Emmenberger is Gulliver.

While Bärlach had been able, barely, to defeat Gastmann, he cannot come close to defeating Gastmann's opposite pole. Only Bärlach's opposite pole is capable of this feat. Bärlach believes in an ordered universe and seeks order in society. Gulliver knows the chaos intimately and navigates smoothly within it. He remains outside the law, operating in the illegality of the international underground, with no respect for bourgeois convention. Through his seeming immortality, Gulliver has attained mythical identification with Ahasverus, the Wandering Jew. He moves in the darkness, shunning the daylight and leaving no trail. Officially dead and thus outside the law, unapproachable by the law, he dispenses Old Testament justice.[9] Gulliver dispatches Emmenberger quickly and efficiently, without philosophical debate or recourse to the protection of a corrupt legal system. As committed in his own way to justice as is Bärlach, Gulliver is equipped, as Bärlach can never be, to fight the most egregious manifestations of evil the modern age can unleash.

Yet, lest the Bärlach novels be misinterpreted as a universal advocation of vigilante justice, Gulliver's final words to Bärlach include a warning. To save the world is not in the hands of the authorities, of a single race, or of the devil, but in God's hands. We can help in small ways, but we cannot hope to do it alone. Gulliver's limitations are the limitations of all humanity. "Therefore, we ought not to try to save the world but to get through it—the only true adventure that remains for us at this late hour" (Q 161).

Das Versprechen (The Pledge)

After the philosophical victory of evil over good and the transparent deus ex machina conclusion to The Quarry, there was only one final, logical act the author could perform: the funeral of the detective novel. This he accomplished seven years later in 1958 with the narrative The Pledge. The previously quoted passage in which Dr. H. rails against the exaggerated logic in detective stories is taken from the novel's rather lengthy frame. Dr. H. makes it clear that detective fiction itself will be the subtext of his narrative. Dürrenmatt places himself squarely into the novel as the first-person narrator, who is soon supplanted in this role by the fictional Dr. H. Dürrenmatt is in Chur to give a lecture to the Literary Society on "the art of writing detective stories." Real place names and the presence of Emil Staiger lecturing on Goethe the same evening give the narrative a deceptive documentary quality. The author places himself good-naturedly into the role of straw-man, seeming practitioner and proponent of the genre at which he is about to aim a lethal blow. Soon the narration is taken over by the fictional retired police commissioner, who proceeds to "correct" the author, first with polemic, later with an example from "real" police work.

Without revealing why, Dr. H. introduces Dürrenmatt and the reader to a drunken, feeble-minded gas station attendant and a slovenly sixteen-year-old girl named Annemarie, who serves them coffee in a ramshackle roadside cafe. Their identities will soon become known, but first Dr. H. holds forth on detective fiction. The problem with the genre, he says, is that it is based on a false premise, logic: "You build your plots up logically, like a chess game; here the criminal, here the victim, here the accomplice, here the mastermind. The detective need only know the rules and play the game, and he has the criminal trapped, has won a victory for justice. This fiction infuriates me" (TP 12). In the real world chance plays a much larger role than probability. "Our rules . . . apply only in general and not in particular. The individual stands outside our calculations" (TP 13). The proof of Dr. H.'s point is the "sad, soused wreck who pumped gas" (TP 14) for them. His name is Matthäi, and he was once one of the best men in the Zürich Cantonal Police Department.

The story which Dr. H. narrates next bears close similarity to the screenplay of a made-for-television film Dürrenmatt had written the previous year. Entitled Es geschah am hellichten Tag (It Happened in Broad Daylight), the film arose out of national concern over the growing number of sexual crimes against children and was intended to alert parents to the danger. On his last day before leaving the force to take an assignment in Amman, Jordan, Matthäi is called in on a murder case. A third-grader, Gritli Moser, was found in the woods near Mägendorf. Her throat had been slit, and there were no clues. The peddler who had found the body and alerted police became a suspect, because he had a police record. Matthäi swears to Gritli's distraught parents "by his salvation" that he will find her killer. Although the peddler confesses after an all-night interrogation, then hangs himself in his cell, Matthäi's instincts tell him that the killer is still at large. Two other girls have been murdered the same way in recent years. Determined to keep his promise, he reneges on the contract with Amman, and undertakes the investigation as a private citizen.

Lacking clues or witnesses, Matthäi constructs a profile of a murderer out of a girl's imagination. Shortly before the murder Gritli had told a friend about a "hedgehog giant," and the last picture Gritli drew in school was of a man taller than the trees, dropping spiny spheres down onto a tiny girl in the forest. In the foreground was an American automobile and a strange horned animal. Gritli, it appears, was acquainted with her killer. Matthäi determines that the animal is an ibis, the emblem of Canton Graubunden in eastern Switzerland. Gritli must have seen it on the license plate, he reasons. Talking with a psychiatrist, he develops a profile of the type of large, slow-witted, and sexually dominated individual who would commit sexual crimes. From a young fisherman he learns that to catch a "carnivorous trout" one must find the right spot in the stream and throw out live bait. Buying a filling station along the main road out of the Canton Graubunden and hiring a housekeeper with a daughter (Annemarie) who looks like Gritli, Matthäi waits all summer for the killer in the American car to come to him. Then one day Annemarie comes back from playing in the woods with a tale about a sorcerer and a pocketful of chocolate truffles—Gritli's hedgehogs! Unable to keep the child who loves him in danger any longer, Matthäi constructs a child-sized doll in the woods and sends Annemarie and her mother off to safety. The following day the police surround the clearing. They watch and wait. The killer appears; there is a struggle. Matthäi is wounded but manages to kill the assailant. Annemarie, who has run away from her mother, suddenly dashes into the clearing and Matthäi intercepts her, distracting her from the grisly scene with a hand puppet. The camera pans back for a long shot.[10] Indeed Matthäi's scheme has been a long shot, but with razor-sharp logic and the luck of the righteous detective, he has carried the day. The credits roll.

It is the ending which Dürrenmatt most radically changed in the novel, and in doing so he illustrated the contention made in the frame. The killer never comes. Matthäi, consummate Dürrenmattian hero, has done flawless police work.

With logic and brilliant inspiration he has pieced together an eerily accurate profile of a killer out of practically nothing. Yet instead of catching a murderer, he reaps only the hate of the little girl, who had once loved and trusted him and now discovers she has been mere bait in an elaborate trap. Unable to comprehend his defeat, he sinks into alcoholism and deep depression, still waiting for the killer to come. "Nothing is grimmer," Dr. H. concludes, "than a genius stumbling over something idiotic. But when such a thing does happen, everything depends upon the attitude that the genius takes toward the ridiculous thing that has brought him to a fall, whether or not he accepts it. Matthäi could not accept it. He wanted his calculations to accord with reality. Therefore he had to deny reality and end in a void" (TP 161).

What is it that has rendered a masterful piece of detection absurd? Dürrenmatt does not have to tell us for the sake of realism, for it is precisely his point that often the police do not find out such things. But the frustrated reader is indeed grateful for any glimpse into the machinations of blind chance, a glimpse denied to the now hopelessly insane Matthäi. An old woman's deathbed confession years later reveals that her feeble-minded husband had murdered Gritli and the other girls. The woman, the aristocratic Frau Schrott, had not reported him because she wanted to avoid a scandal. Her much younger husband had been her gardener and chauffeur. It was an unconsummated marriage, and "blessed little Albert" had lived under the domination of her money and status. Fitting precisely the psychiatrist's profile, Albert Schrott had killed the girls on orders of "voices from heaven." He was on his way for Annemarie, razor and truffles in hand, when he was killed in a car wreck.

Why is it that a master criminologist did not take the possibility of this type of coincidence into his calculations? A check of area hospitals would surely have turned up a corpse matching the description of Matthäi's suspect. The automobile would also have been matched, further investigation would have revealed the weapon, and an the interrogation of the widow would have provided the rest. This omission has prompted the charge that Matthäi was ultimately a victim of his own stupidity.[11] But it is precisely Dürrenmatt's point that a genius can trip over the unexpected. Matthäi had already included the highly improbable in his calculations, a fact which had allowed him to track down a murderer who, according to the psychiatrist Dr. Locher, probably did not even exist. The coincidence over which Matthäi stumbled was simply too trivial and incalculable.[12] Romulus had suffered a similar fate, and five years later a much greater genius, a physicist with much more to lose, would stumble over coincidence in one of Dürrenmatt's greatest theatrical coups. Both Romulus and Matthäi prefigure the physicist Möbius.[13] Each has a logically constructed plan, and each is refuted and rendered absurd by the unforeseen. The difference between Romulus and Matthäi is that the former accepts reality, although it does not conform to his calculations, while the latter cannot accept any solution but his own.[14] Matthäi is logic personified as long as emotion is disengaged. He lives for his work, and he has earned the nickname "Matt the Automat" for his cold professionalism. He is a man not unlike Max Frisch's Walter Faber who, in the novel released the previous year, is shaken out of his complacency at mid-life and forced to confront the fact that the world is disordered. However, it was not Dürrenmatt's intention to echo Faber, nor was Frisch's novel a catalyst for *The Pledge*. Detective Matthäi is rather the next logical step in a progression of Dürrenmattian characters, good as well as evil, who put on the heavy armor of logic only to step into the quicksand of irrationality.

Like Romulus before him, Matthäi is a victim of aborted heroism. Of all the worst possible fates that Dürrenmatt has described, Ulrich Profitlich calls Matthäi's the cruelest. Rather than refuting his goal, coincidence works in the same direction, and, arriving a few minutes before Matthäi, robs him not only of the credit but of the whole purpose of his sacrifice.[15] Matthäi is not even able to bring the identity of the criminal to light. This is accomplished only years later through the confession of Frau Schrott, an ironic twist that parodies the classical criminal novel's denouement.[16]

The sudden intrusion of emotion into Matthäi's character is a problem that has been generally overlooked in interpreting the novel. Stupidity is much too strong an accusation against Matthäi; rather, his judgment is clouded by a depth of emotional involvement in the case which he has never before experienced. Dürrenmatt has added an antithesis to Matthäi's stone-cold logic: compassion. The icy tactician has discovered the soul he did not know he had until he wagered it. He has acquired human emotions. However, the anti-Hegelian Dürrenmatt will not allow a smooth synthesis to develop. Where Matthäi most needs the aid of his human instincts, to protect Annemarie, his logic—the realization that he needs live bait for his trap—overrides his concerns for her safety. Yet at the moment when he most needs a clearly reasoning mind, when the killer seems to reject the bait, Matthäi's rational powers abandon him. His inability to synthesize logic and compassion leads him to precisely the state where the psychiatrist Dr. Locher predicts he will end: madness.

Dürrenmatt, speaking through Dr. H., is careful to emphasize that Matthäi's fate represents the real world, that he must be accepted as a plausible, if somewhat extreme, manifestation of the reality of police work as opposed to the distortions fostered by literature.

You are probably cleverly saying to yourself that you need only make it turn out that Matthäi is right in the end and catches the murderer, and then you'll have a wonderful plot for a novel or a film—that after all the writer's job is to make things translucent by giving them a certain twist, so that the higher idea shines through them, can be glimpsed or inferred; that by such a twist, by showing Matthäi as a success, you would not only be making my degenerate detective interesting, but in fact transforming him into a Biblical figure, a kind of modern Abraham in the greatness of his hope and faith. (TP 157)

Dürrenmatt is describing here precisely what he did in the film version— rewarded Matthäi's faith and made him into the stock detective hero who perpetrates the big lie. He had given the television industry what it demanded, but now, on his own time, he would right the wrong and tell the real story. Transcending the pedagogical, he would teach a deeper lesson about reality. Through the mention of Abraham in the preceding passage, Dürrenmatt underscores his concern that the reader not mistake the failed detective for a kind of Kierkegaardian Knight of Faith. In fact Matthäi's transfigured face and his perpetual droning: "I'll wait, I'll wait, he will come, he will come" (TP 10) are nothing but a pitiful parody of faith. He has not made the most basic movement of faith according to Kierkegaard, resignation. He has not humbly accepted defeat in order to be able to say: "nevertheless." True faith accepts and embraces the absurd. Matthäi merely stumbles over it without recognizing it. No Abraham at Mount Moriah concludes this narrative, only a pathetic wreck on a filling station bench, stinking of absinthe.

Dr. H. summarizes Matthäi's failure in a monologue which echoes tenets of Dürrenmatt's dramatic theory:

The worst *does* sometimes happen. As men we have to count on that possibility, have to arm ourselves against it, and above all we have to realize that since absurdities necessarily occur, and nowadays manifest themselves with more and more forcefulness, we can prevent ourselves from being destroyed by them and can make ourselves relatively comfortable upon this earth only if we humbly include these absurdities in our thinking, reckon with the inevitable fractures and distortions of human reason when it attempts honestly to deal with reality. (TP 161–62)

As Timo Tiusanen correctly observes, this passage is both a warning and a consolation. It is a refutation of his nihilists, who see the world as "entirely void of justice or meaning," and it serves as a corrective to his idealists: "The world is not rational."[17] However, this is not a call to inaction or a defense of resignation. It is a moral imperative that the courageous individual still act.[18] Dr. H. admonishes us: "We nevertheless must act, even at the risk of acting wrongly" (TP 14). Of the extremist characters on both ends of the philosophical spectrum to whom Dr. H's corrective could be aimed, a significant number inhabit plays and novels from the seven year interim between *The Quarry* and *The Pledge*. To them we must now turn our attention.

CHAPTER 5

Two Plays about Ideologies and God's Remoteness

Die Ehe des Herrn Mississippi (The Marriage of Mr. Mississippi)

That Reiß Publishing House did not accept this "blasphemous" comedy for publication in Switzerland was a blessing in disguise for Dürrenmatt. When *Mississippi* opened at the Münchner Kammerspiele on March 26, 1952, it was the author's first premiere outside his native land and an important step toward gaining an international reputation as a dramatist. There have been four revisions and a film version since, the greatest changes (with the exception of the film script) coming between versions one and two. It is the second version, from 1957, that has been translated into English; this version is very close to the final one, from 1980. The most significant changes after the Munich version consisted of softening the shrill religious overtones that had so offended Ernst Ginsberg, as well as redesigning the stage to remove the surrealistic set pieces the author had prescribed for the premiere.[1]

The action takes place in a single lavishly but eclectically furnished room, whose centerpiece is a Biedermeier coffee table. During the course of the play, the room and its furniture are gradually destroyed, with the exception of the coffee table, which is as indestructible as the characters sitting around it. The furniture, a hodgepodge from various historical periods—a gothic grandfather clock, two Louis Quatorze chairs, a Louis Quinze sideboard, a Louis Seize mirror frame, fin-de-siècle wall mirrors—suggests a museum of European culture, a parody of Western heritage.[2] The symbolism of its gradual destruction should not be lost on the audience. "Bewildering" is the view out the windows: "To the right the branches of an apple tree, and behind it some northern city with a Gothic cathedral; to the left a cypress, the remains of a classical temple, a bay, a harbour."[3] No one culture spawns these types. They are universal and timeless.

Dürrenmatt treats the audience to the end of the play at the beginning for "aesthetic reasons." Three men in raincoats enter and execute Frederic Rene Saint-Claude with a bullet between the shoulder blades. Saint-Claude keeps talking as though nothing has happened, and his monologue sets the surreal tone for the subsequent action. A series of portraits lowered in Brechtian fashion from the scenery well aid in his introduction of the characters, one of whom, Count Bodo von Übelohe-Zabernsee, staggers drunk past the windows during the monologue. Saint-Claude tells the audience to ignore him because the windows they see are on the second floor, and therefore it would be impossible for anybody to stagger past them without being able to fly. It soon becomes apparent to the audience that they have never seen anything like this from Dürrenmatt before.

Central to part 1 is the marriage proposal. In a flashback to five years earlier, the state prosecutor Florestan Mississippi, whose wife, Madeleine, has just died of a "heart attack," pays a visit to Anastasia, whose husband has just suffered the same fate. Over coffee around the Biedermeier table, Mississippi confronts Anastasia with the suspicion that she poisoned her husband out of jealousy. Anastasia's husband was having an affair with Madeleine. Confronted with the evidence, Anastasia confesses to poisoning him with a sugarlike substance she obtained under false pretenses from her own lover, Count Bodo, who ran a hospital. But Mississippi is not there to arrest her, rather to propose marriage to her. He confesses to poisoning Madeleine with the same sugary substance after confiscating it from the count. He did not commit murder, he explains, but rather executed an adulteress according to Mosaic law. Their lives together will be just punishment, Mississippi suggests, for both of their deeds. He, in his fervent crusade to reinstate Mosaic law into Western society, will continue to obtain death sentences against all sorts of criminals, and she as the "Angel of the Prisons" will comfort them in their final moments and watch them die. Anastasia has no choice but to accept.

Perhaps the play has its finest moments in this first scene. The text is never this fresh and witty again. It tends to play itself out later in windy, philosophical monologues and lengthy Shavian dialogues, and yet the plot is not easy to summarize. Mississippi is not the only man in Anastasia's life. Saint-Claude (not his real name, as we later learn) appears to enlist the aid of his old friend Mississippi (also not his real name), and immediately enters into a clandestine relationship with Anastasia. Saint-Claude is a Communist revolutionary with whom Mississippi shares a sinister past, that the latter hopes will never come to light. However, as the prosecutor has no inclination to give up his crusade for the Law of Moses in order to join the revolution, he falls victim to Saint-Claude's extortion threat. Every newspaper soon carries the true story: the hated public prosecutor grew up as the illegitimate son of a prostitute and once ran a brothel. Into the equation comes Count Bodo, just returned from Borneo, where he has been ruining his health running a jungle hospital ever since he had to flee in the

48

wake of the poisoning scandal. But his flight has been in vain. After Anastasia's marriage to the prosecutor, Bodo's case was dropped. The count hopes that a miracle will save their love, and he determines to tell Mississippi the truth about the relationship. Finally, there is the only lover who is Anastasia's equal, who can possess her because he truly understands her, a man as amoral as she: Justice Minister Diego.

Saint-Claude's revolution fails, just as Mississippi's Mosaic experiment has failed. Saint-Claude plans to flee with Anastasia and set her up as a whore in his brothel, from which they will exploit the rich until they can foment the next revolution. Mississippi's attempt to tell the truth about the double poisoning lands him in an insane asylum. After escaping, he poisons Anastasia, hoping to ascertain via a deathbed confession whether or not she has been true to him. She has, of course, been sleeping with everyone in the cast, but she denies all to Mississippi and dies with a lie on her lips. Mississippi falls victim to poisoned coffee which Anastasia had originally intended for Saint-Claude. Saint-Claude is caught and executed, so that only the opportunistic justice minister Diego and the hopelessly alcoholic Christian philanthropist Count Bodo are left alive. However, Dürrenmatt is not quite finished with the plot. He resurrects Anastasia, Mississippi, and Saint-Claude immediately after their deaths to warn the audience that their kind is immortal. They will always return.

A number of significant parallels can be drawn between *Mississippi* and *Romulus the Great*. The author himself gave the impetus for this comparison. Accused by Tilly Wedekind of plagiarizing her husband's play *Schloß Wetterstein*, Dürrenmatt stated in his defense that the real model for Mississippi had been Romulus.[4] General similarities abound: Both the emperor and the state prosecutor have appointed themselves judge and jury over institutions in society they perceive as corrupt. Both are loners, following the dictates of their beliefs in the face of growing hostility and isolation. Each is willing to sacrifice his own life and the lives of others in order to realize his goal, and each has married with the explicit purpose of furthering his ambitions. Finally, both are repudiated by history, that is, their sacrifices are rejected and they must confront the absurdity of the world against which they are struggling.

There is, of course, much more than just *Romulus* underlying this unique comedy, which in turn contains germinal elements of later plots and characterizations. Mississippi, Saint-Claude, and Count Bodo all more closely resemble the Anabaptists than Romulus in their ideological fanaticism. Anastasia is a worthy successor to the blind duke's daughter, Octavia: "beautiful as the land of Italy," hedonistic, unscrupulous, a personification of the life force. Count Bodo is a descendant of Knipperdolinck, not only as a failed existence, a fool in

Christ, but in particular as a man of faith and good intentions who follows the dictates of that faith into a type of self-destructive ideological extremism. However, he has more than one predecessor. Like the blind duke he believes in miracles, although it is obvious that Bodo is intended to be a comic counterpart to the duke. Bodo has his sight and thus need not be a fool of faith, yet he continues to tilt against windmills to the end. Mississippi, on the other hand, betrays a much more sinister line of descent. Not Knipperdolinck, but rather Jan Matthisson is his spiritual progenitor, a man whose dogged biblical literalism not only costs him his life but recklessly endangers the entire Anabaptist community.

In one way, Saint-Claude is a new character for Dürrenmatt: the first appearance in his works, drama or prose, of a Communist ideologue. In another way his type is familiar. Paule (alias Mississippi) became an adamant proponent of Mosaic law because he once found a moldy Bible in a cellar and used it to teach himself to read. Equally coincidentally Louis (alias Saint-Claude) once found a copy of *Das Kapital* in the pocket of a murdered pimp. Thus he dedicated his life to the revolution. Their careers would have taken entirely different courses had Louis found the Bible and Paule the Marx text. Ideologies are interchangeable, but ideologues are born.[5] Precisely this fascinated Dürrenmatt. The writer's confession in *The Judge and His Hangman* refers to the nihilist Gastmann, but is equally valid for any ideologue: "It always gives me a thrill to meet a cliché in the flesh" (P&E 207). Mississippi and Saint-Claude, two fanatics who are merely types, differ only in the philosophy that drives them. In the wake of destruction they leave behind they are hardly distinguishable from each other. Underscoring the relativism of their ideologies is their plan to give up politics and go back to running a bordello together.

Mississippi is Dürrenmatt's most self-referential comedy, constructed on elaborate alienation techniques by which the author repeatedly breaks the dramatic illusion and reminds the audience of the play's fictionality. This alienation performs two functions. On the one hand, it parodies Brecht, whose optimistic belief in the mutability of society through communism is also under attack.[6] On the other hand, Dürrenmatt is employing alienation for the same reason Brecht employed it—to prevent the audience from identifying with the characters. Dürrenmatt himself called *Mississippi* "a comedy—employing all technical means of the theater—about ideologies and ideologues, who destroy each other in the struggle over *Frau Welt* (Anastasia), only to rise from the dead again and again" (25:146). Although each character has a past and an individual fate, which could invite identification on the part of the audience, Dürrenmatt wants them to function as representatives of interchangeable ideologies. He resolves this tension by trivializing the individual fates through comic alienation. By reminding viewers that they are witnessing an allegorical struggle among stereotypes, he lessens the danger of their identifying with the characters.

Dürrenmatt claimed to have patterned *Mississippi* after the comedies of Aristophanes, with the exception that the choruses were replaced by monologues given by the male characters (25:146). The most intriguing of these monologues is that of Count Bodo near the end of the first part. The curtain has fallen, the house lights are up, and the audience is already stirring in anticipation of intermission. Bodo staggers in front of the curtain and calls the audience back to attention to listen to what he has to say. Whereas previous monologues have reinterpreted the past, anticipated the future, or delineated the ideology of the speaker, Bodo's monologue discusses the author and his reasons for writing the play:

> Oh, I can well believe . . . that he was concerned to investigate what happens when certain ideas collide with people who really take them seriously and strive with audacity and vigour, with insane fervour and an insatiable greed for perfection, to put them into effect. . . . And I can well believe that the curious author sought an answer to the question whether the spirit—in any shape or form—is capable of changing a world that merely exists and is not informed by any idea, that he wished to ascertain whether or not the material universe is susceptible of improvement. . . . (FP 156)

Bodo claims to have been the only character the author loved with his whole passion, because he alone in the play undertakes "the adventure of love." For this reason, he claims, the author stripped him of his dignity,

> in order to make me not like a saint—saints are no use to him—but like himself, so that he could cast me into the crucible of his comedy, not as victor but as vanquished—the only role in which man again and again appears. And all this to see whether in this finite creation God's mercy is really infinite, our only hope. (FP 157)

The language of the drunken count seems to suggest that he speaks for the author, an assumption generally made and only occasionally refuted, and yet there is a disquieting quality to the language that raises as many questions as it answers. Aspects of his language seem to belie the higher perspective which

Bodo stakes out for himself with his claims of special favor. His monologue contains repeated references to an author who does not seem to know the score, one "concerned to investigate what happens . . . ," seeking "an answer to the question whether . . . ," wishing "to ascertain whether or not . . . ." Certainly an author can seek answers to universal philosophical questions, but how does he ascertain these answers by constructing fictional situations? At best such an author could present various models of reality, but determining empirical validity for one or the other model is not possible within the fictional setting. And how is it possible, as Bodo—speaking for all the characters—claims, that the author "having created us . . . took no more hand in our fate" (FP 157)?

Dürrenmatt is playing with the mind of the audience here as in no other play he wrote. In the manner of the Italian dramatist Luigi Pirandello, he has obscured the boundaries between appearance and reality. From the perspective of the characters, as whose spokesman Bodo functions, they are being used in a grand experiment of the author's in order to ascertain certain elusive truths. Their author has set them adrift in a medium in which they must clash with each other like the chemicals in a reagent glass, while their creator, temporarily in the role of God, merely watches the various reactions without intervening further in the experiment. In reality the outcome is "predestined" by that same Calvinist creator who has scripted every word out of Bodo's mouth. The audience of course is invited to take Bodo at his word and step willingly into the Pirandello trap, in which it is possible to accept the fiction that Bodo and the other characters are indeed in search of their author—that their roles have not been scripted, but rather they are condemned to struggle blindly through what Bodo calls a "ludicrous life" in order to satisfy their creator's "horrible curiosity" (FP 157).

With foreknowledge of how the characters' struggles will end, Dürrenmatt the creator knows better. He is not investigating what happens when ideologies collide, but rather demonstrating it.[7] He has thought the story through to its worst possible conclusion: The ideologues destroy each other and themselves without being able to better the world any more than can committed individuals such as Romulus or Bärlach. Their presence, however, adds to the universal misery. Furthermore, they are eternally recurring—nourished by the indifference of the many, opposed by but a few.

Who has won in the end? Anastasia is dead of the same poison with which she had murdered two husbands. Mississippi and Saint-Claude are likewise dead, although all three corpses will rise again in a resurrection parody, intended to underscore the allegorical nature of the triad and make the cynical statement that such character types will always be with us. The clear winner is the unscrupulous justice minister Diego, who has not only survived the mass dying, but has also increased his material wealth and power considerably. Diego is a political realist devoid of ideals. He fights all ideologies on the same terms and knows how to exploit the anarchy that temporarily arises when ideologies clash. Also left standing, but barely, is Count Bodo. To him Dürrenmatt even gives the honor of the last word. He appears "alone, a battered tin helmet on his head, a bent lance in his right hand, again and again submerged in the circling shadow of a windmill" (FP 197). His final monologue is defiantly hurled at the windmill, whose arms he describes as dripping with the blood of the nations it has hacked to pieces: "Look at Don Quixote de la Mancha, . . . many times battered and beaten, many times jeered at, who yet defies you" (FP 198).

It is a pathetic Don Quixote who rides out to engage the ideologues of the world in battle each time they are resurrected. He has no hope of ever winning, but Dürrenmatt does not condemn his idealism. The author had a special fondness for the Don Quixotes of the world, for with this character we are back to Kierkegaard and his Knight of Faith,[8] and we are also back to Bärlach of *The Quarry,* "sad knight *sans peur et sans reproche,* who went out to slay the evil dragon with the force of his spirit . . ." (Q 156). Bodo cannot save the world any more than could Bärlach, or Knipperdolinck or Romulus. He is a fool for believing he can, and yet this does not diminish the heroism of the attempt nor the affection the author felt for him. This is the reason Bodo is given the last word, whereas the materially successful but morally reprehensible Diego vanishes long before the final scene.

To the final question which Bodo asks on behalf of his author in the monologue—"whether in this finite Creation God's mercy is really infinite" (FP 157)—there is no comforting answer. Dürrenmatt remains a Calvinist; his God keeps his distance, accessible only to those who have undergone that degree of cleansing torment necessary to strip away every last layer of pride. Only in pain and absolute humility can the select few begin to comprehend God's greatness, to partake of his mercy. The "infinite" into which Bodo rides is a "flaming abyss," but there and there alone, in his helpless futility, can he hope to see God's glory "blaze forth."

Dürrenmatt once quipped that the worst possible experience he could imagine would be to walk past a bookstore and see a volume in the window entitled: "Comfort from Dürrenmatt." He continued: "Then I must say: Now I'm done for. Literature must not give comfort. Other things can give comfort. Literature, I believe, may only disquiet."[9] He needed not fear that he might have inadvertently slipped a word of consolation into *Mississippi.* The worldview, despite the brilliant flashes of wit, the crafty reversals of plot, and the profusion of alienation techniques through which he out-brechts Brecht, is uncompromisingly dismal: The world is a whore who goes unchanged through death; an entity that neither ideologies nor courageous individuals can hope to change; a place where only unscrupulous opportunists can flourish, and where God is distant.

Ein Engel kommt nach Babylon (An Angel Comes to Babylon)

Angel, planned as the first part of a trilogy about the Tower of Babel, followed *Mississippi* twenty-one months later at the Münchner Kammerspiele under the direction of Hans Schweikart. The evil star that had shone over Dürrenmatt's efforts to bring the construction of the tower to the stage five years earlier appeared to be wielding its influence once again. Shortly after his train pulled out of Neuchâtel for the trip to Munich, where he would oversee the mounting of the play, the author felt a sharp pain in his forehead. He reached Munich in the company of his wife, unable to sit up. The doctor diagnosed a sinus infection. Bedridden, Dürrenmatt missed most of the rehearsals.

This could have hardly seemed fair given the play's stormy history. With dogged determination Dürrenmatt had managed to gain control of a theme that had nearly driven him mad once before. *Der Turmbau zu Babel* (Building the Tower of Babel) was the working title for the play he had been writing and sending in installments to Kurt Horwitz throughout the summer and fall of 1948. The tower was to rise higher with every act, until only a few actors would be left in oxygen masks. Nebuchadnezzar reaches heaven as the only survivor of the race he had enslaved to build the tower "because he, driven by a tremendous self-loathing, wants to conquer heaven and kill God, the creator of this senseless world" (TB 47). He challenges God to a duel, but only his own words echo in the emptiness. His enemy is nowhere to be found. Only an ancient figure with a long beard appears, pushing a broom with which he sweeps up a few stray atoms. Once, long ago, he too had enslaved a race and built a tower in order to conquer heaven. Where God is, the man does not know. He only knows that now he has found someone to replace him at the endless task of sweeping the attic of the world. It is senseless, Nebuchadnezzar protests. "In nothingness nothing makes sense" (TB 48), the ancient one replies, and hands the Babylonian king his broom. Left alone in the ether, Nebuchadnezzar slowly drops his sword and begins sweeping, gradually disappearing into the blackness of space, only a shadow now, to sweep forever or until another tower builder eventually replaces him.

In December 1948 a thick stack of manuscripts had gone up in flames in Dürrenmatt's fireplace, leaving the author with an immense sense of relief. The *Turmbau* project, too expansive to complete, had been consuming him for months, with new characters and plot lines constantly being added to existing ones. "In the Third Act the tower was only a few stories high, and I capitulated" (TB 49), he wrote. Now the author lay ill in a hotel room in Schwabing while the rehearsals went on under Schweikart's direction. This was a new play on the old theme that had finally found its way onto the stage. No longer trying to show the construction of the tower, Dürrenmatt had limited himself to the background story, more particularly the reason for the tower's construction. This was to be the first of three plays on the subject; the trilogy format would give him more leeway to develop all the plot strands that had once proved too much for a single drama. Only the first act of *Turmbau* had survived more or less intact. Acts 2 and 3 were new and took the plot in a different direction. The author was able to witness a very few rehearsals and was disturbed by what he saw. He called director Schweikart and set designer Caspar Neher to account and learned to his horror that both had "misinterpreted" the play. "I suddenly comprehended that Schweikart saw a satire in *Angel*. He believed that I was a successor to Wedekind or Sternheim" (GW 6:242). It was too late to correct the misconception. Too ill to attend the dress rehearsal, Dürrenmatt dragged himself out of his sickbed to attend the premiere. He was convinced that the play was a failure: "I expected the strongest impact from Act III. It flopped, and with it the play" (GW 6:243).

Who could have imagined that both Hans Schweikart and Caspar Neher would be guilty of grossly misinterpreting the same play at the same time? Schweikart, author and theater director, had been superintendent of the Münchner Kammerspiele since 1947, and had successfully directed *Mississippi* the previous year. Neher had collaborated with Brecht for three decades on his major productions and had been set designer for the Salzburg Festival since 1947. These were two consummate professionals, whom Dürrenmatt was fortunate to have on his team at that early point in his career. If they interpreted *Angel* as a satire it must have been with good reason. There was in fact every good reason to make this assumption. On its way toward its nihilistic conclusion, the play makes fun of everything in sight. Dürrenmatt admitted as much in his fictional conversation with "F. D." in 1981. "F. D. is making fun of someone in this play: either Heaven, or the powerful, or the theologians or all of us, or himself alone. Of whom, is not clear to me" (25:148).

Already as the curtain rises the backdrop sets the tone. ". . . a vast sky is suspended over the whole scene. In its midst hovers the Andromeda Galaxy, seeming oppressively close, as it might look through the telescopes of Mount Wilson or Mount Palomar, and filling up half the background of the stage."[10] The dominating Andromeda Galaxy is an omnipresent alienation technique, for the proximity is soon revealed as an optical illusion. Named by the Angel as the location of Kurrubi's creation, it also contains God's abode. It has taken only moments for the Angel and Kurrubi to fly down to earth from "Heaven," which appears comfortingly close. But the brief journey means eternal separation from her creator for the perfect child who is to become God's gift to the lowliest of men. The Angel tells Kurrubi, barely fifteen minutes old and curious, that since the lowliest men are the beggars, she is to be presented to Akki, the only beggar remaining on earth.

Since replacing his old adversary Nimrod, King Nebuchadnezzar has outlawed beggars. Only Akki continues to defy his order to take a civil service job. The king has disguised himself as a beggar in order to try one last time to convince Akki to give up his profession. The Angel is astounded to learn that there are two beggars on earth. To whom must he give Kurrubi? Akki provides the solution by suggesting a contest. Kurrubi will belong to the loser of the contest, for he must be the poorest of the poor. Of course "Nebby," as Akki calls him, loses badly—he has absolutely no experience in begging—and Kurrubi is presented to the disguised king. Nebuchadnezzar rejects the child, striking her down with his fist. Why has heaven shunned his majesty and bestowed its grace on a beggar? Akki acquires the captive ex-King Nimrod in a clever ruse and trades him for Kurrubi. Temporarily, at least, the token of God's grace seems to be in the proper hands. She is with the intended beggar, but not the one she desires: "I love you all the same, my beggar from Nineveh" (FP 230), she whispers to the disguised king as Akki leads her away.

Act 2 under the Euphrates bridge belongs primarily to Akki and Kurrubi. The bridge vault is adorned with "a hotch-potch of various objects of every period: sarcophagi, heathen idols, an ancient royal throne, Babylonian bicycle and car tyres and so forth" (FP 231)—an anachronistic analogue to the "museum of European culture" which Anastasia's living room represents in *Mississippi*.[11] Sharing this abode with Akki are poets, lepers, pickpockets, and thieves. Since Kurrubi has come to Babylon, everyone has become a poet: the policeman, the workers, the banker, the wine dealer. And everyone wants to possess the beautiful child; she is besieged by one proposal after another. Suddenly the Angel appears. Having completed some scientific investigations, the Angel is convinced that God's creation is perfect. Ignoring Kurrubi's pleas for help, the Angel flies away singing the praises of nature. The supernatural visitation has, however, had an effect. Fearful of God's wrath because the child is in rags, the people determine that she must be taken to the king. Alone again with his poets, Akki is visited by the hangman. However, he saves his life by trading an antiquary shop he had acquired through begging for the hangman's profession.

Act 3, Nebuchadnezzar's act, takes place in the throne room. Utnapishtim, the chief theologian, convinces the king to marry Kurrubi. The prime minister bursts in with the news that the Angel has touched down in the city park and his presence is causing an uprising among the people. There is no time to lose. Kurrubi must be crowned queen in order to consolidate church and state. However, Kurrubi recognizes Nebuchadnezzar as her beggar from Nineveh and refuses to marry him unless he becomes a beggar again. Fancy theological footwork by Utnapishtim nearly sways Kurrubi, before the prime minister reports that the mood of the masses has turned ugly. The appearance of the Angel has undermined the authority of the state. The Angel must be denounced as an impostor, as an actor from the court theater. Kurrubi's refusal to take part in this denunciation and her subsequent rejection of Nebuchadnezzar lead to the sentence of death and her final flight with Akki across the sands of the desert, unaided by the Angel who has vanished from Earth. Shunned and bitter, Nebuchadnezzar vows to build a tower high enough to strike at the heart of his enemy. He will pit his justice against the injustice of God and see which is stronger.

Throughout his career, Dürrenmatt took considerable inspiration from the nineteenth-century Viennese writer and actor of folk comedies, Johann Nestroy. *Angel* is his most Nestroyesque play, teeming with puns, pantofarce, and characters masquerading as someone else.[12] Akki is a traditional Nestroy comic hero, surviving and prospering by virtue of his wits. He continually demonstrates his mental superiority over physically and politically stronger characters whom he confounds through clever, witty language. As uncertain as it is in *Mississippi* whether any character is really speaking on behalf of the author, Akki is clearly Dürrenmatt's mouthpiece in *Angel*. With Akki, Dürrenmatt presents the audience with a character who puts Gulliver's advice from *The Quarry* into practice successfully. "To withstand the world," Akki explains, "the weak must know it inside out, in order not to go blindly down a path that leads astray, or run into danger that leads to death."[13] In a series of *maqamats,* prose narratives with internal rhyme, he tells his dramatic life story, a tale full of reversals of fortune. Akki developed a strategy for the survival of the weak. He became a beggar out of the insight that one must become like the sand in order to survive. The sand does not retain the footprints of the oppressor, it is always transforming itself in shape, yet remains eternal in substance.

Akki is a humanist, not a materialist. He despises mammon, which explains his prodigality with the wealth he begs. He creates opportunities to be a humanitarian, eschewing public acts of heroism which would call attention to himself but nevertheless acting heroically—resisting the mighty by seeming to do their bidding. This admonition could just as easily have come from Brecht: from his Herr Keuner, or *Schweyk in the Second World War,* or even from Azdak in *The Caucasian Chalk Circle,* a survivor in hostile times not unlike Akki. Akki sums up his philosophy of survival best in his final *maqamat.* It is foolish for the weak to try to attack the strong since they lack the weapons. The powerful will always take whatever they want from the weak. The trick is to seem to have nothing that attracts them. One must pretend to be stupid in order to grow old. Put on a humble face and sneak into the abodes of the mighty. Attack from within, and do not be ashamed to hide humanity behind the mask of the hangman.

What Akki preaches in the second act he practices in the third. Humanity behind the hangman's mask is an important theme in the act, though it remains in the background of the swirling events and plot reversals that command the foreground. Akki has relatively few lines, and most of his utterances are ambiguous, intended to keep his identity and subversive activities hidden. Despite numerous death sentences in act 3, nobody is hanged. Thus, while he avoids overt acts of heroism, Akki manages to save whomever he can: the page he was ordered to hang, all the Babylonian poets, and ultimately Kurrubi, with whom he flees through the sandstorm—a visual reminder of the admonition that the powerless must be like the sand in order to survive.

Akki represents one of the two main story lines running through the play. Although he engages primarily in passive resistance to Nebuchadnezzar, he is the active protagonist, while his counterpart Kurrubi, carrying the other story line, remains passive. Around these two positively viewed protagonists swirls a constellation of major and minor characters ranging from ludicrous to shady to villainous. Despite the nihilism and Kurrubi's tragic fate, most of the play is couched in satirical comedy. Perhaps the mildest satire is reserved for the poets. The poets live off of Akki's generosity and are truly the poorest of the poor. A running gag throughout the play is how much various people earn relative to the salary of a poet. The poetry they compose is trite at best and always in doggerel, yet Dürrenmatt treats the poets as a class with dignity. They seem to have a higher understanding and appreciation of Kurrubi's beauty and perfection. We even see a few poets following her through the sandstorm at the end.

In the political philosophies of the rival kings can be found lofty words but little action that benefits the state. There is no difference for the common people, whether the liberal Nebuchadnezzar or the conservative Nimrod is on the throne.

To accentuate this, Dürrenmatt has them often speak the same lines simultaneously in the third act. The doubling of the kings in *Angel* mirrors the doubling of the ideologues in *Mississippi*. Neither king can change society for the better with his imposed social agenda. The apparatus of government has continued to grow unabated. Nebuchadnezzar has outlawed beggars, not poverty, and his grandiose-sounding social program has nothing of substance to differentiate it from Nimrod's capitalist initiatives. Although Dürrenmatt focuses on Nebuchadnezzar, he leaves no doubt that Nimrod would (and did) use his conservative philosophy to justify creating an equally excessive authoritarian society. Nebuchadnezzar's fanaticism about creating the perfect state, regardless of whatever inhuman means have to be employed in the process, places him in the immediate company of Mississippi and Saint-Claude, absolutist ideologues—grotesque types which Dürrenmatt rejects.

Nebuchadnezzar would not be the last to use the term "socialism" to justify acts of aggression against his own people. The Hitler parallels are too intentional, too obvious to be overlooked. Hitler, too, it should be remembered, took the beggars off the street. Misery was something that simply did not exist by definition in the Third Reich. More dangerous than Nebuchadnezzar's reality are his dreams. "The next step toward a rational society is to move against either the poets or the theologians" (FP 261). As theology proves to be a more useful momentary ally than literature, he decides to hang all the poets, and the playwrights too: "The perfect state cannot allow the spreading of untruths. Poets advertise feelings which do not exist, stories they make up themselves, and sentences which don't make sense" (FP 264). The totalitarian state must control the academies to insure obedience: "The study of theology must be insisted on throughout my empire. I shall have all other branches of learning forbidden" (FP 264). The king's answer to any threat to his power: "Mow the people down!" (FP 265). Nor does he feel safe unless he has the hangman near him. Quick to execute real and perceived enemies, to ban all ideas which do not support his theory of the perfect state, and to purge society of intellectuals; driven to conquer the world with his armies; and skilled at perverting the terms "social" and "socialist" into euphemisms for his totalitarian rule, "Nebby" is at best a thinly disguised Hitler—or Stalin.

The prime minister represents that type of survivor who can outlast any internecine struggle in government. "People like ourselves will always come out on top somehow" (FP 274). He is the pendant to Justice Minister Diego from *Mississippi*. A political weather vane, he has all the necessary documents for radical shifts in governmental philosophy drawn up in advance, including a Republican Constitution should the monarchy collapse. Utnapishtim, the chief theologian, is no better. Although he has written volumes against the existence of angels, he eagerly acknowledges them when, as a result of this angel's appearance, membership in the established church skyrockets. His condition for denouncing the Angel as an impostor in order to save the monarchy is half the national revenue. Both the prime minister and Utnapishtim betray Kurrubi as well, by attempting to force her to deny her divine origin: "The Minister betrayed her for reasons of state, the priest for the sake of his theology" (FP 285). The people betray Kurrubi because they cannot posses her on their own terms. The final betrayal is Nebuchadnezzar's, for the sake of his power: "You are alone. Heaven has forsaken you, mankind has rejected you. . . . Hangman. Take the maiden out into the desert. Kill her. Bury her in the sand" (FP 284).

Faced with so many Judases, we are compelled to see Kurrubi as a Christ figure. As a token of God's grace she is given to humanity. Specifically, she is intended to aid the poorest, most downtrodden of the race. Her special creation by God places her between God and humanity, or, in the Angel's words, "as eternal as nothingness, and as mortal as a human" (FP 205). At her creation not one single star but the entire Andromeda Galaxy shines brightly over Babylon. She requires of the king, who would possess her, that he give up all his worldly possessions. As a vision of "heavenly perfection," and created by God directly, not of mortal birth, Kurrubi is sinless, capable only of love and obedience to the will of her creator as she understands it from the mouth of the Angel. And in the end she is betrayed and scorned by the mob who in the previous act was hailing her as their queen, and turned over to the hangman—forsaken by heaven, rejected by humanity. The scene just before Nebuchadnezzar passes sentence on her, in which the crowd rejects her with cries of "Hand her over to the hangman!"—"Witch's brat!"—"She bewitched us."—"Death!" (FP 282) gives the drama unmistakable characteristics of a passion play.

However, these biblical allusions are themselves alienation techniques designed to make the audience attentive to a far different theological message. This is not a Christian play, another parable of humanity's unwillingness to see and accept God's grace. God creates Kurrubi and without a moment's delay gives her into the charge of the Angel. Yet Kurrubi does not come with an instruction book. She has received no guidance from God, and the Angel who brought her knows nothing about the human race or the earth. Worse yet, the Angel can only talk in generalities and platitudes and is unable to give meaningful answers to the child's questions: "What comes from the hand of him who created us we never understand, my child" (FP 205). If a resident of heaven who sees God face-to-face on a regular basis is so ignorant of his ways, what hope does this newly created child have—indeed, what hope does the human race have? Convinced of the perfection of creation, the Angel refuses to accept the fact that his charge is in mortal danger. He possesses the perfect bureaucratic mentality: What Kurrubi is experiencing cannot possibly be true, because by definition the opposite is true. Three times he abandons Kurrubi when she is most threatened, drowning out her cries for help by spouting Leibniz's philosophy of the best of all possible worlds. The affirmation from the Ninety-first Psalm, repeated in the temptation of Christ scene from Matthew—"For he will give his angels charge of you to guard you in all your ways"—is bitterly refuted here by an author who himself has lost patience with God. Christ felt momentarily abandoned by God; Kurrubi has been once and for all. All the semblances to a passion play have only served to emphasize this fact. Years later, referring to the absentminded deity of this play, Dürrenmatt claimed to have "no clue as to what God really means by creating this girl," and added: "We must unfortunately conclude that God does not know either. God's grace is not only unfathomable to us, but also to God" (25:147).

Dürrenmatt reserves his bitterest satire in *Angel* for God, who was growing more and more distant with every play and novel. Now God had finally and irrevocably disappeared behind the Andromeda Galaxy, out of sight and, from now on, out of mind. The Tower of Babel again failed to materialize. The announced sequel to *Angel* went unwritten. There would be no further attempt to strike at the heart of an opponent he no longer felt worthy. Dürrenmatt had shaken his fist skyward for the last time. No other character in play or novel would ever raise a cry to heaven in earnest again.

CHAPTER 6

The Radio Plays

Between 1946 and 1956 Dürrenmatt wrote eight radio plays. Of these, *Die Panne* later became a novella and finally a stage play, and *Herkules und der Stall des Augias* became a stage play. These two will be discussed in later chapters. Unlike stage plays, which are routinely revised and adapted, the radio play is unfortunately a dead genre. Its approaching obsolescence was already evident by the mid-fifties, when Dürrenmatt stopped writing for radio. In the early fifties, however, radio kept war-ravaged Germany together, and the importance of the radio play for a culture-starved populace at that time cannot be underestimated. It was a genre which gripped the imagination in ways conventional multi-sensory theater cannot. Like a well-told campfire story, a good literary radio play transported its listeners out of their immediate reality into an illusion which they helped create, and the imagination of each listener created the scene differently, aided by the engaging dialogue and sound effects. Switzerland's unique position among German-speaking countries in the initial postwar years—its theaters were intact and thriving—prevented the genre of the radio play from attaining the heights of popularity it achieved in Germany and Austria, where radio was allowing such authors as Ilse Aichenger, Ingeborg Bachmann, Heinrich Böll, Wolfgang Hildesheimer, and Günther Eich to reach wider audiences and was advancing their literary careers. Swiss radio stations did not pay as well as German stations. This fact, combined with the voracious appetite of German audiences for radio plays, made Germany a seller's market. All but one of Dürrenmatt's radio plays were first broadcast in Germany, a fact which aided Dürrenmatt's name recognition and popularity with potential German theater audiences. With the exception of *Der Doppelgänger,* all the radio plays are adaptable to the stage without much modification. *Nächtliches Gespräch* was staged in Munich in 1952, *Abendstunde* in Berlin in 1959. What has remained unadapted are museum pieces—monuments to the prevailing conditions in society and to the author's philosophical standpoint at the time of their inception. It is a museum well worth entering, for the pieces on display are some of Dürrenmatt's finer works of art, and it is in this original form that we shall proceed to examine them.[1]

"Thematically, *Der Doppelgänger* belongs to the world of *Die Stadt* and the early dramas."[2] This assertion by Armin Arnold is accurate, but it is also true that *Der Doppelgänger* (The Double) bears the clear fingerprint of Kafka and anticipates *Die Panne (Traps),* as well as *The Visit.* Although it received little acclaim and was rejected by Radio Bern in 1946, it is a seminal statement on the problems of guilt and justice, two of the red threads running through the author's lifework. The play is itself the process of creating a play, as the author, whose conversation with the director forms the frame of the plot, has only a general theme in mind. Several stops and restarts result from objections by the director concerning the logic of the story. Diego, the double of Pedro, enters the latter's bedroom in the middle of the night and informs him that he (Pedro) has been condemned to death by the high court. Diego has committed a murder for which Pedro has been accused, tried, and convicted in absentia. Unlike Kafka's Josef K., Pedro is presented with the guilty verdict at the outset. Analogous to Josef K's situation, however, is the secrecy and omnipotence of the court that convicted Pedro.

Pedro is arrested; his execution approaches. No one believes his story about a double. The second miraculous appearance of the double frees Pedro from his cell. Diego claims to be acting on orders of the high court. In the remainder of this night, Diego promises, he will bring Pedro to the recognition that he is a murderer, by causing him to commit murder. "Whom will I kill?" Pedro asks. "Me" replies Diego. He then takes Pedro to his home, where he springs his trap. Diego's wife Inez has been plotting Diego's murder and tries to enlist Pedro as her weapon. Pedro kills Inez precisely in order to keep from being guilty of his double's death. Diego has skillfully eliminated his wife using the unsuspecting Pedro as his weapon, but to Pedro this is the proof of the high court's contention. Had Pedro only admitted his guilt the first time instead of insisting upon his innocence, the double tells him, he (Diego) would gladly have died in his place. Pedro poisons Diego, then runs through the night back to the court to confess his murders. It is a sentiment of which Kafka would have approved. Everyone is a potential murderer, guilty by virtue of the human condition, condemned rightly in advance by God, who is the unseen highest authority,—or so it seems.

At this point, however, the director stops the play. Incensed over what he sees as an injustice, he demands to intervene and speak to Pedro. The author allows this, but Pedro is not to be swayed, convinced as he is of his guilt. Next the director demands to speak with the court. Author and director follow Pedro and the bailiff into the hall of justice, an impressive rococo palace, where they search for the court in vain. The palace is abandoned, dilapidated inside. The court is a *deus absconditus.* "And I should be content with this?" the director shouts. "We must be content with it" (GH 37), are the author's final words. In the absence of a higher authority, the human being is his own judge and jury. True recognition of guilt and true atonement must come from within.[3] Accepting personal guilt and embracing the consequences is for Dürrenmatt the highest form of justice, which leads to personal salvation. Alfred Ill will come to this realization as well ten years later, in *The Visit.*

Der Prozeß um des Esels Schatten (The Trial of the Donkey's Shadow), Dürrenmatt's second radio play, written in 1951, is based on *Geschichten der Abderiten* (Tales of the Abderites) by Christoph Martin Wieland (1733–1813), universal scholar, proponent of the Enlightenment, and one of Germany's most important classical poets and innovators in the genre of the novel. Dürrenmatt used, most uncharacteristically, a song by Bertolt Brecht, although he replaced this with one of his own in the revision. This is Dürrenmatt's first adaptation, and, as in his later adaptations of Shakespeare and Strindberg, he begins close to the source and ends far away from it. From Wieland is the premise and much of the early dialogue. Dürrenmatt simplifies the plot considerably, however, without diminishing the social satire. His modernizations are obvious, particularly in the emphasis on class-struggle between the proletariat who frequent the Latona Temple and the bourgeoisie who worship at the Jason Temple, an antagonism especially prominent in the speeches of the "Agitator of the Macedonian Workers' Party" and the president of the Senate. Modern, too, is the interest of the weapons industry in supplying both parties while fanning the flames of conflict. And timely six years after the end of World War II, yet timeless in its validity, is the observation of the High Priest Agathyrsus: "It has always begun with the adoration of a jackass and ended with mass murder. We know the symptoms" (GH 67).

As in Wieland's version, the dispute between the donkey drover Anthrax and the dentist Struthion over whether the latter, in renting a donkey for a day's journey, also rented the donkey's shadow, ends up in court. Struthion merely wanted to rest in the donkey's shadow, for which Anthrax demanded two drachmas more. As the Abderite magistrate Philippides suffers from his usual indecision, and as two lawyers happen by at the wrong time and smell a profit, the case escalates. The donkey is confiscated as evidence, and the lawyers promise their clients large settlements for which they charge exorbitant fees. For Anthrax in Dürrenmatt's version this means pawning his furniture and eventually selling his wife. Both parties change their lifestyles to influence the judges, and both use connections to get to the judges more directly. Finally the verdict is a five-to-five split. Two parties form: the Donkey Party, favoring Anthrax, and the Shadow Party, favoring Struthion.

At this point Dürrenmatt takes the plot in a new direction. Once ideologies are involved the story cannot have a harmless outcome. Unlike Wieland's version, in which the people make a scapegoat out of the donkey and thereby save themselves from civil war, Dürrenmatt's Abderites have committed the greatest stupidity possible in the author's eyes: they have succumbed to ideologies. The Shadows have adopted "progress" as their slogan, while the Donkeys stand for "traditional values." When the drunken sea captain Typhis—Dürrenmatt's addition to the plot—accepts bribes from both parties and sets both the Latona Temple and the Jason Temple ablaze in the same night, the obstinacy of the ideologues manifests itself. Half of the firemen are Shadows and half are Donkeys. They refuse to cooperate, for cooperation would mean compromising their principles. As they argue the fire spreads from the temples and consumes the town. Dürrenmatt gives the last word in this satire to the donkey, which is running for its life from the angry mob: "Since I have, in a way, the leading role in this tale, don't be angry with me and answer me honestly with a clear conscience, as I now perish miserably from the arrows of your brothers: *Was I the jackass in this story?*" (GH 87).

Dürrenmatt's shortest radio play is his most problematic. *Nächtliches Gespräch mit einem verachteten Menschen* (Nocturnal Conversation with a Despised Person) with the subtitle "A Course for Contemporaries" is a modern version of a medieval dance of death. This motif will recur much later in the drama *The Meteor.* Here, however, it is reduced to its simplest form: a debate between death and a single victim. Death comes through the window in the form of a hangman sent by the state. His victim is a writer in a time of anti-intellectual repression. As in *Der Doppelgänger,* the death sentence has already been passed by a Kafkaesque authority beyond the comprehension of the reader or victim. The hangman is a valid death figure to the extent that he knows only death. How people live is a matter for curiosity on his part; how they die is his area of expertise. The writer, who has long known the hangman would eventually come, expected a younger, more powerful adversary. The listener can only assume that the victim could easily overpower the hangman, who must be at least seventy years old. That the victim does not resort to violence is a logical result of his intellect. The hangman has not come on his own initiative, but on orders from the state, from whose verdict the writer cannot escape. The other reason the scene proceeds without physical resistance is inherent in the genre. A dance of death has a certain prescribed form it must follow. Foremost is the fact that once the death figure appears, the victim's fate is sealed. Physical force is as useless as the intellectual arguments often advanced by the victim. While Death traditionally takes people of all stations in society,

Dürrenmatt reduces the dance here to one victim and extends the arguments to achieve full didactic potential.

There is, however, a major difference between this play and the traditional dance of death. There Death is exclusively God's messenger; here the hangman is the servant of a Godless state and suffers from a bad conscience. There each person's death fulfills a preordained divine purpose; here the victim has the choice to either die a meaningless death or to give it meaning. Like Josef K., the victim in this play will die in the middle of the night, alone without any witnesses. But whereas Josef K. had to die like a dog, Dürrenmatt's victim has the option to die with dignity. The dialogue with the hangman is a course in how to accomplish this—a course for contemporaries. What the protagonist learns from the hangman is the result of the latter's accumulated experience from fifty years: the virtues of death with humility. Precisely those guiltless victims who die humbly defeat the hangman and the worldly authority whose servant he is. In his final speech he ceases to function as a lackey of temporal tyranny and becomes for a moment the death figure in his traditional theological role. "I can take your body, Sir," he reasons, "that is given over to worldly authority, for everything which crumbles to dust is subjected to it, but that for which you have fought, over that I have no power, for it does not belong to the dust" (GH 108). In the flesh of the violated and abused, by means of which the tyrants construct their castles, is embedded "knowledge of how the world should be, the memory of why God created the earth, and the belief that this world must crumble in order that his kingdom come" (GH 109). As water has the power to reduce rocks to dust, this knowledge will eventually grind the castles of the mighty to sand.

Those who die humbly like children, peacefully, against all logic, reveal "the powerlessness of the unjust, the insubstantiality of death and the reality of truth over which I have no power, which no sheriff seizes and no prison holds, of which I know nothing more than that it is, for every brutal man is imprisoned in the dark windowless dungeon of his self" (GH 109). Death's advice is to concentrate on that which is not under the power of temporal authority, that part of the human being which cannot be broken and ultimately will carry the victory. Grace is possible in this play, as it was in *Es steht geschrieben,* but only to the unique chosen individual to whom God deigns to speak—here through his messenger the hangman—and only at the boundary between life and death where the individual can be receptive to that grace. The year is 1951, two years before *Angel.* Now thirty years old, Dürrenmatt felt the faith of his father burning in him as strongly as it ever had or ever would again. Within a couple years at most it would flicker out.

With *Stranitzky und der Nationalheld* (Stranitzky and the National Hero) it appears we are back in Abdera. After all, Wieland concluded that after the Abderites abandoned their mouse- and frog-ridden homeland, they scattered to the four corners of the earth, multiplied fruitfully, and continue to live among us. The modern Abderites in this play worship a national hero named Baldur von Moeve,[4] whose supposed heroism is never explained beyond the mention of participation in a pair of minor military skirmishes. Moeve underscores his phoniness by quoting the classics, even comparing himself in his suffering to Goethe's Faust. Self-justification by hypocrites through quoting the classics or speaking in classical style is a beloved theme of Dürrenmatt's. Examples include Wood in *Das Unternehmen der Wega*, Petit-Paysan in *Once a Greek...*, Frank the Fifth, and the chorus of Güllener at the conclusion of *The Visit*. In contrast to Moeve are two poor invalids, Stranitzky and Anton, who lost their legs and eyes respectively in the service of their country. They now enjoy a symbiotic partnership: Stranitzky acting as Anton's eyes and Anton as Stranitzky's legs. When the national hero returns from a trip to Ethiopia with a leprous big toe, the entire country goes into mourning. For Stranitzky and Anton, who survive as beggars, the alms cup is suddenly empty. Everyone is contributing to the Moeve fund and buying patriotic Moeve placards instead. Moeve's serialized interview "I Suffer" increases the circulation of the periodical that carries it to four million, and his forthcoming book promises to break records. While the print media fight over rights to publish photographs of the leprous toe, the real sufferers—Anton, Stranitzky, and the other low-income residents of their slum—fade further into obscurity.

Hyperbole makes good satire, and Moeve's toe is a well-chosen model of a triviality that the press can easily sensationalize to sell newspapers, especially where the cult of the personality is involved. This press feeding-frenzy is similar to the one that will follow Claire Zachanassian's every move in *The Visit*. However, there is another aspect to this story as significant as the gullibility of a sensation-starved populace, the exploitation of that populace by unscrupulous journalists, or the misguided hero-worship of the powerful by the powerless. At its core, this play is about responsible action in the face of ill-fortune. Certainly Stranitzky is a double victim: first of a war that took his legs and thereby his livelihood (he was a professional soccer player), and again when the unwarranted attention to the phony hero Moeve deprives him of his only remaining source of income. But Stranitzky is also a fool, the biggest Abderite in the play. When the state offers him a pair of prosthetic legs, he refuses. He also rejects Marie, a woman who loves him and wants to care for him as he is. Suffering from the delusion that society owes him much more, he chooses to beg until he can get his chance at wealth and power. This he erroneously believes has come when reporter J. P. Whiteblacke arranges for him and Anton to meet Moeve. The reporter merely wants a story, but the megalomaniac Stranitzky believes he has been summoned for a higher purpose. This delusion costs him his third foolish mistake, buying new furniture and delicacies for his victory party on credit.

The trip in a Buick to Moeve's hospital suite is a fairy tale, a meteoric ride to apparent fame and glory. The crash to earth comes with the evening news. His sermon to Moeve about the plight of the poor and his offer to help the national hero form the next government is edited out of the tape. Moeve had only been seeking a public relations stunt by giving two invalids pictures of himself. Stranitzky's disillusionment over his brief rise to glory and ignominious crash has fatal consequences. As a result of suicide or bad luck Stranitzky, riding on Anton's back, ends up in the river, unaware or unconcerned that the one person whose love could have saved him, Marie, was chasing and calling to him.

Dürrenmatt's aversion to ideologies, which had been the subject of *Der Prozeß um des Esels Schatten* in 1951, *The Marriage of Mr. Mississippi* in 1952, and *An Angel Comes to Babylon* in 1953, achieved its most cynical manifestation up to that time in the radio play from 1954 *Das Unternehmen der Wega* (Operation Vega). Ideologies have now brought the earth to the brink of World War III. The moon is in Russian hands. Mars has declared neutrality and is strong enough to enforce it. Only Venus remains in doubt. In 1954, of course, nobody knew what lies under Venus's thick cloud layer, and Dürrenmatt can certainly be excused for positing a barely inhabitable environment there. Venus is the penal colony for the entire earth. The Free United States of Europe and America send common criminals as well as undesirables who espouse Communist ideas; while Russia with its allies Asia, Africa, and Australia send common criminals as well as undesirables with Western leanings. The heat, continual rain, sulphurous air and drinking water, volcanos, earthquakes, monstrous animals, and poisonous plants make Venus a hell, and yet the last American and Russian commissars sent to monitor the planet have refused to return to earth.

The mission of the spaceship *Vega* is to convince the inhabitants of Venus to ally with the United States against Russia. They carry promises of amnesty after the war, but they also carry hydrogen bombs for the eventuality that the inhabitants should refuse. What the delegation, led by foreign minister Sir Horace Wood, finds is incomprehensible to them. There is no government on Venus with which to negotiate. There is also no war, no crime, and no ideologies— only cooperation. The colonists live in crude boats on the seas because the land is too unstable. They hunt whales together, the only thing edible on the planet.

They survive without medicine and technology. The great lesson of Venus, that has caused the American commissar Bonstetten and his Russian counterpart to defect, is simply that "the human being is something precious and his life is an act of grace" (GH 237). Amnesty is out of the question, for no colonist would accept it. Told of the bombs, Bonstetten is unmoved. The inhabitants live with death every day. The war back on earth is completely irrelevant to them, Bonstetten assures Wood. There is no way they would side with either ideology. They wish only to be left alone.

Safely back on the ship Wood lets his old suspicions resurface. Inaction is too risky. They could, after all, still ally with the Russians. Predictably, Wood orders the bombs dropped, after promising Bonstetten he would not do so. In the name of his ideology Wood becomes a mass murderer of an innocent civilization—one that has created a paradise out of a hell. It is easy for Wood to appease his conscience afterward. He was, after all, just following orders—an excuse so transparent in the wake of the Nürnberg trials that no listener should be fooled by Wood's false-tragic stance.[5] The bombs were on board by direct order of the president, and Bonstetten really could not be trusted. But Wood's life will soon get easier. As a government official he has a comfortable bomb shelter. There he looks forward to spending the war in peace reading the classics.

In his final radio play, Dürrenmatt turned his satirical wit on his own profession. *Episode on an Autumn Evening* (*Abendstunde im Spätherbst*) is essentially a dialogue between the Nobel Prize–winning mystery writer Maximilian Friedrich Korbes and the detective Fürchtegott Hofer, although other characters intrude briefly. The play is elliptical, in that its opening paragraph is also its closing one. The scripted introduction with which the author Korbes begins the play is theoretically not written down until the end, because the subject of the play is the event leading up to its writing. This last radio play betrays the mature Dürrenmatt. It is most consistent with his method of operation in the masterworks. A particular *Einfall* (witty idea) forms the point of departure, here the fact that a Nobel Prize–winning author of mysteries committed all the murders about which he wrote. The detective Hofer can only be commended for his brilliantly constructed case against Korbes. He has spared no expense, ruining himself financially in order to reconstruct twenty-two murders and link all but one to the author. However, the "worst possible turn" trips Hofer at his triumphal moment, because he belongs to that class of Dürrenmatt's refuted heros who, according to Ulrich Profitlich, achieve unqualified success, only to find that their heroic efforts have been a "superfluous waste of energy."[6]

It is Hofer's misfortune to come from a small village and only to read reputable newspapers. He cannot know what everyone knows who reads the tabloids, and so he has proven what needed no proof. Hofer may be the last person alive to come to the realization that Korbes's novels are based on personal experience. Hofer's weak attempt to blackmail Korbes is equally futile, because the latter's murders are sanctioned at the highest levels. No court in the world would prosecute him. He gives the reading public that for which it thirsts, realistic bloody murder. Korbes's study is full of letters from women of all social classes offering to be his next victim. But none of them will be, because Hofer has just given Korbes an idea for a radio play, and Korbes needs money.

There are a number of reasons to assume that Dürrenmatt identifies with Korbes. They have the name Friedrich in common, as well as a visceral animosity toward critics. Kenneth Whitton notes that Korbes's house is an exact replica of Dürrenmatt's house in Neuchâtel.[7] Korbes's statement that he must write a radio play because he needs the money has an autobiographical ring to it. The telling fingerprint, however, is Korbes's correction of the term *Dichter,* with which Hofer addresses him, to *Schriftsteller.* Both words mean "author" in German, but *Dichter* implies a writer of poetry, or at least a writer of a higher, idealistic form of literature. In an essay published the same year as the radio play, 1956, entitled "Schriftstellerei als Beruf" (Writing as a Profession), Dürrenmatt differentiates the terms at the outset and proclaims himself a *Schriftsteller,* implying that the term *Dichter* was often used among members of the profession to imply that the individual could "compose" but could not write.

That Dürrenmatt is polemicizing through this radio play is obvious. But what is his agenda? In the above-mentioned essay he discusses the plight of the writer in Switzerland. Writing is a business. On the one hand, the writer wants and needs to be free, not bound to one acceptable norm like writers in the Communist bloc. On the other hand, the price of this freedom is the necessity to compete on the open market. The Swiss, he wrote, like their literature full of high ideals, in contrast to their daily lives in the business world. But Switzerland is too small, so the writer is forced to export his products to markets with different standards. In particular he mentions West German radio and television as being hungry for material. He concludes with the pragmatic warning: "In general the writer does well to be guided by the marketplace. He learns to write thus, to write artfully, to do his thing under imposed conditions. Earning money is a writer's stimulant (GW 7: 418)."

"Once I'd grasped what the world wants, I proceeded to deliver it," Korbes proclaims. Before learning that lesson, he had tried it the other way around. "As a young man I tried being a literary stylist. All it got me was a few pats on the shoulder from some minor local editors. Aside from that, no one gave a damn."[8] Dürrenmatt is being his most provocative self in the essay and through his fictional mouthpiece Korbes. His target is Swiss critics who wanted to hold him to the classical ideals demanded of writers by the Zürich literary pope Professor Emil Staiger. Ten years later Dürrenmatt and Staiger would be at each other's throats in the famous *Zürcher Literaturstreit* (Zürich Literary Dispute), which Dürrenmatt seemed to be already trying to provoke.

Korbes has long since put the critics behind him. Dürrenmatt's warning between the lines in the essay, that writers rejected in Switzerland can make more money marketing their wares in Germany, mirrors what Korbes has done in the play. He has gone from local rejection to international acclaim, precisely by abandoning the straightjacket of stylistics and lofty classical ideals and giving the public what it wanted. *Episode* amounts to a gauntlet thrown down to the critics. He threw it at a point in his career when he could finally back it up. Nineteen fifty-six was the year that Dürrenmatt achieved international fame, the year in which *The Visit* premiered. However, unlike Korbes, Dürrenmatt never got rid of the critics.

CHAPTER 7

Consolation from Dürrenmatt

A Romantic Fairy Tale: *Grieche sucht Griechin (Once a Greek...)*

In 1955, at the same time he was working on *The Visit,* Dürrenmatt wrote this romantic fairy tale about reality. Its protagonist, an intolerable ideologue, has few illusions about changing the world, but he is quite convinced that the world can never change him. *Once a Greek*... is as unambiguous a statement on the nature of love and grace as Dürrenmatt ever wrote: unique in its simplicity and even more so in its optimism. Love and grace finally come down to earth, though certainly not in the way Kurrubi came down to earth. No Andromeda Galaxy hangs over the fictionalized Paris of the novel as it did over the anachronistic Babylon of the play. The gift of grace that comes to the protagonist in the novel is not sent, she comes of her own free will. She is not perfect creation, preprogrammed to goodness; rather, she is totally of this world, a mistress of sensuality. The symbol of the grace that permeates this work is no longer the broad expanse of heaven but the narrow confines of a *Himmelbett* (canopy bed).

The basic plot of *Once a Greek*..., stripped of its social, political, and religious satire, is as straightforward as its message. In a fantastic European city in which opulence and decay are both in abundance, a humble and religious man of Greek origin places a personal ad in the newspaper seeking a Greek woman to marry. Chloé, the woman who meets him at Madame Bieler's cafe that Sunday morning and announces her intention to marry him, is beautiful and well-dressed, but she is able to convince her naive partner that she is a servant girl. Archilochos, the young Greek, lives in poverty himself, holding the lowest level job in a huge industrial concern and supporting the family of his unemployed brother, Bibi. During the next two days Archilochos rises to a director level in the company and experiences so much other good fortune that he cannot comprehend what is happening. At his wedding, however, attended by all the dignitaries in the city, he realizes to his horror what has taken place. He has married a courtesan, and all her former customers have given him wealth and power as their wedding gifts. Disillusioned, he attempts suicide but is rescued by the notorious anarchist Fahrcks (a former customer of his bride), who convinces him to avenge himself on society by assassinating the president (also

Chloé's customer). Archilochos does not throw the grenade at the decisive moment, however, because the president is not in his bed, but rather in the kitchen having a midnight snack. There he and Archilochos talk, and the president convinces him that he has been blessed, and if he can accept the love that his bride wants to give him unconditionally he can make something beautiful out of something ugly. At the conclusion of the novel Archilochos returns to find not his bride at home, but the family of his ne'er-do-well brother carousing in his house. Enraged, he beats his brother senseless and throws the family bodily out of the house. In an alternate ending Archilochos goes to Greece and finds his bride again. Although there is a difference of opinion among critics and scholars on this point, the endings are not mutually exclusive. The second ending simply carries the fairy tale further to its obligatory happy conclusion—not Dürrenmatt's usual worst possible ending—and contains Chloé's final, important statement on love. The reader should not be fooled by the disparaging title: "Ending for Lending Libraries."[1]

Arnolph Archilochos—his name immediately brings to mind the German word "Arschloch" (asshole)[2]—is only a Greek by a long stretch of the imagination. His most recent ancestor from Greece died alongside Charles the Brave fighting the Burgundians at Nancy in 1477. He looks anything but Greek with his "plumpish, graceless, rather northern-looking frame."[3] He speaks no Greek, nor does he profess Greek orthodoxy. Yet for Archilochos the most important thing is order. Everything must fit neatly into a category. His identification is with his name and a little-known ancestor from the distant past. We almost hear the words of Nebuchadnezzar, another great stickler for categories: "It is of utmost importance to mankind that everyone should stick to his own name. Everybody should be who he is" (FP 210). Thus, Archilochos will only consider marrying a Greek woman.

Archilochos has assembled an "ethical cosmos," a hierarchy of role models, whose pictures he has on his wall: The president of the republic is number one, followed by Bishop Moser of his church; Petit-Paysan, the owner of the company that employs him; and a number of other luminaries including the lawyer Maître Dutour, a modern artist named Passap, the American ambassador, and the Rector Magnificus of the university. The final position of honor is held by his parasitic and criminally inclined brother, Bibi. The latter's presence in the ethical cosmos results from a congenital blind spot Archilochos has toward his family. Bibi, he argues, is a good and sensitive human being, if one looks past the exterior to the core. The discrepancy between the reality of each of the figures in his moral pantheon and his own hagiographic projection of them is greater in some cases than others, yet in every case the protagonist is in for a shock. With a naivete rivaling that of the Christian ideologue Count Bodo or the Angel, Archilochos transfers his ideal view of innate human goodness onto those in power, and even onto brother Bibi, transforming them in his mind into paragons of his very own brand of morality.

Religious dogma is very important to Archilochos. As a member of the Church of the "Old-New Presbyterians of the Penultimate Christians," he draws fine but vital distinctions between his beliefs and those of the "Old Presbyterians" or of the "New Presbyterians." Even in his rare moments of passion his priorities are always straight: "Chloé," he groans, as his fiancée draws him toward her onto the canopy bed, "I haven't yet explained to you the fundamental dogmas of the Old New Presbyterian Church" (OG 121). Besides regular church attendance—he is there more often than the pastor—he practices vegetarianism and strict abstinence from alcohol and tobacco. His abode is more than humble. Even at his paltry salary as the lowest bookkeeper, he could afford better than his garret next to the public toilet, were it not for his sense of Christian duty in supporting Bibi's family. With such a Spartan lifestyle and such rigid rules to live by, Archilochos relies on his "ethical cosmos" to give him a beacon by which to guide.

Chloé Saloniki comes into Archilochos's world from the opposite end of the reality spectrum. She knows exactly how immoral the world really is, and she longs to change that reality for herself. The name Chloé suggests one knowledgeable in love: Chloé, beloved of Daphnis, whose name in Greek means the one who is germinating or budding. Saloniki suggests the salon, the elegant world from which she enters this fairy tale.[4] She has no intention of deceiving Archilochos: "I came in my best clothes. As I wanted to accept you as you were, I meant you to accept me as I was" (OG 176). Chloé, the best-known and highest priced courtesan in the city, becomes for the starry-eyed Archilochos a Dulcinea figure in reverse. Quixote's totally subjective transformation of the Toboso pig-girl into noble lady finds its inverse in the idealization of a rich prostitute into a poor and humble paragon of virtue. Chloé's tall tale about abject poverty, of growing up a street urchin before being taken in as a servant girl by world-renowned archaeologists, is ludicrous in contrast to the fur coat and jewelry she wears to their first meeting. What the rest of the city knows, fails to register with Archilochos. One is tempted to call him stupid; however, it is a combination of naivete and dogged idealism rather than low intelligence that holds him back. Chloé, for her part, is a keen enough judge of human nature to realize that the truth up front would destroy the man she loves. Her task is to educate Archilochos not only about love, of which he knows nothing, but also about the nature of the world. The second lesson contains the serious risks.

Chapters 4 through 20, the fairy tale within the fairy tale, chronicle Archilochos's meteoric rise to general director of two divisions of the Petit-Paysan Machine Company, member of the World Consistency of the Old-New Presbyterians, Honorary Doctor of Medicine, Honorary Consul of the United States, and millionaire with a small baroque palace. The careful reader will have figured out Chloé's profession and its connection to Archilochos's fortune by the end of chapter 10 at the latest. By chapter 16 everyone understands it—except the protagonist. His improbable rise begins on Sunday morning when, for the first time in Chloé's company, Archilochos is unexpectedly greeted by all the luminaries in his moral world order. Since he believes Chloé's fable about her humble origins and status as a maid to the British archaeologists the Weemans, it does not occur to him that she could be the catalyst for this sudden recognition. The discrepancy between Chloé's story and her appearance is now obvious to the reader. Madame Bieler estimates that Chloé's jewelry must be worth hundreds of thousands of francs, not to mention her fur coat and perfume. Chloé's embarrassed pauses at key moments add further cause for suspicion: when Archilochos first calls her a *Mädchen,* (a word for girl implying innocence) for example, or when she is trying to invent the details of her life story and cannot immediately come up with the name "Weeman." The reactions of several of the luminaries who greet Archilochos and Chloé are also comically transparent: Bishop Moser slinks away into the nearest side street, while Maître Dutour and the Rector Magnificus wave barely perceptibly, because they have their "enormous" wives at their sides.[5] And at the end of the magical evening, as Archilochos takes his bride home to the palace where she lives, Chloé even stands illuminated by a red light hanging in the portal.

In the face of overwhelming evidence—presented with charming wit and irony—Archilochos remains steadfastly ignorant of Chloé's identity. Passap's intimate acquaintance with Chloé's anatomy and the fact that he painted her nude causes only temporary wonderment. Believing the baroque palace he has just been given formerly belonged to the Weemans, Archilochos cannot figure out why Chloé is sleeping in Mrs. Weeman's bed, or why the gaunt, boyish Mrs. Weeman would have pictures of naked men and women on her walls, or what the mysterious trail of stars and comets leading to the bed could possibly mean. Even when two servants in the palace tell him that they work for "Mademoiselle Chloé," he passes it off as a misunderstanding, nor does the fact that Maître Dutour is well acquainted with the rear exit of the palace arouse any suspicion. When Arnolph asks Maître Dutour "'Oh . . . you know my dear fiancée?'" the duplicitous reply seems directed right past him at the reader: "I have had the pleasure" (OG 112).

After his two transforming experiences—the disillusionment of discovering Chloé's true identity and the healing discourse on love that he hears from the president—Archilochos begins to drink alcohol, to smoke, and to eat meat; symbolic of the break with that extreme dogmatic religiosity which had been a symptom of his emotional immaturity. The final step in his maturation process is his refusal to put up with Bibi and his entourage any longer. Archilochos is transformed momentarily into a Hellenistic hero: Odysseus. In a battle of mock-Homeric proportions Archilochos cleans house of Bibi, his whole family, and their murdering, thieving compatriots. In his tattered wedding tuxedo, Archilochos stares out of swollen eyes, his glasses lost. Indicated here are not only the glasses he wears for nearsightedness, but more importantly the metaphorical rose-colored glasses that had been obscuring his view of reality.

A vertical cross-section of society is represented by the administrative skyscraper of the Petit-Paysan Machine Company. The Kafkaesque atmosphere of the lower floors, where the legions of bookkeepers and assistant bookkeepers work at glass and steel tables in rows, the impersonality (everyone has a number rather than a name), and the intense jealousy and paranoia infecting the work force at every level make for excellent satire. Dürrenmatt reserves his most uncompromising barbs for the man at the top: Petit-Paysan. His name ("little peasant") is ironic and harmless sounding, but behind it lurks a very dangerous man with his false modesty and even falser humanism. In his penthouse office with the priceless art treasures on the wall, Petit-Paysan is ignorant of much that goes on even a few floors below him. The existence of Archilochos's division, obstetric forceps, is a total surprise to the boss. He thought that the Greek worked in the atomic cannon division. So he merely combines the two divisions and makes Archilochos director of atomic cannons and forceps, justifying the merger with an absurd rationalization: "I suppose it is more or less a humanitarian division. Good to think that in addition to things that remove human beings from the world we also manufacture things that bring them into it" (OG 66).

A weapons manufacturer with such perverse powers of rationalization is a dangerous man indeed. However, Petit-Paysan also draws solace from literature, which he misinterprets. He greets Archilochos with a volume of Hölderlin's poetry in his hand. One poem has particularly moved him. "The Archipelago" is a beautiful homage to Greece's golden age and a dream of its restoration in modern times. The poem's central figure, a merchant, is declared to be as beloved of the gods as are the poets, for his motives are pure. His vessel is a symbol of unity, distributing the gifts of the earth, uniting near and far. By misinterpreting the adjective *fernhinsinnend* (thinking of far away), Petit-Paysan

76

transforms the peaceful merchant into a "far-sighted" industrialist, who over-looks individual fates in order to concentrate on the big picture: crushing the competition at the highest levels. Hölderlin's peaceful merchant vessel becomes a gunboat on the high seas of the international arms trade, and the poem is perverted to justify Petit-Paysan's ruthless business practices.

The novel treats love and grace, the two elusive virtues which, in *Angel,* were combined in the figure of Kurrubi and subsequently lost to the human race. Between the last play and this novel, however, lies a caesura. Dürrenmatt has come down to earth. Whereas previous to *Once a Greek . . .* the question always turned on "God's love" or "God's grace," for which humans strived, it is now and henceforth simply "love" and "grace." Although the concepts have lost nothing of their wonder, are still incomprehensible and thus retain a certain numinous quality, they have lost their connection with theology and have become human terms. Even Bishop Moser, from whom a theologically grounded justification for Archilochos's miracle could be expected, fails to mention God once in his explanation.[6] Senior director in Petit-Paysan's company and member of the World Church Consistency in the same day—and now the bishop is being called upon to explain how this could be happening to such a "lamentable existence" as Arnolph Archilochos's. In place of the expected God's-ways-are-unfathomable speech, which Kurrubi heard from the Angel, the bishop walks skillfully around the question, managing not to lie. The reasons, he says, are unimportant, for they lie in the human sphere. What is important instead is what all this means: "You are a blessed person" (OG 89), the bishop tells him. How he accepts these blessings will determine whether he was really worthy to receive them.

This is self-serving advice—the bishop has also slept with Chloé—but this fact does not detract from its value for Archilochos or invalidate it in general, because it is the author's advice as well. If "grace" could only be "God's grace," definable only in a teleological context—that is, existing only as the conscious act of a benevolent deity—then it could not possibly lie "in the sphere of human beings," and the bishop's advice would be absurd. However, this is no longer Dürrenmatt's definition of the concept. He equates grace with chance. "For me, grace is also related to coincidence. Actually it always occurs in my works in a contrary sense. Just look at Kurrubi's development. . . . Grace has to do with chance, for if anything is incalculable, it is grace. I would say that for me, grace is an existential signal."[7] If grace is an elemental experience for the author, fundamental to his existence, then he can rightfully call it, as he does, a "religious" experience. However, as he is quick to emphasize, "religious" always belongs in quotation marks.[8] A grace that goes hand in hand with coincidence can hardly be grounded in teleology, and absent divine supervision, with only chance pulling the strings, there is truly reason for Archilochos to fear that this grace could at any time and for any reason turn into nemesis.

In this fairy tale, however, chance is not the final instance, and it is this fact which affords *Once a Greek* . . . its unique status among Dürrenmatt's works. What happened to Archilochos was initially brought about by chance. Chloé decided to retire from her profession and dedicate her love to just one man at the very moment when Archilochos published his intention to marry a Greek woman. Further, when she saw him in his naivete and helplessness, she unexpectedly fell in love with him. What occurs later—everything in the first half of the novel which appears to the protagonist to be coincidence—is a direct result of that other component of grace: Chloé's love. It is the president who adds this second part to the equation, while reiterating the bishop's admonition about grace:

A grace has been conferred upon you. . . . There are two possible reasons for this grace, and it depends upon you which of them is the valid one: love, if you believe in that love, or evil, if you do not believe in that love. Love is a miracle that is eternally possible; evil is a fact that is eternally present. Justice condemns evil, hope longs to reform it, and love overlooks it. Only love is capable of accepting grace as it is. There is nothing more difficult, I know. The world is terrible and meaningless. The hope of finding a meaning behind all the meaninglessness, behind all the terror, can be preserved only by those who nevertheless can love. (OG 164–65)

The president, and through him Dürrenmatt, has in few words defined love as infinite possibility, as the catalyst to all that is good and just—in many ways similar to the Pauline definition of love from the Letter to the Corinthians, with one very significant difference. Paul's *agape* is love between human beings and God which, in the context of the Christian community, extends to love of neighbor, often translated as "charity." Theologian Karl Barth, whose early and powerful influence on the author has already been discussed, writes in his exegesis of the *Letter to the Romans*—a treatise Dürrenmatt devoured as a student—little of a comforting nature about humanity's ability to love God. Distilled to its essence, Barth's message is that the ability to love God is not given freely to us. Those few privileged to do so are those "who are called according to his purpose." God has opened a wide gulf between himself and his creation and "deprives man of every possibility save one of returning his love." Barth speaks in good Calvinist terms of the "foreordained," those select few who even before their birth were ordained to seek and know him.[9] Thus God chooses who can love him, and for those not selected, no human initiative can bridge the chasm.

Clearly a time came when Dürrenmatt simply could no longer tolerate Barth's (or Calvin's) theology of exclusion, the same brand of theology with which he was raised, a theology which eliminates most of the human race from participation in *agape*. The point in his literature at which this rejection became obvious is *Angel*. Kurrubi wandering through the sandstorm is an extreme caricature of the Barthian perspective, God's love with too many strings attached, seeking in vain for the elusive elect, so narrowly defined that it has ceased to exist. In *Once a Greek . . .* for the first time love and grace are freed from the fetters of theology. The courtesan succeeds the Angel, *eros* replaces *agape,* and Archilochos enjoys, at least in the second variant, that which Nebuchadnezzar was denied: a happy ending. The great ability of love to transform life triumphs in the fairy tale, a power at last that can accomplish what ideologies cannot.

In *Once a Greek . . .* Dürrenmatt has succeeded in secularizing grace and love—almost. Both remain elusive concepts in the final analysis. Is coincidence really blind? In Dürrenmatt's dramatic theory it functions to bring about the worst possible turn of plot, and in this role it seems to have a sixth sense about when to strike. And can Chloé's love for the overweight, naive, and helpless Archilochos really be understood? She herself is not able to put it into words if she does understand. It was something which happened unexpectedly: ". . . and when I saw you sitting at the table, . . . I fell in love with you" (OG 176). It is a miracle that is always possible, but a miracle nevertheless. So grace and love remained in a certain way "religious" experiences for Dürrenmatt— but please, always in quotation marks.

CHAPTER 8

The Corruption of Justice

Der Besuch der alten Dame (The Visit)

"Would you commit a murder for a million dollars if you knew you could not be arrested?" Most people would immediately reject the possibility of murder for money out of either a religious or humanistic sense of morality. Although the question becomes trickier when conditions are added—"Would you commit murder for a million dollars if you were very poor?"—most people would answer as does the mayor of Güllen: "We would rather have poverty than blood on our hands."[1] Taking this question one step further in order to render the moral dilemma more acute, one might ask: "Would you, for a million dollars, kill the person directly responsible for your (and the community's) poverty?" Most people still would not go as far as murder. From here, however, the distance is not so great to that final rationalization which renders the question in this form: "Are you willing to execute an evildoer and rid society of an injustice in exchange for a million dollars?" With each succeeding variant of the question, the individual's degree of moral guilt appears to lessen. When changed from individual guilt to participation in collective guilt, this already decreasing moral burden becomes even further diluted. Thus Dürrenmatt poses the question to his audience: "How much rationalization is required before murder becomes justice?"

A second, related question asked in the first act is: " Can justice be bought?" "I'm giving you a million and I'm buying myself justice" Claire announces.[2] The mayor replies, astonished: "Justice can't be bought." "Everything can be bought" (V 36), the old lady answers. Dürrenmatt spends the next two acts proving her right, but the townspeople are blind to that proof because the powers of rationalization have put a veneer of respectability on the transaction. Justice is another of Dürrenmatt's "religious" concepts. Through the early plays he was literally wrestling with divine justice, which was inextricably joined with the concept of God's grace. Humans could neither comprehend it, nor approximate it on earth. They could only attempt to play God, an endeavor doomed to failure from the outset. Now, in The Visit, justice comes under scrutiny as in no other previous play, examined as intensely as was the concept of love in Once a Greek... There love was distinguished as to its lower and higher forms: blind love based on illusion, and ennobling love that sees and overlooks faults, and which alone can be given unconditionally. In *The Visit* Dürrenmatt achieves the same dichotomy within the concept of justice. "The play posits justice twice: as the result of guilt it can be demanded, and is thereby corruptible; as insight into guilt it can only be effected by the guilty" (25:149). So justice is corruptible, but only in its common form. Dürrenmatt makes each form of justice the basis of its own plot line and sets them masterfully on a collision course.

On its surface, the plot of *The Visit* is one of Dürrenmatt's least complicated. Claire Zachanassian, the richest woman in the world, returns to her impoverished native village to demand justice for a wrong done her in her youth. The shopkeeper Alfred Ill, the most popular man in town, had impregnated and abandoned her forty years before, causing her to be run out of town. She demands his death and will pay the town a million francs as soon as the deed is done. At first the town stands by its beloved citizen, but soon deficit-spends itself into a crisis. Rationalization and greed eventually outweigh humanitarian values, and the town carries out a ritualistic murder for the sake of financial prosperity.

The progression of *The Visit's* theme from early narrative to stage masterpiece offers fascinating insight into Dürrenmatt's dramaturgical way of thinking. The prose narrative *Mondfinsternis (Lunar Eclipse),* the first version of *The Visit,* remained unpublished until 1981. Despite several obvious superficial similarities, the narrative remains a distant, poor relative of the drama. There is next to no character development, and the story drags on much too long after the decision to kill for money is made. Wauti Locher returns to the village of his youth in the Bern uplands, having made his fortune in Canada and sporting the Americanized name Walt Lotcher. He had left forty years earlier when his girlfriend married his rival Mani Döufu. He has brought a million Swiss francs for every family in the village, but upon hearing that his girl friend was pregnant when he left and that he now has a grown son, he decides to make the money conditional on the villagers killing Mani. The murder must take place in ten days at the full moon. Walt Lotcher then takes a room at the inn, where he spends the next ten days in an endless orgy of alcohol and sex with every wife and daughter in the village.

For all intents the story is over now before it really begins, and as ten days must pass before the murder can occur, the body of the narrative includes several static subplots: Attempts to keep the pastor, the schoolteacher, and the policeman from finding out about the conspiracy; the revelation that the pastor is an atheist; the affair between the schoolteacher and the pastor; and the outing to the agricultural exhibition, where pages are wasted in intricate technical descriptions of the latest farm machinery. On the morning after the murder, government officials arrive to inform the villagers that their village has been selected as the site of a new health spa. "God has blessed us," the mayor contends. Perhaps the best element of the narrative, which carries over smoothly into the drama, is the exposé of money as the root of all evil. The villagers are portrayed as ignorant and superstitious without many ideals, but the few they have vanish immediately with Lotcher's offer.

While this improbable tale contains the germ of *The Visit,* the characters were too unmotivated and three-quarters of the text too static to sustain a stage drama. Dürrenmatt did well to keep *Mondfinsternis* in his desk drawer until he could think it through dramaturgically. He described in *Stoffe I–III* how this stage idea came to him. On his numerous trips between Bern and Neuchâtel his train would stop in Ins and Kerzers, two tiny towns with "wretched" stations. Dürrenmatt had his entry point. Someone is coming, the expectation is so great that the whole town is caught up in it. Festivities are planned which could be disrupted if the expected dignitary came too early or too late. He opted for too early, and as he continued to think in terms of stage possibilities, he had his first act.

The train station retains its significance as the center of the action throughout the play. Each act has a pivotal scene there. The transformation of the mountain village into Güllen allowed the development of depth to the characterization. Güllen—the name is from "Gülle," a Swiss dialect word meaning liquid manure—is not isolated from the rest of the world. Its people are not illiterate, superstitious, or otherwise backwards. The town had industry at one time. It has a high school, a mixed chorus, a gymnastics club, a small, dilapidated, but architecturally interesting minster—in short, it is connected to European culture. There is a Goethe arch, a Brahms square, and the hunting lodge of "Prince Hasso the Noble." Despite, or perhaps because of, their recent, unexplained financial crisis, the people have clung to that small degree of culture which their poverty will still allow them. Güllen has a history which in recent memory of most of the population was better than the present, a past to which they long to return. The Gülleners are three-dimensional. They are people who put up a credible fight against overwhelming temptation. "The Gülleners who swarm around the hero are people like the rest of us. They must not, emphatically not, be portrayed as wicked" (V 107). Dürrenmatt admitted he did not know whether he would have acted otherwise under the circumstances. "We are Gülleners," declares Timo Tiusanen,[3] and Urs Jenny analyzes how Dürrenmatt draws us in: "Like them we await the visit, like them we are astonished and fascinated by

82

the old lady's pompous arrival: like them we react with spontaneous indignation to her outrageous demand for revenge."[4]

Claire Zachanassian's revenge has been planned carefully over many years and is directed not only against Alfred Ill, but also against the townspeople, whom she considers guilty by complicity in the crime perpetrated against her. Driven out of town in shame, branded a whore because of the unjust verdict against her, Kläri (Claire) became a prostitute in Hamburg. There she lived Archilochos's miracle in reverse. Instead of the rich prostitute marrying the poor man, a rich man married the poor prostitute. In any case, it was grace that Kläri willingly accepted. The name of the Armenian oil magnate Zachanassian, a construct composed of parts of the names of three real billionaires—Zacharoff, Onassis, and Gulbenkian[5]—stands in ironic contrast to her maiden name, "Wäscher" (washer), which implies proletarian origins but also contains the implication of "whitewashing." This is what Alfred Ill accomplished forty years earlier with his bribed witnesses, and this is also what the town has done with this unsavory chapter of its history in the intervening years. Claire is prosthetic, not only as regards her leg and arm of ivory—souvenirs of a plane crash and a car wreck—but also her heart. Since her betrayal by Ill she has been unable to love anyone else. Long aware of this herself, Claire uses men only as means to her various short-term ends. Her long-term goal, to live out her life in Capri by the sea with the corpse of Alfred Ill in a mausoleum, requires no more husbands. Alfred will be true to her in death as he never was in life.

As a purveyor of Old Testament justice Claire is another manifestation of Dürrenmatt's fascination with the subject. Like Gulliver, Claire is grotesque in appearance and was a victim of injustice herself; however, she lacks Gulliver's humanitarian dimension. Neither is she driven by ideology as is Mississippi. She is driven purely by personal revenge. Claire's attitude toward justice is prefigured in the retinue she brings with her to Güllen. She has demonstrated that justice can be bought by paying a million dollars each to have two condemned killers released from Sing-Sing. Also, she has literally bought the judge who ruled against her in the paternity suit, and turned him into an agent of her personal revenge against Ill and Güllen. Finally she has administered Old Testament justice to Jakob Hühnlein and Ludwig Spahr, the false witnesses against her. She has had them castrated and blinded—that is, she has taken their manhood as they destroyed her womanhood, and their sight since their perjury had blinded the court to the truth.[6] All people in the entourage, including the various husbands, have lost their identities and function only as extensions of Claire. Thus she has given them dehumanizing, rhyming names.[7] They are, as one scholar has noted, "victims of the depersonalizing power of money, a state towards which the Güllener are rapidly moving."[8] In Claire, Dürrenmatt created such a monumental character that he would later complain his most performed play was his most misunderstood. He was at pains in a postscript, added later, to peel back the allegorical layers critics had added to his character: "Claire Zachanassian does not represent Justice or the Marshall Plan or even the Apocalypse, she's purely and simply what she is, namely, the richest woman in the world and, thanks to her finances, in a position to act as the Greek tragic heroines acted, absolutely terribly, something like Medea" (V 106).

Alfred Ill is as far away from Mani Döufu as Claire is from Walt Lotcher. He is guilty of a real crime, one that has gone unpunished for forty years. He must run the entire gamut of emotions from denial and anger through fear, to admission and calm acceptance of the conditions of atonement. If Dürrenmatt seems to deny universal allegorical significance to Claire, he has granted this to his hero. It begins with his name. Ill resonates very closely to the French pronoun *il* (he). We are compelled, and not for that reason alone, to treat Alfred Ill as an "Everyman."[9] Death, in the form of the old lady, has come to claim Alfred. Once the most popular man in Güllen, he is abandoned in due course by all, including his family. He is a sinner, but so are all the townspeople. All his good works flee him as well in the final hour. The fact that his store has fed their hunger through the lean years, that he has always extended them credit and borne their inability to repay, counts ultimately for nothing.

The question arises whether Dürrenmatt has not made a Christ figure out of Alfred Ill and cast *The Visit* as a thinly disguised passion play. A number of tempting parallels exist in the text.[10] Ill's agonized days and nights spent pacing back and forth upstairs in the third act function for Ill like a Gethsemane experience, from which he emerges strengthened and resolved for the coming ordeal. He has the opportunity to speak on several occasions and save his life, but he does not do so. In answer to the pastor's helpless "I'll pray for you" Ill utters his last words: "Pray for Güllen" (V 96)—a faint echo of Christ's exhortation to the women of Jerusalem: "Do not weep for me, but for yourselves and for your children." The rest of this prophecy concerning the days of tribulation to come has already been uttered, not by Ill, but by the schoolteacher, the last humanist left in Güllen: "I know that one day an old lady will come for us too, and then what happened to you will happen to us" (V 77). Finally, Ill willingly assumes the role of sacrificial lamb, dying for the good of the community. His anguished cry at the town meeting, "My God!" (V 94)—here an expression of incredulity, not an appeal to heaven—hints at Christ's penultimate words from the cross.

Working against these Christ parallels is the fact that Ill dies for a real and serious crime. Thus he cannot be considered an innocent victim. Second, and more important, is the fact that his death serves only the material betterment of Güllen.[11] On the spiritual level it has the exact opposite effect. Güllen is left financially rejuvenated and spiritually dead.[12] Ironically, Ill's only chance to save the Gülleners' souls would have been to refuse the role of sacrificial lamb and flee, as the pastor entreats him: "Lead us not into temptation with your presence" (V 58). By accepting the role, Ill partakes in a secular passion play with only distant and ironic connections to the biblical one—an "anti-passion play" similar to the one in *Angel,* quite in keeping with Dürrenmatt's theological skepticism.

Another biblical motif Dürrenmatt weaves into his text is the worship of the golden calf. It begins with Claire's taking up residence in the "Golden Apostle." From its balcony she oversees the town in the second act and waits for her temptation to take hold of the people. She herself is the apostle of this worship of mammon she has introduced in Güllen. The manifestations among the people begin with the proliferation of yellow shoes, found first on the patrons in Ill's shop, then on the policeman, and finally on the mayor. From the mayor we learn that they have been specially ordered from Kalberstadt (City of Calves). The policeman is sporting a new gold tooth. A placard with a huge golden sun hangs over the train station in act 2, inviting the Güllener to travel south, and even the autumn leaves blanket the ground "like layers of gold" (V 84) on the day the citizens murder Ill. To this golden calf they offer a human sacrifice. The murder itself is a ritual in which all participate, spreading the individual guilt as thinly as possible, preventing the possibility of future reprisal, and hallowing in the name of community that which would be profane in the name of the individual.[13]

Arguably the most important dramatic moment in the play comes in the train station scene at the end of the second act. It is a scene fraught with ambiguity, more a mind game than a physical confrontation, as Ill attempts to flee Güllen for his life. Two distinct plot lines intersect in this scene. The first is the moral dilemma of the townspeople. It traces their descent from the lofty position taken at the end of the first act, when they unanimously reject Claire's offer of a million francs for Alfred Ill's murder, through their spending spree on credit in act 2 that leads to the crisis in act 3, and finally to the rationalization that in killing Ill they are ridding their town of an ancient evil. The second plot strand is Ill's maturation process, from complete denial of guilt through fear for his life and attempt at flight, and culminating in his final acceptance of guilt and atonement. This concluding scene of act 2, placed strategically before intermission, is an important convergence of these plot strands.

From the moment of Claire's offer at the end of act 1, there is immediate denial on the part of both the citizens and the proposed victim. Ill is moved by the mayor's rejection of the offer and the unanimous applause it solicits. He truly believes that the town is on his side. Claire's ominous and prophetic "I'll wait" (V 39) sets the two plot lines in motion, putting the town and Ill on their collision course. Yet it is Ill who gets out of the starting blocks first in the sense that he gains an early lead on his adversaries in the realization of what is actually happening in Güllen. He maintains this advantage throughout the play, sizing up the situation long before the townspeople do, realizing the danger he is in. While the Gülleners squander the entire second act in denial, Ill realizes almost from the start that the course of action the townspeople have embarked upon can only end in his murder. It is a time advantage that should enable him to save his life. After all, his adversaries are telegraphing their intentions to him long before they can admit these intentions to themselves. The scene in which all the mounting anguish of uncertainty comes to a head for Ill, in which he finally comprehends that he will surely be murdered if he stays in Güllen, is situated near the end of act 2. Unfortunately for readers of the English translation, Dürrenmatt added this scene to the final revised version in 1980, and no English translation has been performed on this final authorized version. (In the English version, however, the killing of the panther functions as this moment of final recognition for Ill.) Having seen his friends indulge in increasingly lavish credit spending, and having witnessed the symbolic hunt for and killing of the black panther, Ill realizes that his only hope lies with Claire. She must publicly call off the bounty. For the last time in the play, Ill shows aggression. When his entreaties fail he threatens Claire with his rifle. This tactic too is unsuccessful, and she disarms him with a reflection on how he had betrayed her trust and love years before. The soliloquy not only confirms her intentions to have Ill killed, but also sows the seed of guilt in Ill that will paralyze him later.

Thus, Ill knows when he arrives on the train platform in the next scene, that he is facing a life-or-death situation. What he does not know is that the townspeople have not yet come to this understanding. For them it is still a harmless game, for they still naively believe in human perfectibility. They first learn the truth in the opening scene of the third act in Peter's barn. With the revelation that Claire already owns the factories, that it was she who shut them down to force the issue, comes the horrible certainty that the town is sitting in a trap. All the careless deficit spending, done in the belief that they would get Claire's money without having to commit murder, has now made the latter imperative. Only now does Ill's fate begin to be sealed. The actual decision process takes much longer, precisely because it involves intense systematic rationalization. The teacher's later admission that he and the others were slowly becoming murderers, although none of them could yet admit it to themselves, witnesses to the gradualness of this transformation.

So at the moment Ill reaches the train station, suitcase in hand, pursued by the rest of the citizens, only he is in possession of the truth. Whereas Ill, propelled by an exact awareness of his situation, has a compelling purpose, the townspeople betray their ambivalence. Something in each of them welcomes Ill's departure, and yet their financial plight requires them to try to hold on to the one sure card they have to play. They have not yet considered how to go about this. In their presumed unity is total disorganization. Ill could almost certainly have escaped, for his urgency far outweighed that of the citizens. Their ambivalence was ripe for the exploiting. Positioned as it is between Ill's learning the truth and the town's learning the truth, the train station scene marks the first point at which escape becomes necessary and the last point at which it would be possible—an ideal window of opportunity lost forever.

Dürrenmatt planted the seeds for this scene a decade earlier in the short story "Die Stadt." A man who has just participated in a failed rebellion against the government capitulates to authority by accepting a low-level position with that government. He is to be a guard in the subterranean prison, in which the guards are dressed exactly like the prisoners in order to create a state of paranoia and insure order. As he has nothing to do in the long hours but sit and think about his situation, the guard eventually happens upon the notion that he could perhaps be a prisoner himself. He constructs numerous scenarios in his mind, each of which raises more questions than it answers. Walking out the door unimpeded would at once reassure him of his guard status. However, being stopped by someone else would reveal that he was a prisoner, and that realization would be more than he could bear. He resolves to sneak unnoticed along the glassy wall to the door, but as he approaches the final niche, he encounters a form coming in the opposite direction—his own mirror image. Frightened, he retreats into his niche and slowly goes insane. In fact, he has become a prisoner by his inability to walk to the glass door and out to freedom. Each time he comes close to accepting his role as guard on faith, a new possibility occurs to him and his courage fails. An act of faith falters when subjected to rational scrutiny, for as Kierkegaard states, "faith begins precisely there where thinking leaves off."[14]

Ill's dilemma at the end of act 2 is prefigured in this existential nightmare in the subterranean prison, for the only person standing between Alfred Ill and the train is Alfred Ill. Claire added a dimension to his anguish in the previous scene by engaging his conscience. With the increasing comprehension of his own culpability, Ill has taken the first step which will eventually lead to acceptance. However, he is still far from reaching that point. The anchor holding Ill back on the train platform is forged from his overactive intellect. While this ability to assess every situation and deduce a response has placed him at an advantage over the Gülleners, the inability to suspend rationalization at the decisive moment and act robs him of this advantage. Ill tortures himself instead with scenarios. Why did the chief constable in Kaffigen not answer his letter? Why does the station look newer than it had before Claire arrived? Why is the town building new structures? Why are the people wearing new trousers? Why have they all come to the station at once? Why are they crowding him? Some-one will hold him back. Which one will it be? . . . And so Ill thinks and talks himself out of escaping. Can he get on the train or will they hold him back? Is he free or is he a prisoner? Like the guard, Ill has encountered in himself an adversary he cannot defeat. As the unlocked glass door is for the one, so is the waiting train for the other: an unattainable goal only a few feet away.

After the prophetic words on the train platform "I'm lost" (V 62), Ill never again puts up a struggle. He becomes in the third act "a man who in recognizing his guilt lives out justice and who, in death, achieves greatness" (V 107). Thereby Ill joins the list of "courageous people," in whose breasts the lost world order is restored.[15] Is he, then, a tragic hero? Despite some critics who would see him in this light, the majority of scholars have recognized that Dürrenmatt does not grant him this privilege. Despite the personal courage Ill shows, the insights he gains, and the calm with which he accepts his death, his sacrifice plays out against a background of baseness and moral depravity that are not ameliorated, only increased, by the sacrifice. He is surrounded by buffoons and fools, none of whom learns anything, and he remains, as Kenneth Whitton wrote, "the ac-tual tragic character in the actual comic situation."[16] We are reminded once again of Dürrenmatt's admonition in "Problems of the Theater," written a year before *The Visit:* "Comedy is the only thing that can still reach us."[17]

Nowhere is the power of rationalization more in evidence than in the final scene, performed in Sophoclean choral style by the well-dressed, wealthy Gülleners on the platform of their modern train station. Güllen has not mur-dered its most popular citizen, it has purged itself of an injustice. It has not acted out of greed, rather it has purified itself in order to be worthy to accept Claire's gift. And so the self-satisfied citizenry can pray with a clear conscience that God will protect their sacred possessions. This garland-draped happy end-ing is the truly sad conclusion to *The Visit*.

Dürrenmatt did not consider *The Visit* one of his best plays. He was suspi-cious of its worldwide success, believing much as Brecht did about *The Threepenny Opera* that such success can only be a result of a weak play.[18] International audiences and critics worldwide were of a different opinion. This remains Dürrenmatt's most famous, best-loved, and most quoted work. That it is his "most misunderstood," as he claimed, is also possible simply because, as a parable, the play invites so many varied interpretations from the Freudian and Jungian, to the Marxist, to the religious and antireligious, to the legal or historical. Most fitting in conclusion are the words with which Murray Peppard opens his discussion of the play: "Even the most exhaustive critique cannot raise all the possibilities of interpretation or explore all the lines of suggestibility contained in the play, and the lengthiest commentary cannot provide adequate compensation for the pleasure of new discoveries that can be made by every new reading of the text."[19]

Die Panne (Traps)

Leaving aside a made-for-television drama and an Italian film, the story of Alfredo Traps appears in three different versions: as a radio play (1955), as a novella (1956), and as a stage play (1979). The stage version has not been translated into English. Such exploitation of a theme demonstrates the author's depth of fascination with the problems posed by the plot. As the novella thinks the plot of the radio play further, Dürrenmatt writes, so does the play think the novella a step further. The first two versions fall into the same time period as The Visit, and deal with common themes: the recognition and acceptance of guilt, and extralegal justice. The German title means "the breakdown." Translators Richard and Clara Winston chose instead the name of the protagonist as the English title.

The simplest, purest version of the plot, and perhaps the most provocative, is the radio play. It begins with a mechanical breakdown. Travelling sales representative Alfredo Traps's Studebaker stalls in a small, unnamed village. Traps, who must wait for repairs until the morning, could take the train home to his wife and children. He prefers, however, to spend the night in the village, where he hopes for an amorous adventure. Since a small livestock breeders convention has booked all the guest rooms, Traps is referred to a villa on the outskirts of town owned by a retired judge named Werge. Invited to have supper with his host and participate in a stag evening with three of the judge's retired friends, Traps believes he has stepped into a fairy tale.

The judge and his friends—a retired prosecutor named Zorn; a retired public defender, Kummer; and a former hangman, Pilet—meet regularly to play at their old professions. All their game lacks is a defendant. The mock trial will be played out over the course of the evening. The lodging is free, and the room Traps will be assigned will depend on the sentence he receives. Traps is intrigued by the game but doubts his own role in it. After all, he is guilty of no crime. The old men only smile. Everybody is guilty of something; they will bring a crime to light. The sense of living a fairy tale intensifies as the meal is served in ever more lavish courses and the wine flows in older and older vintages. Traps immediately begins to boast of his new Studebaker, his well-paying profession, and of his membership in the "Utopia Club" (*Schlaraffia*), where his nickname is "Marquis de Casanova." Then, sometime late in the evening, after the wine has worn down his inhibitions, the food has made him sluggish, and the skilled oratory of the prosecutor has planted suggestion after suggestion in his mind, Traps confesses to murder. The simple fact that Traps was driving a new Studebaker, when he had recently owned an old Citroën, aroused the prosecutor's initial suspicion. From the few facts that Traps willingly and innocently tells him—Traps hated his boss Gygax, had an affair with the boss's wife, and told a friend about the affair; Gygax died of a heart attack; Traps took over his position and since then has had nothing more to do with the widow—the prosecutor constructs a *dolo malo* murder charge against him.

As this is not an ordinary court, neither bound by judicial convention nor having any authority, the jurists believe that they can serve a purer form of justice than can the heavily encumbered legal system. The trial actually begins long before Traps realizes it, masked as innocent conversation during the serving of the first course. Despite the defender's whispered warnings to weigh every word carefully, Traps speaks the naked truth in a carefree manner. "Don't worry about a thing, my friend," Traps tells his counsel, "Wait till the interrogation begins. I won't lose my head, I assure you."[20] "He didn't catch on, he didn't catch on," (GH 260) the judge sniggers amid raucous laughter of the others. In a scene reminiscent of Kafka's novel *The Trial,* the defender takes Traps outside into the garden and tells him that his case is going very badly. They stand a good chance to lose it. At this particular time Traps, who has been babbling on innocently about his life, still has no idea of what the charge is against him.

Traps doggedly insists on his innocence, but with equal vehemence the prosecutor draws long suppressed intentions out of the recesses of Traps's mind. He had successfully rationalized all his individual actions. He had the affair with Gygax's wife because he loved her. He told the friend, knowing it would get back to Gygax, because he despised secretiveness, but he did not tell his own wife, because after all, he had children to consider. He stopped visiting "Käthi" after Gygax's death in order not to give her a bad reputation. He knew about Gygax's heart condition, and hoped that the revelation would "damage" him, but he never thought it would kill him. The prosecutor refutes each of these weak alibis in turn until the light goes on in Traps's head: "I realize it now.

I am a murderer" (GH 279). Of course he is not legally culpable. Traps, like Alfred III, is out of reach of the judicial system. But neither Ill nor Traps—who significantly share a first name—is dealing with a legally constituted court. While Ill faces his fear and comes to the recognition of his guilt after a period of denial, Traps is helped much more quickly to his confession by the four strange old men, "who had illuminated his world with the pure radiance of justice" (T 108).

Suddenly as convinced of his guilt as he had been of his innocence moments before, Traps refutes all exculpating arguments of his defense attorney. The weather had been terrible the night Gygax died: hot wind and violent storms, the worst kind of weather for people with heart conditions. The prosecutor had played mind games with Traps to exact the confession, but the real reason for Gygax's death lay in his careless lifestyle and the pressures of the job, which had weakened his heart. The weather and coincidence did the rest. Traps's animosity against Gygax was understandable after all he had suffered at his boss's hands. That he wanted to avenge himself on Gygax with the latter's wife is only a natural response. Traps may be ruthless, as the laws of his profession dictate, but he is no murderer. Traps has used all these arguments to alibi the situation to himself. With his new insight, however, he no longer can accept them. Just as the teacher could not convince Ill to fight for his life after he had admitted his guilt, neither can the attorney convince the enlightened Traps of his innocence. "I am a murderer. I didn't know it when I entered this house, didn't want to know it, now I know it. I dared not think about it, obviously I was too much a coward to be honest, now I have the courage. I am guilty. I acknowledge it with horror, with amazement. Guilt has opened my eyes, like a sun it illuminates me, burns inside me" (GH 282–83). Before passing sentence, the judge asks Traps the question which the mayor asked Ill: whether he will accept the verdict. Traps has murdered, says the judge, but not with a weapon, rather thoughtlessly, with the most natural instinct of his profession, "to drive another man to the wall, to proceed ruthlessly, come what might" (T 107). The sentence is death.

The scene in which Pilet, the hangman, shows the drunken Traps to his room is masterfully done, full of double meanings and outright misunderstandings. They climb the stairs past medieval torture instruments which the judge has collected. In the room itself is a guillotine from the judge's collection. Pilet demonstrates the guillotine, then takes Traps's coat off him and loosens his collar. Traps steels himself for the inevitable, but Pilet just wants to put him to bed. The game has ended happily for all except the defense attorney and the disoriented Traps: "But I'm a murderer, Mr. Pilet, I must be executed, Mr. Pilet,

I must—now he's gone—turned out the light. But I'm a mur- I'm a—I'm—I'm tired, it has all been only a game, a game, a game! (falls asleep)" (GH 286). The next morning as he rushes to pick up his Studebaker from the garage, the game is but a distant, vague memory, about which he can now laugh ("Imagined I had committed a murder. Such nonsense"). Eagerly he drives off on his next business trip, ready to bleed his next victim dry: "Now I'll act ruthlessly, ruthlessly. I'll ruin him. No mercy!" (GH 287).

At the same time hopelessly cynical and true to life, Alfredo Traps's experience presents one possible and all-too-frequent reaction to guilt. Traps has learned nothing from his confrontation with himself. The long look inward, an agonizing path to an execution that was only symbolic, cleansed and enlightened him only for the duration of the game. In his reality before the game, Traps considered himself righteous. In the game his consciousness was raised until he comprehended his own capacity to commit murder. The fairy-tale-turned-nightmare had been a unique opportunity for Traps to reform. Leaving the game and entering reality again, Traps had essentially three possibilities: he could renounce the game completely, remain trapped within the game, unable to reorient to reality, or synthesize what he has learned about himself into the life he must lead beyond the game—in short, he could become a more humane businessman, aware of the dark side of his nature and able to combat it. This third possibility, a dialectical synthesis, is the ideal. Traps, however, is incapable of synthesis. He takes the first option, rejecting the game as fiction. That he had been taken in temporarily was only the result of the alcohol. The breakdown of the Studebaker was a moment of grace, but like so many with Dürrenmatt, one that is rejected.

The connection between the name "Traps" and the English "trap" is obvious. The protagonist walks into one after another. In fact he trudges into the prosecutor's traps awkwardly, with a heavy, clumsy footfall, as the German verb *trapsen* suggests.[21] Werge, the judge, echoes the word *Zwerg* (dwarf), and in fact he is very small of stature, but also *Wergeld,* which means reward money for bringing in a criminal. Given the luxurious villa in which he lives, the expensive wines he drinks, the lavish dinner parties he frequently throws, and the elaborate collection of medieval artifacts he possesses, it is apparent that he has made out quite well from the legal profession. The prosecutor is named Zorn (anger) and the defense attorney Kummer (worry, grief). Gygax is probably a reference to the legendary Lydian tyrant and usurper Gyges. Hephaiston, the fabric Traps sells, refers to Hephaistos, the blacksmith among the Greek gods, who spun a fine net to capture the adulterous Ares and Aphrodite in the act. Ironically it is Traps who stumbles under the artful snare fashioned for him by the old jurists.

The differences between the radio play and the novella are not great, except for the conclusion. Naturally the radio play, limited by time restrictions, is the most compact form the plot can take. The addition of the authorial voice in the prose narrative gave Dürrenmatt much more liberty to expand, comment, and editorialize. A subtle but important shift in emphasis in the novella concerns the motivation for Traps's ultimate acceptance of guilt. In the radio play Traps is awe-struck at the realization that he is a murderer. He has held fast to the illusion of his moral innocence to the bitter end. His admission relieves him of a great subconscious burden. Subsequently he clings to his guilt not because he enjoys the thought, but because, like Alfred Ill, he has accepted it, albeit under the influence of the game. Thus he acknowledges his guilt "with horror, with amazement." In the novella, this horror and amazement are replaced by a sense of newfound self-respect. Flattered by the words of the prosecutor that he has committed a crime "that merits admiration, astonishment, and respect and may deservedly be considered one of the most extraordinary crimes of our century" (T 96), and impaired judgmentally by the large amount of wine he has consumed, Traps insists on his guilt as a point of honor. Instead of a sudden recognition of a past crime, Traps's confession in the novella amounts to an ex post facto reinterpretation of actions that had seemed innocent at the time as a cunning, premeditated murder.[22] As Kummer's argument threatens to reduce him from the lofty status of the century's most genial murderer to unknowing victim of society and the pressures of the business world, Traps loudly condemns the assault on his self-esteem, for that Traps is an egotist is clear from his incautious boastfulness during the trial. Furthermore, he has come to respect the four old men deeply and values greatly their respect in return.

With this changed outlook toward his guilt, the new Alfredo Traps of the novella is primed for the altered ending Dürrenmatt gives his story. Earlier in the evening, when Traps was still protesting his innocence, he complained of momentary disorientation: "The game threatens to flip over into reality" (T 56). By the time the verdict is announced, the game has become so important to Traps that it has completely replaced reality for him, and he remains entrapped in it. Unlike the protagonist of the radio play, this Traps cannot fall asleep with the words "only a game" on his lips. With his last strength he hangs himself in his room. The widely held assumption that his suicide reinforces his acceptance of guilt in the manner of Alfred Ill is a premature conclusion. The game has given him something neither the superficial camaraderie of the Utopia Club, nor his lonely cutthroat profession, nor his loveless marriage have yet given him: warmth, human contact, and personal dignity. He does not regret his crime, as Ill did—he revels in it. So the suicide that ends the novella is not about justice or the expiation of guilt. Rather, in his judgmentally impaired state, Traps believes the only way to hold on to the fairy tale that has given his wretched existence meaning is by playing the game to the end according to the rules.[23] The retired jurists have done to the psychologically weak and susceptible Traps exactly what they accused Traps of doing to Gygax with his weakened heart: indirectly caused his death.[24] For Traps it has all been a terrible misunderstanding, a communications *Panne.*

Between the novella and the stage play lie twenty-two years. At Egon Karter's urging Dürrenmatt adapted the novella for the stage in 1978, and the following year Karter's players took *Die Panne* on the road around Germany and Austria. For his opening scene Dürrenmatt employs a tactic which proved successful in *Mississippi.* The play begins with the epilogue, centered around Traps's coffin and bursting with flashes of wit, but having little to do with the plot of the play. Finally the judge turns to the audience and introduces himself as the actor Karl-Heinz Stroux. The explanation he gives for the scene just presented is that those actors and actresses in it with small parts did not want to wait for hours in strange dressing rooms in strange towns night after night just to make brief appearances. Thus they have performed the ending of the play first. Those characters take their curtain call, Stroux gives them flowers, Traps climbs out of the coffin, the actors playing the retired jurists put on Greek masks, and the real play is about to begin.

With the exception of introducing the character of the judge's nymphomaniac daughter Justine, which Dürrenmatt could easily have done some other way, there seems to be no justification for this admittedly humorous epilogue/ prologue that adds fifteen minutes to an already very long play. Once the actual play begins, an audience familiar with the radio play or the novella will still not immediately recognize the plot. Justine explains to Traps that her husband, an aristocrat named von Fuhr, had killed himself three years ago. His castle burned to the ground; only the wine cellar remained intact. Justine explains why he killed himself: "He shot himself, in order to become guilty. He thought it indecent not to be guilty." Traps's reply is prophetic: "I would have to shoot myself then too" (16:86).

Justine, of course, is lying. She is under her grandfather's spell, his victim and, as Dürrenmatt writes in the introduction, his "amorous murder weapon" (16:64). Justine killed her husband by setting his wig on fire as he slept. Since Justine was smoking in bed at the time, it was ruled an accident. In fact, she had acted on the instructions of the judge (named Wucht in the stage play), who coveted the von Fuhr wine cellar. Wucht, Kummer, and Zorn are corrupt; all have taken bribes or worse in order to amass the fortunes they now possess, and all enjoy Wucht's ill-gotten wine cellar with impunity. This overt corruption of the court is a new twist in the play, and it taints whatever "justice" may be imposed on Traps.

Another modification in the plot calls into question a very important premise of the radio play and the novella with respect to Traps's guilt or innocence. For Traps to have acted *dolo malo* in causing Gygax's death, the affair with Käthi had to be unmotivated by anything other than the expected shock to Gygax's weak heart. The prosecutor works hard to establish this as the sole motivation. The bombshell that Traps drops amid the defense arguments, unwillingly, coaxed by the defender, removes this fragile moral link altogether. When Gygax died he was not at home, as the prosecutor had postulated, but rather in bed with Traps's wife. The affair had been going on for some time; Traps knew and felt helpless rage. Thus the motivation was revenge: adultery for adultery, repayment in kind, not premeditated murder. The prosecution's case against Traps collapses in that moment, although Traps continues to protest his guilt. Later revelations of Traps's sexual insecurities even cast reasonable doubt as to whether Traps was capable of having an affair with Käthi. Furthermore, it is shown that Käthi was having affairs with several men. Traps seems less of a murderer and more of a pretentious blowhard with each succeeding revelation.

Traps gets the death sentence he desires because, as the judge says, in this world of shameless crimes in which no one wants to take responsibility, in which crimes have become essential to keep the world operating, "one who declares his own guilt deserves to be rewarded and celebrated" (16:161). In practically the same breath, however, the judge issues a second verdict: acquittal. The guilt in which Traps wants so earnestly to believe is a fiction, not because he did not wish Gygax dead, but rather because his wishing had nothing to do with reality. Chance has replaced fate in this world, where everyone is guilty and innocent at the same time, Wucht tells Traps. "It was not your deed which did your boss in, rather a simple storm. It wasn't intent which linked your wish with its fulfillment, but coincidence" (16:163). Two contradicting verdicts; Traps must choose. Mired as he was in the novella in what Dürrenmatt called "the hopelessness of a fixed idea, which sees something extraordinary in crime," Traps shouts "I shall prove my guilt to you!" (16:164).

In the forties and fifties, in particular in *Der Doppelgänger* and in the earlier versions of *Die Panne,* humanity was guilty by nature and only had to accept that fact. Now, in 1979, Wucht replies that Traps's guilt or innocence is equally unprovable. "What was this night? A high-spirited stag party, nothing more, a parody of something which does not exist but which the world is tricked into believing in again and again, a parody of justice, of the cruelest of the fixed ideas, in whose name human beings slaughter each other" (16:165). Dürrenmatt has thought his argument from "Problems of the Theater" on the inefficacy of tragedy in modern times a step further. In a world in which collective guilt has replaced individual guilt, *justice* is no longer possible. There must, then, be two verdicts for Traps, because in a chaotic universe everyone is both guilty and not guilty.

Finally, the jurists puts on their masks again for one final act: the execution of the "truly guilty ones," the gods—the perfect ones who created imperfection, the guilty who cast us into guilt. They fire volleys at the planets—Jupiter, Mars, Saturn, Venus, Mercury—reciting vitriolic, blasphemous sounding verses. The destruction they cause in the village thereby is unintentional. Justine had bought live ammunition for the pistols as a prank. Dürrenmatt for his part cannot resist adding one final *Panne.* Traps shoots himself with one of these pistols that should have been loaded with blanks. However, Dürrenmatt also found the grotesque figure of Traps hanging from the chandelier indispensable. So he had Traps shoot and hang himself at the same time. What he gained in the way of a grotesque scenic image—the corpse hanging above while Wucht and Pilet continue to enjoy their wine at the table below—compromised his stated premise that Traps's death was accidental because the gun should not have been loaded. There is no indication that the rope should also have been defective, but this flaw in logic did not seem to bother Dürrenmatt.

While the radio play won an award and the novella is considered one of his best narratives, the stage play will not contribute much to Dürrenmatt's fame as a dramatist. After *Die Panne,* a very disillusioned Dürrenmatt would write only one more play before turning exclusively to prose.

Frank der Fünfte (Frank the Fifth)

Dürrenmatt's comedy about a private bank exists in three versions. It has not, however, been published in English translation.[25] Although the author considered it one of his best plays, critics and audiences did not, and it had a short run in 1959. The original version with a few minor changes was published in book form in 1960. A planned revival of the play in Bochum in 1964, for which Dürrenmatt made considerable textual revisions and cut out some of the songs, was canceled by the theater manager after four weeks of rehearsals. The final revision for the *Werkausgabe* in 1980 radically changed the ending, but otherwise added nothing new to the plot. Failure in German-speaking theaters, however, was partially compensated by the play's success in France, and also in Eastern Bloc countries, where it was seen, like *The Visit,* as a parable of the evils of capitalism.[26]

The story line of the first published version, subtitled "Opera about a Private Bank," with music by Paul Burkhard, can be summarized as follows. The play begins at the cafe Chez Guillaume next to the Frank Family Private Bank. Päuli Neukomm and Heini Zurmühl, looking to make quick money, plan a bank robbery. Gottfried Frank, the fifth-generation bank director, sees them and offers them jobs. Frank tells them he is dying, and two days later Päuli is literally digging Frank's grave. After the funeral, Frank's widow Ottilie catches Päuli hiding a key to the vault in his pocket. Praising him for the attempt, she declares him a full-fledged member of the company. Päuli realizes that he has joined a gangster bank. He immediately has another revelation, as Frank emerges from a closet. He has faked his death. Ottilie will follow, and soon the gangsters will liquidate the bank and divide the profits. In the coffin is Päuli's friend Heini, who had tried to blackmail Frank.

Frieda Fürst, a prostitute in the service of the bank, is in love with Richard Egli, the chief of personnel. They dream of a life together and children after the bank is liquidated. Meanwhile, Frank stands in his villa surrounded by pictures of his ancestors. He sees the Frank family empire ending, because he is "not a bank director" but rather "unfortunately a good man through and through."[27] Frank and Ottilie reveal that they have a son and daughter. Herbert is studying in Oxford and Franziska in Montreux. Neither knows what the parents really do. Ottilie admits she hates the criminal life, and only carries on for the sake of the children. The bank, however, is in financial trouble. The gangsters have been robbing the till, two "perfect" scams go awry costing them millions, and a mysterious extortioner is blackmailing them. Frank and Ottilie call a staff meeting. Everyone is ordered to return all their "savings" to the bank at once along with their keys to the vault. Only Frieda Fürst refuses, counting on her fiancé Egli's support. Forced to choose between Frieda and the bank, Egli takes Frieda into the cellar and kills her.

Emil Böckmann the chief clerk, on his deathbed with cancer, calls a priest to make a confession. Instead, Frank shows up in a priest's robe with Ottilie, who kills Böckmann with an injection of poison so that he cannot confess. Paranoia reigns in the bank. Each suspects the other of being the blackmailer. Herbert and Franziska introduce themselves through a song. He is the blackmailer, she Frieda's replacement. They have known about the bank and have been waiting for the opportune moment. As Frank and his employees huddle in the cellar next to the vault, keeping their eyes on each other, Herbert appears and forces his father into the vault. Frank's mistake, Herbert tells him, was trying to run the bank the way his ancestors did. That is no longer profitable. There is a fortune to be made legally in this business.

Horrified at what her children have become, Ottilie goes to the Presidential Palace to confess the bank's criminal activities. In a Gilbert-and-Sullivan-style ending, the president can only smile and forgive. It is really not so bad, he tells her. Just stop killing people. The banking industry is all connected, the president explains. If the Frank Bank failed, it would set off a devastating chain reaction. Instead of justice for her crimes, Ottilie receives a check to cover the whole debt of the bank. There is nothing for Ottilie to do but to run the bank with her children. Instead of the desired justice, only a foul grace:

> The penalty denied, the verdict a sham
> And justice wasn't worth a damn. (FF 88)

In the final revised version from 1980, Herbert does not kill his father, but merely identifies himself as the blackmailer. Frank and Ottilie both "abdicate," and go off together to live out their lives poor but honest. Herbert, now Frank VI, will run a "legal" banking operation, just until the climate again becomes suitable for profitable gangsterism. Egli predicts that this time will soon come.

One scene deserves particular consideration, because Dürrenmatt considered it the best scene he ever wrote, and described it as the central scene of the play. "Whoever takes me at my word here," he stated, "to that person the entire play will begin to speak. Whoever does not understand me in this scene, does not understand me at all" (6:165). The scene is the murder of Böckmann. Instead of Father Moser to hear his last confession, Böckmann gets the false priest, Frank. Under no circumstances can Frank let Böckmann confess, since even this confidentiality could be breached by a loose word. Facing death, Böckmann has been enlightened, not unlike Alfred Ill. He sees that he has been living a lie and tells Frank that none of their crimes were necessary. When Frank protests that their heritage had made it impossible to turn back, Böckmann replies: "You lie. At any hour we could have turned back, at any moment of our evil lives. There is no heritage that could not have been rejected and no crime that had to be committed. We were free, false priest, created in freedom and abandoned to freedom. Leave my deathbed, you specter, and cast yourself back into your grave . . ." (FF 60). There is no comedy in this scene. Dürrenmatt has never been more serious, his message more clear. This is not moralizing, but it is a stern rebuke for all who would alibi foul deeds by denying their fundamental freedom to choose another course, be it within a gangster collective, a youth street gang, a political party, or a lynch mob. But here, too, there is a catch. "Everything happens out of fear," Dürrenmatt wrote in the notes to the 1964 version, "but also, naturally, out of mistrust. This makes it necessary for the bank to continue to murder; above all, the criminals must eliminate each other. Whoever would be free, must die, a simple observation that leads to the conclusion that a gangster democracy is an impossible thing" (6:154). Does the fact that whoever would be free must die exempt the gangsters from responsibilities for their actions? Not once they have made the conscious choice to become gangsters.

Bank director and gangster, the combination is not unprecedented. Macheath tells Polly in act 2 of *The Threepenny Opera:* "Between you and me it's only a matter of weeks before I go over to banking altogether. It's safer and its more profitable."[28] The key word is "altogether," implying that Macheath already has one foot in the door, and that the distinction between gangster and banker is one that can easily be bridged. Dürrenmatt, of course, would not be pleased with this comparison. Almost from the moment the play premiered on March 19, 1959, in Zürich, he began defending himself against accusations he had repackaged *The Threepenny Opera*. Not Brecht, he insisted, but Shakespeare provided the inspiration for *Frank.* "A historic play of Shakespeare is the story of a monarchy, *Frank V.* is the story of a firm. Here as there the people are classified in a hierarchy. Frank the Fifth is just as bad a banker as Richard the Third is a bad ruler, both are monstrous, both criminals" (6:153). Though he mentions *Richard III,* he is not claiming to model his play exclusively on it. He also mentioned being influenced by *Titus Andronicus.*[29] More than individual dramas, one should look for the spirit of Shakespeare's historical plays behind *Frank.* Let us take him at his word.

The play contains several scenes in which the characters must choose whether to risk their place in the hierarchy by betraying their fealty to King Frank. Likewise Frank deals as a tyrant would with anyone who becomes a threat to his eminence. The murder of Böckmann to prevent him from confessing, that is, betraying the King's secrets, is one such masterful scene. Another is the tragic dilemma in which Egli finds himself after his beloved Frieda has defied Queen Ottilie. It is the classic choice between duty and inclination. Richard Egli, ever the true vassal, sacrifices his fiancée, even does the deed himself, in order to repair the relationship with the Crown that Frieda's defiance had damaged. Like Lady Macbeth, Ottilie is the dominant partner in the marriage. Frank is a coward, a sensitive, somewhat reluctant tyrant, who assuages his conscience with the study of Goethe and Mörike. It is Ottilie who commands the moment whenever something embarrassing or painful must be said. She tells Böckmann the truth about their role in suppressing the cancer diagnosis, after Frank falls speechless. It is Ottilie who rises "majestically" to deal with Frieda's defiance at the board meeting, after Frank whines helplessly "You say something!" (FF 55), and it is Ottilie who gives Böckmann the deadly injection, while Frank sings in the background. Finally the play contains the son's obligatory usurpation of the throne through treachery, which ends, as it must, in patricide.

Unquestionably King Richard III and Frank the Fifth are two of a kind. They use people under the guise of loyalty, then dispose of them. Is this not equally true of Macheath, however? His move to the banking profession will necessitate the jettisoning of the band of hoodlums who have brought him this far. For years they served him with medieval fealty if not always with the greatest skill, but in a couple weeks he will deliver them all up to the police chief. The Brechtian parallels do not stop with Macheath. "Who does not think of Richard the Third?"[30] Brecht asks, when introducing his other great gangster, Arturo Ui.

Certainly aware of how close he was treading to *The Threepenny Opera,* Dürrenmatt made an immediate conscious attempt to distance himself from Brecht through parody. The opening monologue contains a direct refutation of the premise of *The Threepenny Opera* without mentioning it by name. It includes a reference to "inflated ticket prices," an ironic reversal of Brecht's reduced price of three pennies, which even beggars could afford. "If we came at you with beggars, every dog would howl," Dürrenmatt wrote a few lines later, because "only from a million up is there classical art" (FF 8). So right from the outset Dürrenmatt draws the battle lines. An audience expecting Brecht will not get him. Why, then, did critics find it difficult to take him at his word? Because there is a nagging feeling that Brecht is still right there below the surface. Part of the similarity lies in the structure. Descriptive scene captions establish the link. Both plays feature songs, usually with verses and a refrain, during which the play stops and the action is reflected upon, or some aspect of a character's personality is revealed. There are striking textual similarities as well. When Päuli sings "Who would want to live in goodness, but miserably?" (FF 18), we cannot help thinking of Macheath's dictum "One must live well to know what living is."[31] Päuli's lament "If you plan to do good, it just doesn't work out" (FF 48) comes straight out of Peachum's "Song of the Insufficiency of Human Behavior," and the sappy love duet of Richard Egli and Frieda Fürst, that ends with the mock tragic "Farewell, Frieda. Farewell, Richard" (FF 23), calls to mind Polly and Macheath's "Moon over Soho" duet. Finally Peachum, who calls himself "the beggar's friend," hides behind the Bible, sporting a verse for every occasion; while Frank, who introduces himself to Päuli and Heini as "Frank the Philanthropist" (FF 12), hides under the cassock of a priest. It is clear that the comedy contains numerous references to its Brechtian counterpart, and that these references were purposefully placed.

The logical conclusions from *Frank* and *The Threepenny Opera* are, for the most part, the same ones: society is corrupt to the core, capitalist equals gangster, the financial magnates are beyond the reach of the law. Dürrenmatt would not protest. He would say instead that it is the right of audiences or critics to draw any conclusions they please. However—and here he would differentiate himself clearly from Brecht—he denies intentionally writing these assertions into his play. "I do not begin with a thesis, but rather with a story" is point 1 of the "21 Points to *The Physicists*," and in the afterword to the 1959 version of *Frank* he wrote that it is the critic's responsibility to do that which he, the author, refuses to do: "to discover the world within my possible worlds" (6:157). The general, particularly German, belief that the moral is the most important thing about a play has ruined many stagings, he asserts. Directors stage plays around the moral and not around the plot.

> The director (or the critic) often makes the mistake of believing that the dramatist must always start with a problem. . . . The dramatist can begin with subject matter that contains problems. There is a difference. . . . It is all the same to me as a dramatist—in the moment of writing—what assertions the critic deduces from it, certainly I do not contest his right to do so. But all the less should the stage production be concerned with these possible assertions. (6:158)

Finally, he states his view of the role of the playwright so as to draw a clear distinction between himself and Brecht: "The author is neither a cynic nor a moralist. He puts neither his person nor his beliefs up for discussion, neither his convictions nor his doubts, although he knows that this all plays a subconscious role" (6:159). Eschewing as he did the role of moralist in his dramas, Dürrenmatt could not have written anything like Brecht's moralizing conclusion to *The Threepenny Opera:* Do not persecute the small injustices of the poor, but rather concentrate on the great injustice that keeps them confined in coldness and darkness. However, in his own closing lines, he intentionally calls to mind their counterpart in *The Threepenny Opera*. His chorus speaks a horrifying vision of an "ice-world" permeated by "foul grace," where a person is "only a number," a world that for them has already become reality.

Dürrenmatt demonstrates the vast distance between his dramaturgical theory and Brecht's, between the foul grace by which Macheath is saved from the gallows and that by which the Frank Family Private Bank is saved from ruin.

101

Brecht proclaimed that the fairy-tale endings were only reserved for the rich and corrupt, and that the poor, who may be dishonest out of necessity, can never expect to be pardoned by the queen's mounted messenger. Nevertheless, society can change this, if educated properly to the plight of those who live in the shadows. That is the message of a dramatist who writes intentionally toward a moral, for whom the stage is an ideological pulpit. For Dürrenmatt, who begins with a story he wants to tell rather than a moral he wants to illustrate, the emphasis shifts to thinking that plot through to a conclusion. That means letting the plot take its worst possible turn, brought about by coincidence. The common thread in these worst possible turns is that they cause their victims to accomplish exactly the opposite of that for which they were striving. Frank ends up dead in the vault. The remaining gangsters, who had expected to retire to enjoy the spoils of their misdeeds, must now continue to labor. Finally, Ottilie, who wanted justice in the form of condemnation for her past sins, must instead accept a pardon. A female Romulus, Ottilie has given up her integrity and her health (she is a morphine addict) for the sake of a future generation, only to learn that all has been in vain. When her final sacrifice is rejected, she must live on in the realization of what she has done. Within the fiction of the play, then, we may conclude that justice has been achieved. Ottilie and Frank received due punishment for their years of thieving and murdering.

In a very important way, *Frank* anticipates the next play, the worldwide success *The Physicists*. Frank the Fifth and Ottilie make the decision to hide their true identities from their children. Placing their full resources behind the effort, they feign normal parenthood under an assumed name. The plan, they believe, is foolproof. However, the unforeseen has long since rendered it all a senseless charade—two years earlier Herbert had found pictures of his ancestors, the Franks I through IV, in a lexicon. Dürrenmatt's next protagonist, the physicist Wilhelm Heinrich Möbius, will have a just cause, noble intentions, and a foolproof plan. He will sacrifice his marriage, and his freedom, and ultimately commit murder to keep a secret, but nemesis from the most unlikely source will strike him too. Dürrenmatt's worst possible turn thwarts the just and the unjust.[32]

By the 1964 revision, the Brechtian parallels were gone. However effective Dürrenmatt had hoped they would be in accentuating the differences between his dramaturgy and Brecht's, the effect had been lost on audiences and critics. On balance, however, *Frank* does not stack up favorably against Dürrenmatt's masterpieces. As several critics have noted, it lacks a central idea and suffers from a shallowness resulting from the author's failure to give a clear picture of what he is trying to accomplish.[33] The play consists of clever scenes that do not form a very cohesive whole. The proximity to Brecht rightly or wrongly detracts from the perception of originality, and the question of whether the real world is contained in Dürrenmatt's "possible world" of the Frank Family Bank is not satisfactorily answered.[34] As Timo Tiusanen noted: "Every spectator recognizes himself as a Güllener; nobody recognizes anybody as a member of Frank's gang."[35]

CHAPTER 9

Of Heroism, Failure, and Resignation

Die Physiker (The Physicists)

"Should you then, in time, discover all there is to be discovered, your progress must become a progress away from the bulk of humanity. The gulf might even grow so wide that the sound of your cheering at some new achievement would be echoed by a universal howl of horror."[1] When Brecht's Galileo Galilei makes this prediction to his erstwhile pupil-turned-teacher Andrea Sarti, he is an old man, nearly blind, a prisoner of the Inquisition. Galilei has disillusioned a generation of scholars; all scientific inquiry in Italy has threatened to cease. But Galilei has managed to save his Discoursi from the Inquisition. The revelation of the copy, made at night and hidden, which Andrea is now to smuggle across the border to the scientific free air of Holland, exhilarates the pupil, who believes in the limitless power of science. Galilei, however, has lived too long and seen too much to share in Andrea's unbridled exuberance. He has seen pure science defiled, knows firsthand the corruptibility of the scientist, and so he follows his first warning with a second: "For some years I was as strong as the authorities, and I surrendered my knowledge to the powers that be to use it, no not *use* it, *abuse* it, as it suits their ends. I have betrayed my profession. Any man who does what I have done must not be tolerated in the ranks of science" (124).

Galileo ends on an optimistic note. The scientific era has dawned. Society will no longer burn witches when the superstition that makes this atrocity possible is debunked. The poor will no longer passively accept their misery when it can be proven that their poverty is not cosmically ordained. Brecht, however, who more than once left the curtain down and all the questions open, tempers this optimism with Galilei's solemn warnings. Enter Dürrenmatt with a post-Hiroshima, pessimistic answer to Brecht. More than three centuries pass, and Galilei is living under an assumed name: Wilhelm Heinrich Möbius. Galilei's first warning has become reality. Science has progressed from the acceptance of a heliocentric universe to the ability to unleash a destructive power "brighter than a thousand suns." With Möbius, who has solved the problem of gravitation, worked out the Unitary Theory of Elemental Particles, and discovered something called "The Principle of Universal Discovery," science has advanced to that point Galilei predicted. Möbius has discovered all that the human mind can fathom, which is only a small part of a greater mystery:

In the realm of knowledge we have reached the farthest frontiers of perception. We know a few precisely calculable laws, a few basic connections between incomprehensible phenomena and that is all. The rest is mystery, closed to the rational mind. We have reached the end of our journey. But humanity has not yet got as far as that. We have battled onwards, but now no one is following in our footsteps; we have encountered a void.[2]

Möbius knows that "new and inconceivable forces would be unleashed, making possible a technical advance that would transcend the wildest flights of fancy" (P 75), were his discoveries to be made known. Dürrenmatt, his creator, also knows something else. Science has eliminated old superstitions, but it has not changed the power structure in society. Worst of all, it has replaced old myths with a new, potentially deadly one: the myth of the infallibility of science. The blessed assurance that science not only can but will solve all our problems, eliminating society's ills, has created precisely that gulf between science and society that Galilei predicted and Möbius laments. Society's eagerness to dump all its problems in the lap of science renders it no better off than it was when yielding to the Inquisition's demand that it leave its problems in the hands of God. Society has a new god, to which it can abdicate all responsibility. However, the threat of science falling victim to ideology is as great now as it ever was, and an ideology is no less insidious when it consists of political rather than religious dogma. How should a modern scientist with a conscience, who has heard Galilei's warnings, continue to work in the face of intense pressure to sell out to exploitive commercial or political interests? No less a dilemma faces Möbius.

Möbius is a patient in Dr. Mathilde von Zahnd's mental hospital Les Cerisiers (The Cherry Trees). Once a promising young physicist, he had begun to see and hear King Solomon and was declared insane. Sharing the suite with Möbius are two other physicists, one claiming to be Sir Isaac Newton and one who believes he is Albert Einstein. Newton and Einstein have both recently strangled their nurses. Möbius's wife has divorced him and married a Protestant missionary. Soon they will leave Europe forever, and so she brings their children to say good-bye. Möbius interrupts the session with an insane outburst, and under a hail of curses the family flees the asylum. Nurse Monika Stettler tells Möbius that she believes he is not insane. She also believes he is a brilliant physicist, and she has secured his release from the asylum and a post at the university. Monika loves Möbius and wants to marry him. Their train will leave this evening. Act 1 ends with Möbius strangling Monika.

Inspector Voss begins the second act as he did the first, investigating a strangling. He demands that Dr. von Zahnd hire male nurses for the physicists. She complies. Over supper, each physicist reveals his identity. Newton is a Western secret agent, Einstein an agent from an East Bloc country (clearly the USA and USSR). Both are after Möbius, whom they believe to be the greatest physicist of all time, and they are right. Möbius admits to having made startling discoveries that could destroy the world if they fell into the wrong hands. He has feigned delusions and chosen the asylum as the one place he can think and write without danger of being taken seriously. Each man has had to murder a nurse who got too close to the truth. Now, if they are to escape, they must act together. But Möbius does not want to escape, and he convinces the others that for the sake of the human race they must continue their charade. However, all have deluded themselves. The room was bugged, their conversation recorded. Dr. von Zahnd has been drugging Möbius for years and copying his manuscripts. She claims King Solomon ordered her to steal Möbius's discoveries. Now she has built up an international trust and will rule the world. Möbius and the others can do nothing, because in the eyes of the world they are deranged killers. They are trapped in the asylum forever, and the world is in the hands of a madwoman.

After an unsuccessful foray into epic theater with *Frank der Fünfte,* Dürrenmatt is back in his element. As with *Romulus, The Physicists* adheres to strict Aristotelian form. While beginning where Brecht's *Galileo* leaves off, Dürrenmatt employs a technique designed to insure his independence from his predecessor. Möbius becomes a mirror image of Galilei—every situation is reversed. Galilei wants his Discoursi to reach the outside world and uses deception to achieve this goal. Möbius likewise employs deception but to the opposite end: to keep his discoveries from the world. Galilei was imprisoned because he initially resisted the demands of the Inquisition that he suppress his research. Möbius flees into a kind of prison to escape the pressures of the authorities in the scientific community demanding that he publish his research. Finally, despite the fact that the Inquisition is confiscating them, Galilei smuggles his manuscripts out, to the benefit of humanity. Möbius's manuscripts also find their way out of the asylum, to humanity's great detriment, precisely because they are being confiscated.[3]

For the second time in as many plays Dürrenmatt has drawn heavily on Brecht. In *The Physicists,* however, he lays down the lines of demarcation much clearer than in the gangster comedy. Brecht provides the original impetus; he does not continually reappear as the object of unfocused parody. Once the curtain rises, it is exclusively Dürrenmatt's play. The characters act according to the rules of his dramaturgy, not Brecht's.

Alongside the importance of *Galileo* for the background of *The Physicists* stands a second, more contemporary inspiration. Moments before the final twist of the plot that renders all of Möbius's actions futile, the three physicists celebrate their decision to remain in the asylum with a toast:

NEWTON: Let us be mad, but wise
EINSTEIN: Prisoners, but free.
MÖBIUS: Physicists, but innocent. (P 84)

Möbius's implication is staggering. To be a physicist is to partake in the universal, original sin with which all members of the profession have been stained since that July 1945 morning in the New Mexico desert, when "Trinity" exploded, and, bathed in "the radiance of a thousand suns,"[4] theoretical science forever lost its innocence. Möbius has his own plan to reverse the process, by which he and his two companions can revert to the conditions that prevailed before the fall. Though each has committed murder, all three nevertheless stand guiltless with clear consciences, because they have severed all ties with the scientific community and with the political agencies which control it. The lives of three nurses are but a small price to pay to save the world.

Möbius has argued forcefully enough to convince a CIA and a KGB agent to betray their governments and to give up their freedom for an ideal higher than ideology. There is much talk of freedom in the second act, a pressing theme carried over from *Frank*. If only existential freedom exists in a gangster collective, is the situation any better in the scientific community? Neither Newton nor Einstein can truthfully say that it is. In the real world the scientific establishments of both hemispheres have sold out to politicians in the name of national defense. Only in the prison of their insane asylum can they be truly free to pursue pure research. Paradise seems regained—a *locus amoenus* for pure science—not in a primordial garden of apple trees, but in the tranquility of the insane asylum Les Cerisiers. Möbius has managed to convince the audience as well. Until his confession he has been an enigma: how could he have betrayed his wife and children and murdered the nurse he loved, who would have been his ticket out of the asylum? Although these questions linger, and even threaten the high moral ground he claims in the second act,[5] we are more able to understand and empathize with his dilemma after his confession. Möbius appears to be an extraordinary man for extraordinary times: "There are certain risks that one may not take: the destruction of humanity is one. We know what the world has done with the weapons it already possesses; we can imagine what it would do with those that my researches make possible, and it is these considerations that have governed my conduct" (P 80). Möbius has convinced everyone, it seems, except his creator, for the story does not end here. Dürrenmatt has resolved the ethical dilemma only to thwart the resolution. The apparent denouement has been a false trail, for the author did not believe that the problem could be solved in this way.

The Physicists had been fermenting in the author's mind since at least 1956. That year Swiss historian Robert Jungk had chronicled the development of nuclear weapons in a book entitled *Brighter than a Thousand Suns*. The book is more a story of the bomb's creators than of the bomb itself. Most compelling are the descriptions of the struggles of conscience waged by the scientists and of the miscommunication and mistrust that drove the military establishment to push for a weapon against Germany that it never would have needed. Dürrenmatt reviewed Jungk's book shortly after it appeared, and its influence on him was significant. He wrote: "The idea on which the atom bomb is based, the deep insight into the structure of matter, is a thought of the human race, represented as it were by a small elite group of researchers, and not to be appropriated by a nation. It is likewise impossible to keep secret that which is capable of being thought. Every thought process is repeatable." (In these last two sentences we hear almost verbatim the words of Fräulein Doktor Mathilde von Zahnd.) "The problem of atomic power—the atom bomb is just a special case within this problem—can only be solved internationally" (28:22). The question is how the physicist must act in today's world, and not only the physicist. Thinking can perhaps become more and more dangerous in the future" (28:23). The mistake which the elite group of scientists made during the war was not in thinking radical new thoughts. In fact, these had to be thought—their time had come. The mistake was "that they never really comprehended the unique position in which they found themselves, that they refused to make decisions. Science was afraid of power, and thus it delivered itself into the hands of the powerful" (28:23). Scientists hoped that the politicians would be able to exert the self control that they could not, but "the world was prepared for everything, just not for the atom bomb. . . . Basically nobody knew what to do. What was technically 'sweet' seduced most of them, and it was often simply not possible to remain innocent" (28:24).

It is likely that in this moment of philosophical insight for the author Möbius was born, for he, too, cannot remain innocent. The catastrophe erupts, as it must according to the tenets of Dürrenmatt's dramaturgy. The accident that dooms Möbius, just when his plan seems foolproof, is that he has fled into the one asylum where the doctor is herself mad—power-hungry and ruthless. The reason he cannot be considered "innocent," however, is his betrayal of knowledge, represented metaphorically throughout the play by King Solomon. The doctor's accusation is accurate. Möbius has "betrayed Solomon" by attempting to keep hidden something impossible to hide: an idea. When the knowledge of a particular age speaks through a human mind, that thought is common property, because it is now thinkable and can easily be thought again. Points 16 through 18 of the "21 Points to *The Physicists*" most nearly sum up the insights which Dürrenmatt gleaned from Robert Jungk, and have the most direct bearing on the fate of the three physicists in Les Cerisiers: (16) "The content of physics is the concern of physicists, its effects concern all men"; (17) "What concerns everyone can only be solved by everyone"; and (18) "Each attempt of an individual to resolve for himself what is the concern of everyone is doomed to fail."[6]

So Möbius's chilling example must not be ignored. Science is light years ahead of politics. The world is truly not ready for Solomon's revelations. But his revelations have already been made, and if the mistakes of the past are not to be repeated, those who have stewardship of this knowledge must act together, courageously and wisely, as citizens of the world community. Jungk portrayed the cold war as the product of science abdicating its responsibility to politicians and selling out to ideology. Dürrenmatt demonstrates the foolishness of scientists trying to avoid responsibility by retreating into the ivory tower. Once again, as he has often done in the past, Dürrenmatt shows that the individual acting alone cannot save the world, no matter how pure the motives or how foolproof the plan.

Despite its weighty ethical questions, two dead bodies, and the takeover of the world by a madwoman, *The Physicists* is subtitled "A Comedy in Two Acts." What else could it be? Möbius has none of the qualifications for a tragic hero. His closest affinity among Dürrenmatt's protagonists is with Romulus. He has attempted to solve a problem of society as an individual, sacrificing his family in the process, only to find that he has achieved the opposite of his goal, and now he must live with the consequences. The comedy relies largely on grotesque visual effects—such as the hunchbacked psychiatrist and the serving of a gourmet meal to the patients while the body of Monika Stettler lies where she fell—but also on irony. The first scene of act 2 is a mirror-image reversal of the play's opening scene. There the inspector is off guard and uncomfortable in the situation, wants a cigarette and schnapps, and insists upon using the words "murder" and "murderer" instead of the more clinically acceptable "accident" and "assailant." Here it is Doctor von Zahnd who is off guard, needing a drink, and committing the politically incorrect faux pas.

As we have come to expect, Dürrenmatt has not pulled his characters' names out of thin air. While not overtly satirical, some are mildly ironic or simply fit the personality of the character. Möbius has as a namesake the nineteenth-century German mathematician August Ferdinand Möbius. However, it is not the man but his most renowned invention that bears on Dürrenmatt's character: the Möbius Band, a paper ring with no inside or outside, which shows only one side no matter how one twists or turns it.[7] For the past fifteen years Möbius has shown only one side of his personality, the false side, while hiding his real nature even from his family. Doctor von Zahnd (*Zahn* = tooth) has several German expressions associated with her name. To have "hair on your teeth" means to be tough and independent, while to "show your teeth" means to show your readiness to fight. If the "tooth of time gnaws on you" it means you are showing the ravages of time. Sister Martha Boll is a *Bollwerk* (bulwark, rampart) against anyone who would try to get past her to her patients or to break the rules of the asylum. Inspector Richard Voss is a probable reference to the most popular animal fable of the Middle Ages, *Reinke de Vos* (Reinhard the Fox). If so, then this reference is ironic. The inspector is outfoxed by Dr. von Zahnd and ends up eating out of her hand, ordering exactly what she wants, male nurses for the physicists. Finally, the name of the asylum itself, Les Cerisiers (The Cherry Trees), has, in addition to the Garden of Eden / *locus amoenus* of pure science implication, definite overtones of Chekhov. His *Cherry Orchard,* like *The Physicists,* is a play about an age of innocence carelessly lost, and there are definite similarities between the triumphant tirade by the villain Lopakhin and Dr. von Zahnd's exultant ravings, in particular the images of eclipsing one's ancestors and of plundering resources for profit. Like Lopakhin, Dr. von Zahnd has figuratively chopped down the cherry orchard around Möbius and his colleagues, depriving them of their Garden of Eden, their last refuge of innocence.

To mask his true intentions, Möbius has chosen to feign a delusion, but he has selected his delusion with care. By choosing King Solomon, who is already a universal symbol for wisdom and by extension for knowledge, he has provided himself with a metaphor that allows him to speak on two different levels at the same time. When Möbius begins to claim that Solomon is dictating his manuscripts to him, a literal-thinking person would immediately assume that Möbius was delusional. This is the result he wants, and so he is committed to the asylum. Understood on the metaphorical level, knowledge comes to him in moments of inspiration, wisdom appears to him in flashes of insight. During his first-act tirade against his family, Möbius expands the metaphor from the Golden King (beneficial knowledge) to a pathetic image: "He has cast away his purple robe. Now here in my room he crouches naked and stinking, the pauper king of truth, and his psalms are horrible" (P 43). Knowledge has become debased through its commercialization and the inhuman purposes to which it has been put in the twentieth century.

Manned space flight was in its infancy in 1961, but it had already gripped the universal imagination after Yuri Gagarin's orbital flight on April 12 and Alan Shepard's suborbital hop on May 5. The space race was on, and it was quickly becoming a propaganda weapon in the cold war. Möbius's "Song of Solomon to be Sung to the Cosmonauts"[8] must be understood in this context. To his family it is the final proof of his incurable insanity. Metaphorically it is a scathing indictment of the use to which our knowledge is being put. Humanity's whole recent intellectual journey is summed up in this meaningless voyage into outer space,[9] through the hellishly hot regions of the solar system out into unforgiving cold, until we no longer know or care where we are, searching for meaning we ironically have left in that speck fading into oblivion behind us.

The next extensive use of the Solomon metaphor occurs in the dialogue between Möbius and Nurse Monika Stettler. Monika understands that Möbius is speaking metaphorically, even if she cannot fathom the implications of all he says. "I believe in King Solomon," she tells him. "That he appears to you. . . . Day in, day out" (P 48–49). Since she knows that he is sane and tells him so, this can only mean that she understands him on a metaphorical level. When Möbius tells her "It is fatal to believe in King Solomon" (P 49), he means it again on two levels. Literally he is warning her that she is in mortal danger if she persists on her present path. Figuratively he is stating a veiled truth about the dangerous type of knowledge in which he deals. Accused by Monika of betraying Solomon, Möbius goes on the defensive: "I have always remained faithful to King Solomon. He thrust himself into my life, suddenly, unbidden, he abused me, he destroyed my life, but I have never betrayed him" (P 53). Möbius is not dissembling. He cannot imagine that hiding his knowledge could be treasonous, since he believes that publishing it would amount to a betrayal of humanity. Finally, after Möbius strangles Monika, he alibis the crime to Dr. von Zahnd: "King Solomon ordained it" (P 62). While this is the expected excuse of a hopelessly delusional patient, on the metaphorical level the murder was an intellectual decision, necessary to safeguard the knowledge contained in his manuscripts.

Finally it is Fräulein Doktor's turn to reveal her own experience with King Solomon. Occasionally scholars have mentioned in passing the possibility that

Dr. von Zahnd might not be insane.[10] This is an intriguing idea which no one has seriously argued. Dürrenmatt, of course, confirmed what critics had believed by declaring her "die verrückte Irrenärztin" (the crazy psychiatrist).[11] When Dürrenmatt interprets his own work, it is risky to question that interpretation. However, he also gave the critic the responsibility of finding the real world within his possible worlds. Could this not include finding an element the author did not consciously intend, or that he reinterpreted after the fact? If insanity is the explanation for the psychiatrist's behavior, it stands as the revealed motivating factor for the worst possible turn of the plot. However, let us postulate that Dr. Mathilde von Zahnd is not insane. Certainly the element of coincidence is not compromised—Möbius has still fled into the one asylum where his ruse cannot work—however, accepting the premise that the psychiatrist actually suffers from the exact delusion Möbius invents and feigns requires too much suspension of disbelief. It also compromises the function of coincidence as warning exemplum that it has in Dürrenmatt's other plays.

If Dr. von Zahnd is not really delusional, then what is she saying with her many references to King Solomon? Assuming that she is an astute psychiatrist, it is not much of a reach to assume that she has been on to Möbius right from the beginning. Able to distinguish a real delusion from a feigned one, Dr. von Zahnd must have wondered why Möbius was withdrawing from society in this way. Once she cracked the simple metaphoric code, Solomon = knowledge, it required no stretch of the imagination to deduce that the secret lay in Möbius's manuscripts. Then the brilliant idea struck her to appropriate Möbius's knowledge, while letting the physicist sit in his own trap. For fifteen years, during which the psychiatrist had been stealthily spinning her many webs to insure that Möbius and anyone else who came after him would stay locked up in Les Cerisiers for life, Möbius believed he was fooling her with the Solomon metaphor. She had willingly let him believe this. Now, however, it is time for her great revelation. As she begins to explain the truth to Möbius, she makes full use of his metaphor. "The Golden King came floating toward me" (P 88) [I suddenly had a brilliant idea out of nowhere]. "Möbius betrayed him" (P 89) [Möbius tried to hide the knowledge he had been given]. "What Solomon had found could be found by anyone, but he wanted it to belong to himself alone, his means toward the establishment of his holy dominion over all the world" (P 89) [Anyone can acquire knowledge, but its goal must be the attainment of power for world domination]. "And so did he seek me out, his unworthy handmaiden" (P 89) [Since Möbius has failed, knowledge has sought her out. She will inherit the opportunity Möbius has failed to exploit]. "Let me put it in language you can understand," she seems to be saying between the lines. Möbius believes that she is insane because he ironically fails to recognize his own metaphor being thrown triumphantly back in his face. When Möbius asks her: "Don't you see you're mad?" she replies: "I'm no more mad than you are" (P 90). If we take this line seriously, we can understand the rest of Dr. von Zahnd's speech for what it is: a magnificent, consequential use of metaphor, not insanity.

The last word, however, and the last irony, belongs to Möbius. The metaphor has become reality. He now fully identifies with King Solomon, but not the Golden King, "immeasurably rich, wise and God-fearing." He is "poor King Solomon," whose wisdom destroyed not only his fear of God, but also his wealth: "Now the cities over which I ruled are dead, the Kingdom that was given unto my keeping is deserted: only a blue shimmering wilderness. And somewhere round a small, yellow, nameless star there circles, pointlessly, everlastingly, the radioactive earth. I am Solomon. I am Solomon. I am poor King Solomon" (P 93–94).

Herkules und der Stall des Augias (Hercules and the Augian Stables)

"What concerns everyone can only be solved by everyone. Every attempt by an individual to resolve for himself what is the concern of everyone is doomed to fail." While this moral from his blackest comedy to date still rang in the audiences' ears, Dürrenmatt prepared to bring a play to the stage that would probe this dilemma from the opposite side. Möbius had tried to act alone in the name of society and had failed. If any hope still exists, it is that all those affected by a problem can work together to solve it. This is the theme of the next play, for which Dürrenmatt only had to adapt an existing radio play from 1954, *Herkules und der Stall des Augias*. This radio play, which already contained most of the scenes and verbatim dialogue of the stage comedy, experimented with motifs the author had planned to employ in the aborted sequel to *Angel— The Accomplices:* "All are against the tower, and nevertheless it is built." In the radio play and subsequent stage comedy all are against the manure, and nevertheless it remains.

Hercules, the Greek national hero, is in debt. For that reason only does his fiancée, Deianeira, at the behest of his secretary Polybios, succeed in convincing him to accept Augias's offer of three hundred thousand drachmas to rid the land Elis of its mountains of manure. Sizing up the situation, Hercules plans to divert two rivers and wash the manure into the sea. However, the manure covering the land proves not to be as big a problem as the manure in the heads of the Elier. One by one the members of the parliament have reservations. (Elis is a democracy and Augias is not a king, just the president.) Although all swear that they want the manure removed, the bureaucracy is too weighty and the

113

Elier keep appointing more commissions to study the matter from all sides. Meanwhile Deianeira has fallen in love with Augias's son Phyleus, and Hercules has had to take a job in the circus in order to pay the bills. When the circus folds before Hercules can be paid, and more and more parliamentary commissions block the manure removal, Hercules leaves Elis to take on his next task, the extermination of the Stymphalian birds. Deianeira follows him, leaving a distraught Phyleus at the altar. Elis remains hopelessly buried under growing mountains of manure, but Augias shows his son the way to individual redemption. For years he has been secretly tending a garden, patiently converting manure to humus, and so making at least his small corner of Elis habitable. Now he hands the garden over to his son with the words: "Dare to live, and to live here amid this formless, desolate land: the heroic act I impose upon you now son, the Herculean task I heap upon your shoulders."

Between the radio play and the stage version, Dürrenmatt added some elements to the plot. Out of the love triangle Hercules—Deianeira—Phyleus, Dürrenmatt constructed a love rectangle by adding a seductress for Hercules. From the Hercules legends he drew the character of Iole and turned her into the fourteen-year-old daughter of Augias. Iole sneaks into Hercules' tent and is rebuked and sent home by the hero, but later she follows him to Stymphalia to thwart the reconciliation of Hercules and Deianeira. True to the Hercules legend in spirit, although not in the detail, is a future vision that the author interposed into the middle of the play. We see foreshadowed Hercules' death at the hands of a jealous Deianeira. The hero is now living with Iole. Deianeira sends him a shirt dipped in the blood of the centaur Nessos, which proves fatal. Immediately after the premiere, Dürrenmatt changed the play's optimistic ending. Phyleus rejects Augias's offer of the garden and rushes off to defend his honor against Hercules for taking Deianeira from him. The impetuous lover will die in this foolhardy attempt to prove "Elian heroism."

Dürrenmatt's Hercules is only a pale shadow of the hero of Greek legend. He is an all-too-human bungler who is completely out of his element. He is a would-be hero cursed to live in an unheroic age—our age, barely camouflaged. The Dürrenmattian worst possible turn constantly nips at his heels. None of his tasks have worked out as they were intended: the Nemean Lion turned out to be a dwarf mountain lion, the Hydra sank in the Lernean Marsh, the Cerynean Hind got away, and the Erymanthean Boar fell into a glacial fissure on Mount Olympus. Since Dürrenmatt has made a glorified bounty hunter out of the hero, a failed quest means no reward money. Hercules stands at the edge of bankruptcy.

Dürrenmatt begins the radio play version by citing his source. Gustav

Schwab, he says, described the fifth labor of Hercules as cleaning out the Augean Stable in a single day. The error was not Schwab's fault, he adds. He was relying on Greek poets, and in this case his sources had tended to underestimate the task. Out of the manure in the Augean Stable Dürrenmatt makes mountains of manure that cover the entire land of Elis. Out of King Augias he makes President Augias, the wealthiest farmer in a land of farmers and the most powerless of presidents in a small parliamentary democracy. Augias enjoys a warm relationship with his son,—no talk of banishment as in the Greek legend—and in the stage version he gains a daughter. None of this bothered Dürrenmatt, because he was not retelling the Hercules myth, but rather demythologizing Hercules in order to make him the antihero of a modern parable.

Although it deserved a better fate, the Hercules comedy managed to offend critics and audiences alike. No one attentive to the rhythm into which Dürrenmatt had fallen should have been surprised by the failure. Following the success of *Mississippi* had come the disappointing reaction to *Angel*. After the worldwide acclaim accorded *The Visit* followed the disaster of *Frank*. Now *The Physicists* was casting the long shadow. Only thirteen months had passed since its premiere, and it was still setting records in Switzerland and Germany and picking up momentum worldwide. It would have taken another play of that caliber to satisfy the critics' expectations. *Hercules* is not in the same league with *The Physicists*. As an unresolvable dilemma, manure simply does not arouse the same concern as nuclear annihilation; nor can the audience properly empathize with the thwarted heroism of this anachronistic hero. Möbius locked away in a mental hospital after a failed attempt to save humanity is fodder for ethical debate. Hercules lifting weights in a circus is at best a cause for laughter.

Still there is philosophical depth to be found in the coarse comedy. Deianeira and Phyleus represent the spirit of human potential. When Deianeira recites a poem from *Antigone,* the uneducated Phyleus replies: "I understand these words. Human beings should rule over the earth" (8:76). Deianeira elaborates: "The earth was given to us for that purpose: That we should tame fire, use the force of the wind and of the sea, that we should shatter rocks and out of their rubble build temples and houses" (8:76). Such energy and idealism could have served the country well, but against the overwhelming inertia in Elis they have no chance to prevail. Deianeira cannot bear to live in a land where the elements hold sway over the human spirit, and so when the manure removal project fails, so does the chance for the union of the young lovers.

For much of the comedy, however, farcical elements dominate. Several jokes arise from Hercules' sexual impotence and the resulting ruse he contrives to keep his reputation as a womanizer intact. He forcibly bathes Augias's stable

115

servant Kambyses and puts him in his tent as a decoy. Half the women of Elis sneak into the tent and sleep with Kambyses, believing he is Hercules, before the servant gives out from exhaustion. One running gag concerns Hercules' temper tantrums, each of which results in a new injury to Polybios, until the poor secretary, still loyal because he is waiting for his overdue salary, winds up in a body cast. Most of the jokes, however, revolve around the manure in ever new, creative variations. Hercules slogs through it cursing, Polybios slips down a mountainside of it and crashes through the roof of Augias's stall, and the members of Parliament arise as a group out of it whenever they have a meeting and sink back down into it when the meeting is over.

Although references to Swiss culture and politics are a trademark of Dürrenmatt in general, nowhere are they more openly and satirically presented than in *Hercules*. Behind and through the masks of the Elier grin obviously for all to see not Hellenes, but Helvetians. Elis's mountains of manure are described in alpine terms. All of the Elier are dairy farmers, and there are four times as many cows and three times as many pigs as people, accounting for the massive amount of agricultural byproduct. Politically they are "liberal-patriarchal" (Swiss women were still nine years away from getting the vote), and the Elier boast of being "the oldest democracy in Greece." Symbol of Augias's presidential authority is a cowbell. Elis's army is specially trained for "manure warfare" (*Mistkrieg*), an allusion to the Swiss Army training in alpine terrain combat. Any remaining doubt is removed by the names of the Elier: Pentheus von Säuliboden, Kadmos von Käsingen, Sisyphos von Milchiwil, and from the 1980 version, Kleisthenes vom Mittlern Grütt.

The Swiss immediately saw their own patriotism, moral and material values, and political institutions held up to ridicule, but they sensed still more. Dürrenmatt seemed to be attacking their own icon Wilhelm Tell through the character of his bungling "national hero." Dürrenmatt was recasting the "Tell myth," as he called it, for the unheroic twentieth century. The Tell of legend fires the arrow which fells the tyrant, but the revolution succeeds because a well-planned conspiracy is already in place, and the individual patriots can be counted on to put aside their personal differences and fight together for the common good. Hercules has no weapon against the enemies of progress in Elis. The manure removal project fails, not because the hero lacks the will or the courage, but because the Elier cannot put aside parochial concerns and ideological differences. Lip-service to patriotism is in abundance, for example, in slogans like "Whoever doubts the manure removal doubts the Fatherland!" (8:95). However, it is a patriotism based on a presumably glorious past of which no one has any tangible record. Nobody knows whether Elis's art treasures really exist under the mountains of manure. If they do not, then possibly the glorious past does not exist either. This fear creates indecision, much like Ill's indecision about boarding the train, which is expressed with vintage parliamentary equivocation: "And since, if we do not remove the manure, the question of whether they [the treasures] exist or not remains open—which, speaking with all political candor, is as good as if our sacred treasures were there—I come to the conclusion that we must carefully consider the question of manure removal, although, as I have said, I remain completely convinced of its necessity" (8:94–95). It is typical for nations insecure about their future to cling to the myths about their past, aided by slogan patriotism. It is a tall order to expect any nation voluntarily to peel back the layers of "manure" in its collective past and take an honest look at what may or may not lie underneath it all, but Dürrenmatt is daring to suggest no less.

So *Hercules* offended the Swiss greatly, and the critics railed. The Helvetian satire and the disrespect for Wilhelm Tell were not appreciated, but what everyone found most offensive was the manure, realistically created on stage by Teo Otto, growing higher with every act.[12] Unfortunately the all-too-obvious identification of Elis with Switzerland hindered the audiences from seeing that Switzerland was just the first and easiest target. How unlike Dürrenmatt to write a play exclusively for the purpose of satirizing his homeland. If we are all Güllener, why should we not also all be Elier? The manure is universal. There is not a single event in the world that stood as a model for the conditions in Elis. The play is rather a simple observation on the inability of representative democracies to do what they know to be right and reasonable.

Taken together *The Physicists* and *Hercules* do not leave much room for the optimistic view that society will straighten out its messes in time. When individuals try to act together in a just, common cause, there is no more hope of reaching the solution than if one person tries to solve the problem for everyone. This, too, is an answer to Brecht without the obvious reference to him. We can see in the fruitless dickering of the Elian parliament an indirect refutation of Brecht's *The Caucasian Chalk Circle*. There, reason triumphs, as it always must according to Brecht, when reasonable people, imbued with Marxist ideology, talk to each other. For Dürrenmatt such debates are doomed to devolve into a hopeless quagmire of self-interest and indecision.

Of the Elier, only Augias and Phyleus comprehend the impending disaster. "It is beautiful to have a homeland one can love," Phyleus says to Deianeira. "I cannot love mine. We don't rule over our land any more. It rules us with its brown warmth. We have fallen asleep in its stalls" (8:76). Phyleus fears the manure removal too, because he is a realist: "Because we do not understand how to live without the manure. Because no one will show us the potential of the human being, his capacity to accomplish great and beautiful, true and brave deeds. I fear the future, Deianeira" (8:76). After Hercules leaves, Phyleus asks his father why the manure remains when everyone wanted it gone. The answer: "Because the Elier fear what they want and what they know is reasonable, my son. Because reason requires a long time to assert itself, and because removing manure is not a matter of one generation, but of many" (8:113). Augias has known all along that his countrymen would fail, and so he has patiently carved out a small success for himself and, he hopes, for his son. Had Phyleus accepted this gift and remained to tend his father's garden, the play would have ended on a note of optimism. That would have meant that the flash of insight which leads to personal salvation is transferable. It would have raised Augias's garden from the level of personal, heroic, existential revolt to a symbol of hope for the future. This could not be Dürrenmatt's ending. His courageous individuals are always loners. Their insight is grace, but grace does not come over nations or even families, only individuals. Augias can do no more than try to make Phyleus understand:

I am a politician, my son, no hero, and politics works no miracles. It is as weak as the people themselves, a likeness of their own fragility and doomed to repeated failure. It never creates good if we do not do good ourselves. And so I did something good. I transformed manure into humus. It is a difficult time in which we are able to do so little for the world, but we should at least do this little bit: our own contribution. The grace, that the world might become brighter, cannot be obtained by force, but you can create the conditions, so that grace—if it comes—will find in you a pure mirror for its light. (8:115–16)

Happiness in one's own small corner—a final retreat into the Biedermeier ideal in the face of a senseless world, yet one which represents life amid desolation. Augias's garden amid the manure is a practical application of Gulliver's admonition: "So we should not seek to save the world, only to survive it, the only true adventure which still exists for us in this late age." In direct contrast to Möbius's flight into the asylum, Augias's retreat stands as a life-affirming, positive action, the acceptance of individual responsibility for that small parcel of reality over which one has any control.

CHAPTER 10

Improbable Grace

Der Meteor (The Meteor)

Up to this point in Dürrenmatt's work, grace has been a rare and delicate gift, found by only those few brave persons, the seekers and strivers who gain personal enlightenment by refusing to capitulate—courageous individuals, beaten down by chance, ridiculed by reality. Although Dürrenmatt insisted that grace cannot be earned, each of his characters to date who has received it, culminating in Augias, has been somehow worthy. While grace is always existential, coming in the form of insight, heightened faith, or late-found meaning for one's existence, there has at least been a correlation between striving and attaining, righteous idealism and reward. *The Meteor* represents a radical deviation from this pattern.

Wolfgang Schwitter, Nobel Prize–winning dramatist and reprehensible human being, experiences the miracle of resurrection twice, while nearly everyone who crosses his path dies. In contrast to all the just and unjust characters who fall in his wake, Schwitter is the only character who truly longs to die. At death's door for months and clinically dead for several minutes, Schwitter wakes up and walks out of the hospital, determined to die in the garret where he had lived forty years earlier as a struggling painter. The garret is now rented by an equally struggling artist, Hugo Nyffenschwander, from whom Schwitter temporarily rents the space for two hundred francs. Pastor Emanuel Lutz, barely forty, who was with Schwitter when he "died" the first time and who has come to witness the miracle of resurrection, is the first victim. The excitement is too much for his heart. Schwitter shocks the eighty-year-old "Great Muheim," landlord of the garret, by claiming that he had once had an affair with Muheim's wife. Then he burns his unpublished manuscripts along with one-and-a-half million francs, most of which his son would have inherited. Finally he sends his fourth wife, the former call girl Olga, away in tears and sleeps with Nyffenschwander's wife Auguste, in whose arms he "dies." By five minutes into act 2, after he is eulogized by star critic Friedrich Georgen (and after Auguste has left Nyffenschwander), Schwitter is alive again, but the dying around him becomes epidemic. Muheim, unable to come to terms with his wife's infidelity years before with Schwitter, rages out of control and throws Nyffenschwander

119

down the stairs. Only after the painter's body is found and the police are leading Muheim away does Schwitter admit that he made the whole story up. Professor Schlatter, the discredited doctor who had twice diagnosed Schwitter's death, runs off to commit suicide. Olga poisons herself because of Schwitter's rejection; and Olga's mother, Frau Nomsen, dies of a heart attack while bringing Schwitter the news. Finally, the Salvation Army enters, praising the miracle and singing hallelujah. As the curtain falls, Schwitter, now the picture of health and strength, screams: "Why don't you let me die in peace!"[1]

Structurally the play most closely resembles *The Physicists*. After the open form of *Hercules,* Dürrenmatt returns to a tightly constructed two-acter with strict adherence to Aristotelian unities. The entire comedy takes place in the attic garret in a realtime frame. With the first resurrection having occurred less than an hour before the opening curtain and belonging, as do Schwitter's months of terminal illness, to the play's prehistory, the only time lapse is between Schwitter's second "death" and the eulogy that same afternoon. This hour is compressed into intermission. Schwitter never leaves the stage, and there are no subplots. All the action is directly motivated by Schwitter's futile attempts to die.

Meteorically and with no warning Wolfgang Schwitter falls into the seemingly ordered world of Hugo Nyffenschwander and his wife Auguste, of Professor Schlatter, the great Muheim, Pastor Lutz, Frau Nomsen, and the others. Meteors are natural phenomena that illuminate, if only briefly, everything in their path. Although Schwitter does this, the title is also ironic. A meteor consumes itself in seconds, and although its end is dramatic it disappears as it arises. This is quite the opposite of Wolfgang Schwitter's situation. His extinguished flame continues to relight. By the play's end he appears to be farther away from death than he has been in months. There is something of an elemental force about Schwitter, who bears a kinship to Anastasia from *Mississippi*. With his own vitality ebbing, Schwitter seems to draw the life force out of everyone around him. There is no scientific explanation for his miraculous recoveries, and this fact brings into the play the element of numinosity which so intrigued critics and angered theologians.

Dürrenmatt had not provoked the religious establishment for some time. A few scholars continued to cling to the illusion that Dürrenmatt was still a devout Calvinist who planted Christian messages of hope and salvation behind the failures of his protagonists. However, there were others who recognized that Dürrenmatt had long been pursuing a "theology without God."[2] Dürrenmatt scholars in the nineties have an advantage denied to those in the sixties: the author's complete works containing later autobiographical writings, and a number of published interviews. Even so, it remains a source of wonder that scholars could have searched for the Christian message in this play. To see it as a study in humanity's tragic inability to recognize and accept God's grace is to read the play with blinders on, for one thing which *The Meteor* is not is a Christian play.

The critics had not been kind to Dürrenmatt after *Hercules*. Dürrenmatt, in turn, felt more anger toward the critics than he had ever felt before. It took him three years after the *Hercules* failure to venture back to the stage. When he finally did return with *The Meteor* in 1966, he accompanied the play with a rather defensive set of "20 Points." Whereas the "21 Points to *The Physicists*" has gained validity as a defining document for Dürrenmatt's drama theory beyond the individual play, these twenty points seem more aimed at trying to keep the critics at arm's length. The first two points are directed at them and have nothing to do with dramaturgy or the interpretation of the play itself: (1) "Criticism is not possible without analysis"; and (2) "Of importance is the question: 'what does the author depict?' and not the question: 'what did the author intend?' What the author intended is his business, what he depicts, the objective result of his efforts. Criticism must concern itself first of all with this result" (9:159). Point 19 returns to the critics for a final admonition: "This is the idea of the play in its discussed form. Only on the basis of this can the play be criticized, that is, examined" (9:162). In between he interprets the play, revealing much of what he "intended" beyond that which is immediately evident in the text, and thereby compromising point 2.

In summary, he writes: "The idea of the play is the story of a man who rises from the dead and does not believe his resurrection" (9:160). Such a miracle is either proof of God for the believer or an accident of nature for the unbeliever. The resurrected individual who does not believe his resurrection is a double vexation, applying to the believer and the nonbeliever. Such a person is "in a higher sense a comic individual" (9:160). Dürrenmatt makes the controversial claim that honest Christians no longer believe in the resurrection, and therefore Schwitter symbolizes modern Christianity, which has become a vexation to itself. "The Meteor is a play about not being able to believe" (9:161). Schwitter cannot believe the others who tell him he was dead, therefore he is isolated. Death for Schwitter becomes something insurmountable. Since he does not believe in his own resurrection, he does not believe in any. "That he must die is his despair. If he wants to overcome his despair, he must give meaning to death" (9:162). Thus, he sets death as the absolute and denies life. This is an extreme response, but *The Meteor* is an extreme play.

As a resurrected person, Schwitter belongs to the living—as one who does not believe in his resurrection he counts among the dead. He becomes isolated in society, a total individual among relative individualists. Such an individual becomes dangerous because the death, in which he believes, does not occur. Schwitter gains not eternal life, but rather eternal dying. (9:162)

Autobiographical elements provide the basis for much of the comedy, specifically Dürrenmatt's own dabbling in art and his battles against theater critics. Schwitter like Dürrenmatt is a painter-turned-writer. Nyffenschwander is a talentless painter hiding behind the euphemism "artistic revolutionary," whose entire repertoire consists of infinite variations on one model, his naked wife. Dürrenmatt is having good-natured fun with his past, especially as it regards the lowly position of the struggling artist in society: "Yes, I had a rotten time in this studio too. Nobody will give credit to a talentless painter. I had to bluff my way through, Nyffenschwander, bluff" (M 11). Being denied credit and bluffing his way through are accurate autobiographical confessions.

A masterpiece of irony is the scene in which Dürrenmatt invites the audience to witness his funeral. Left for dead by the critics after *Hercules,* he writes his own eulogy as he imagines the critics would write it:[3] "Brilliantly defined and viciously spoken" (M 36), damning with faint praise, rendering him obsolete before the coffin lid is closed. "Star Critic" Friedrich Georgen's platitudinous eulogy places Dürrenmatt's cultural pessimism, which many theater critics considered immoral and dangerous, in opposition to the optimistic worldview—Schiller's theater as moralistic establishment—upon which they insisted.[4] However, Dürrenmatt has the last laugh on the critics, as he rises from his bed, alive and feisty. Rumors of his death have been premature.

The fact that the writer had also painted in his youth and given it up to pursue writing full-time, coupled with the details of Dürrenmatt's dramaturgy criticized in the eulogy by critic Georgen, inevitably gave rise to speculation that Schwitter equals Dürrenmatt. Certainly Dürrenmatt has injected some of himself into the character of Schwitter, but the portrait is a masterpiece of ambiguity. The author himself once stated: "naturally I share many of his views, and he has a fur coat just like mine, but one can hardly call it a self-portrait."[5] Dürrenmatt was not obsessed with dying, nor would he declare his whole life an artistic sham. Certainly Dürrenmatt is not retracting his life's work, which Schwitter does by burning his manuscripts in the first act. The play is a comedy, albeit a very black one, and Dürrenmatt uses an extreme, fictional representative of his own profession to poke a little fun at himself, his colleagues, and above all at the critics.

In addition to the destructive force which emanates from Schwitter, leaving so many corpses in his wake, is a second quality which can only be partially explained away by his celebrity status. Nobody can say no to him. With a hypnotist's precision he exerts absolute control over not only his wife and his publicist, but also over the total strangers whose lives he disrupts. Under this spell Pastor Lutz helps him throw one-and-a-half million francs into the fire and even abruptly stops praying on command. When the caretaker Glauser sees the body of the pastor on the bed, he knows he must call the police, but at Schwitter's orders he helps the others carry it into the hallway. This type of commanding, mesmerizing presence, coupled with the death force Schwitter projects, begs for an allegorical interpretation.

Schwitter may seem well-suited to the role of Death; however, this is no conventional dance of death. Dürrenmatt has taken a literary model and has proceeded—as is his custom—with his tongue firmly embedded in his cheek to turn the model inside-out. *The Meteor* can at best be considered a modern, secular dance of death. The victims represent a cross-section of twentieth-century society. Schwitter has immortality in common with the medieval Mors, but he lacks the divine mission. Schwitter denies the existence of God: "I have no soul, there was never enough time for that. You try writing a play every year. — Here is a man dissolving into his basic elements, Water, Fat, and Minerals, and you come in serving up God and miracles. And to what purpose? So that I will see myself as an instrument of God? So that I will confirm your faith? I want to die honestly without fiction and fabrication" (M 16–17). While Mors informed his victims of their imminent deaths in verse, Schwitter, totally indifferent to the fates of his victims, is only concerned with trumpeting the news of his own impending demise. Yet the result is the same. One by one his victims perish, while Schwitter continues to be denied the one thing he seeks. In the middle of the twentieth century, in enlightened times, Dürrenmatt stages a mini-plague of death and destruction as incomprehensible as the Black Death must have been in the Middle Ages. However, here Death appears in the form of an arrogant, bumbling clown figure who treats his victims not with derision or even pity, but indifference.

Frequently scholars have recognized the criticism of ideologies that underlies *The Meteor.* It has been termed a "dance of death of ideologies," in which "relative individuals," secure in their belief in one or more basic values, discover in their confrontation with the "total individual"—the absolute ideologue whose power lies in his monomaniacal death fixation—that their lives are built on sand.[6] Schwitter's dying awakens his victims to the consciousness of "the worthlessness, the falseness of their uniform, conformist lives."[7] Another persuasive interpretation, which tries to give the choice of victims meaning, contends that Schwitter, who alone is aware of the meaninglessness of existence, comes face-to-face with individuals who have escaped into the deceptive illusion that meaning can be found in the exploitive institutions of capitalist society, "religion, art, science, prostitution, sexuality and marriage." One by one Schwitter, the judge, confronts them with the illusoriness of their lives and "condemns" them. In this way, the play takes on the character of a modern allegorical "theater of the world" (*Welttheater*).[8] Although this interpretation works well on a symbolic level, it cannot establish a causal nexus between the philosophical differences Schwitter may have with his various conversation partners and the nature of their deaths. Schwitter does not condemn them in any concrete sense, nor do they condemn themselves. All but Olga, whose tragic suicide is the result of Schwitter's indifference, die absurd, grotesquely comical deaths as the victims of Dürrenmatt's favorite nemesis: chance. So with this modern, secular dance of death we are back in the world of Traps and his *Panne,* where: "We are no longer threatened by God, by justice, by fate as in the Fifth Symphony, but by an automobile accident, a dam breaks as the result of faulty construction, the explosion of an atomic plant through the error of some absentminded technician, a wrong setting on an incubator" (T 8).

The most criticized ideology in *The Meteor* is Christianity. Dürrenmatt attacks it primarily on one vulnerable flank. Years later he would attack it on all flanks in *Turmbau.* For now, however, he seems to accept Christianity as "essentially an existential question." He continues: "What science has helped us to understand is that numbers and figures are constructions of the mind. God is too. But Christ exists. In my neighbor. In man."[9] Where he primarily attacks Christianity is in its organization, as a bourgeois institution affirming the status quo and a hypocritical, narrowly defined morality. This is the provocation of the religious establishment in which he revelled his whole life. In 1976 Dürrenmatt expressed his views on organized religion to Heinz Ludwig Arnold, views that were already well-established ten years earlier when *The Meteor* premiered: "I am totally against the church. For me the church is among the worst things that can exist, because the church imposes a constraint, because it only has the appearance of belief, a pretense of religion, a mock-Christianity, only an empty show of faith."[10] Schwitter is a vexation to Christian moralists; he drinks, whores, lies, and blasphemes his way through two acts, yet he experiences resurrection twice and is hailed by Pastor Lutz and the Salvation Army as the "chosen of God." This is a most exaggerated example to prove the point. "Grace is given to the most grotesque object. That is the most strongly expressed dialectic idea the play has theologically."[11] The church, of course, played into his hands by expressing outrage. Dürrenmatt countered by accusing his accusers of smug theology—"As if grace were granted according to human certificates of moral conduct."[12] Dürrenmatt had his scandal, and the play went on to enjoy successful runs in Germany, England, and on Broadway.

Much has been made of Schwitter's inability to accept God's grace, placing the character in a line extending from the Pilate of *Die Stadt* through Nebuchadnezzar of *Angel*. A Christian interpretation would make of Schwitter a tragic character for this reason: He cannot believe in his resurrection. He is clearly unworthy to receive the grace of eternal life, claims a prominent Dürrenmatt scholar, but the play illustrates a basic tenet of Dürrenmatt's cosmic order, that grace does not go hand-in-hand with justice.[13] The weakness of such an interpretation is its presumption that what Schwitter receives is actually grace. Schwitter made a conscious decision amid incredible suffering. On a hospital slab under glaring lights with Professor Schlatter cutting him to pieces, Schwitter gave up wanting to live and began to desire death:

And suddenly I was face to face with myself, there was no escape into fantasy any more, there was nothing there but my old bloated, putrid body. Nothing but horror. (Short pause) And I embraced this end, I rushed towards it. I let go and fell, I fell and went on falling. Everything had become a matter of complete indifference to me. And nothing had weight any longer, nothing had sense, nothing had meaning or value! (Pause) Death is the only reality. (M 60–61)

Schwitter has made an existential decision. What he wants is merely the inevitable, that which someone with his degree of critical illness has a right to expect. Becoming a medical miracle is the farthest thing from his mind and the last thing he desires. From Schwitter's perspective, then, the worst possible turn has struck. Schwitter has realized the exact opposite of that which he wanted, indeed which he believed he must realize. For the believing Christians it is God's grace; for Schwitter it is a curse. He is less a modern Lazarus, his son's derisive name for him, than a modern Ahasverus. The agent of this curse is ambiguous. How each audience member interprets Schwitter's recurring resurrections reflects his or her own beliefs. Schwitter is a nonbeliever, who cannot give a theological interpretation to his situation. If he could, he would still see it far differently than the pastor or the Salvation Army members do from their detached, comfortable positions. Schwitter, if he sensed divine intervention at all, would only be able to perceive a sadistic deity, the torturer-God from Dürrenmatt's early prose. What we are left with is Dürrenmatt's most horrifying theological scenario since those early nightmare visions. Everybody dies except the one man for whom life itself is an anathema; grace is revealed as a curse; and modern man is left with only two options, atheism or belief in a sadistic God.

Finally, Dürrenmatt contends through *The Meteor* that miracles are no longer sufficient to prove the existence of God. In a simpler, more naive time miracles were enough to gain converts. In modern times most of what used to be considered miraculous is now commonplace. The modern rational mind will seek first a logical, scientific explanation. The biblical parable of the rich man and the beggar Lazarus, however, attests to a basic human skepticism about miracles even in biblical times. Dürrenmatt never mentions this parable, but he thinks it through to a still more extreme conclusion. Abraham's answer to the rich man in hell, "If they do not hear Moses and the prophets, neither will they be convinced if some one should rise from the dead," becomes in Dürrenmatt's modern parable for the rationalists "neither will they be convinced if *they themselves* rise from the dead." The existence of God cannot be proven through miracles because the true believer does not need them, and the nonbeliever will not see them as miracles. *The Meteor* is in the final analysis another Dürrenmatt play which challenges and provokes without providing solutions. There is no justification to call *The Meteor* a Christian play in any conventional sense. It is more an attack on the state of modern Christianity by one who already stood far out on its existential fringe.

CHAPTER 11

The Adaptations

Die Wiedertäufer (The Anabaptists)

Four of the five plays Dürrenmatt wrote between 1967 and 1970 were adaptations: two of Shakespeare, one of Strindberg, and one of his own first play, the expressionistic epic *Es steht geschrieben*. True to the author's dictum that "comedy is the only thing that can still reach us," each adaptation recasts its original as a comedy. In 1967 Dürrenmatt revisited his own Anabaptist drama from twenty years earlier, looking at the same historical event in a different way. While the earlier version had painted Bockelson as an evil genius, the adaptation made of him an unemployed actor who is at the same time a frustrated, would-be theater director. It is the clever idea behind the adaptation— that the tragedy of Münster during the reign of the Anabaptists was in fact a comedy being staged by their leader for the benefit of the princes, the cardinal, and Bishop Franz, who were besieging the city.

The adaptation, entitled *Die Wiedertäufer,* is considerably shorter than the original. Gone are most of the monologues, and those remaining have been shortened without being compromised. Dürrenmatt rewrote other scenes with an eye to comic effect. His religious cynicism comes through not only in the very serious character of the bishop, but also in comic scenes such as the return of Johann von Büren and Hermann von Mengerssen to their camp after their stinging defeat before the walls of Münster. The Protestant knight von Büren proclaims his conversion to Catholicism: "I'll convert on the spot. March Field Chaplain! Convert me to the beliefs of the only true church! Pour holy water over me by the bucketfuls, let me embrace statues of the saints, pile mountains of indulgences on my sinful head . . . !" (10:66). Meanwhile the Catholic von Mengerssen has limped onto the stage proclaiming: "Monk, you are hereby named a Protestant Field Chaplain. Convert me quickly to the faith of the great Martin Luther, box my ears with the Catechism, shout hymns into my ear, drum grace into me!" (10:66).

Out of a very short dialogue in *Es steht geschrieben,* Dürrenmatt evolves a long, satirical scene which exposes in somewhat Brechtian fashion—the parallels to *Mother Courage* are compelling but general in nature—the commercial motivations for war. With the superscript "The war is saved," the scene exposes that fact that the siege of Münster has already lasted months too long. The monk has swum the river, scaled the city wall, and returned unchallenged. "For months now Münster would have fallen if you had only attacked" (10:105), he reports. To the monk's protests that it is inhuman to starve the people any longer, von Büren replies: "Münster is surrounded, the booty secure, and as long as we don't take the city the Bishop has to pay our salary" (10:105–6). In the adaptation the monk is the lone voice of reason, suggesting logical and humanitarian solutions to problems (which go universally unheeded) until an absurd misunderstanding leads to his execution. Although a minor character, the monk prefigures the Bastard in the *King John* adaptation.

When the Vegetable Woman appears with a cart of delicacies from Bremen to be delivered to Münster for King Bockelson, von Büren and von Mengerssen stop her and demand the usual bribe of twenty gold pieces to let it through. The Vegetable Woman, however, has learned how the game is played, and now she is holding the cards. With bravado worthy of Mother Courage, she reminds the two generals that without the provisions Bockelson will starve, and that will result very quickly in capitulation. The two generously offer to let her through for ten gold pieces, but they have not yet comprehended. It will now cost *them* to save their war, and before she is through, the Vegetable Woman has extorted twenty-five gold pieces from them to deliver the food to Bockelson.

That decisions to declare war are economic rather than moral is the message of the scene with Emperor Charles the Fifth. In the intervening twenty years since *Es steht geschrieben,* much had happened to raise the question: What causes a nation to commit troops to hostilities in a far away place, when its own borders can hardly be seen to be threatened? Out of a very simple dialogue between the emperor and Bishop Franz in *Es steht geschrieben,* that fails to bring about the desired result—the troops the bishop seeks for his campaign against Münster—Dürrenmatt evolves a scene that exposes the real motivation for a war on foreign soil. Three new characters in the scene—the prince elector, the Hessian landgrave, and the cardinal—all share the emperor's isolationist views. Each has his own parochial interest that takes precedence, and for that reason each tries to belittle the threat of the Anabaptists by making them out to be harmless, devout Christians. The bishop makes several compelling arguments: the Anabaptists behead people daily in God's name, King Bockelson is promoting polygamy, and innocent women and children are suffering under Bockelson's tyranny. The cardinal and the Protestant landgrave coldly refute all the arguments. It is not their war, and they will not get involved. Finally, in desperation, the bishop swallows his moral scruples and plays the winning card: "Then think at least about yourselves, about your lands, your palaces, your indentured servants, your wealth. The Anabaptists have introduced communal property" (10:78–79). There is stunned silence followed by outrage. Dürrenmatt, through the bishop, has introduced the Red Menace. Communism must not succeed, or be perceived as succeeding, even in such an out-of-the-way, provincial place as Münster in Westphalia. Within moments the bishop has four thousand soldiers for the siege.

It would, however, be an oversimplification to see *Die Wiedertäufer* as merely a satire on the cold war and the capitalist response to the threat of communism. As Münster languishes in hopeless deprivation near the end of the siege, a brainwashed butcher uses Nazi terminology to justify his irrational belief in victory: "Now we believe in you, . . . in the Anabaptists and in the final victory (*Endsieg*)" (10:103). Bockelson also has distinct Hitlerian traits.[1] That Bockelson, like Hitler, is a frustrated artist—in this case an actor—is a thread which runs through the play. The emperor very pointedly declares frustrated artists of any kind dangerous. One of his bothersome duties at the Diet of Worms is to appoint members to the Art Academy in Vienna. A local Viennese painter has applied but clearly lags behind the others in talent and inspiration. The emperor makes an astute decision: "Accept him graciously. As a member of the Imperial Academy he can do no damage, except to art" (10:82). By contrast the bishop, the cardinal, and the landgrave all know they should have engaged the actor Bockelson when they had the chance, for he is now showing the full extent of the damage a frustrated artist can perpetrate.

Es steht geschrieben was a chaotic comedy, a world-cabaret. *Die Wiedertäufer* posits on the stage of history a diabolical actor/director with a sense of the absurdity of existence. Bockelson's virtuoso performance in the adaptation ends with the capitulation of the city. There remain only the curtain call and the accolades. In his curtain speech to the princes, Bockelson emphasizes that his gluttony, lasciviousness, and arbitrary justice have all been for theatrical effect, all in the spirit of comedy:

> The play is done, oh Princes without peer
> I only wore your mask, was not your equal here. (10:119)

He turns over the starving populace for the princes to kill, but for himself he demands "a laurel wreath and not the hangman" (10:119). The cardinal, the prince elector, and the landgrave rush to embrace the actor for whose services they will compete in the future.

It is the final scene which emphasizes the theological gulf between the original and the adaptation. In *Es steht geschrieben* the spotlight is on the God-seeker who, in his extreme despair at the edge of existence, has finally become receptive to divine grace. Now, twenty years later, such an extreme manifestation of grace no longer has any validity for the author. Dürrenmatt's mouthpiece, Bishop Franz, has seen too many injustices—the God-seeker broken on the wheel, the seduced slaughtered, the seducer pardoned—and suddenly the realization of his own culpability for the absurdity prompts a rebellion. The bishop, whose final response in *Es steht geschrieben* was resignation but who nonetheless saw the providential hand of God behind the suffering of the condemned, finally resolves in the adaptation the inner conflict he has been nurturing throughout the play. He has been admitting to himself in stages that his eighty years in service to the church have been a sham, that he is no better than the people he persecutes in God's name, and that the sum total of his efforts has been the defense of a rotten status quo. In his soliloquy with Matthisson's severed head it is clear how much he admired the prophet: "Your defeat is better than mine" (10:69), he says. Matthisson had acted foolishly, but he had done so out of an obsession with justice and hope. How petty and misguided the bishop's own partisan political struggles suddenly seemed to him.

Physically and symbolically rising from his wheelchair and standing on his own legs, the bishop declares his independence from the ideological crutch he has leaned on for eighty years. He declares himself free from servitude to the Catholic church, which had forced him to subjugate his conscience to the dictates of hierarchical authority and to preserve a corrupt system—free to follow the dictates of his own conscience as a humanist. Thus, the bishop joins the ranks of Dürrenmatt's courageous individuals. That these are dangerous ranks to join, that these loners do not have a smooth path, is by now well known. The play must end, because the bishop has no idea how to proceed from here. He has courageously declared independence from his lifelong spiritual homeland—despised territory to be sure, but the only firm ground under his feet—and entered the *terra incognita* of those inhabitants of Dürrenmatt's universe who would change the world for the better. "But how? But how?" Brecht believed that he knew how, and so he could direct this question to the audience members at the conclusion to *The Good Person of Szechwan,* confident that they would not only answer it, but go and act on their insight. For Dürrenmatt, as we have seen repeatedly, the question had no simple answer.

König Johann (King John)

When the curtain rose on the premiere of Dürrenmatt's *König Johann: nach Shakespeare* (King John in the Manner of Shakespeare) on September 18, 1968, in Basel, the audience, quite used to Dürrenmatt's iconoclasm, was nevertheless in for somewhat of a shock. The traditional three loud knocks which herald an Elizabethan play had emanated from behind the curtain. After the curtain rose it became clear that the knocks had been beheadings.[2] Three heads lay in three baskets beside the blocks, and soldiers were just dragging the last bloody corpse off stage while others covered the heads in the baskets with towels and carried them off. All this was happening in the same room where King John, Queen Elinor, Blanche (Blanka), Lord Pembroke, and Chatillion were discussing France's claim to the English throne. As the last head was removed the dialogue began.

There is more grotesquerie to come, for example the double wedding feast amid the rubble of the razed city of Angers. Littering the stage are the corpses of the townspeople, and in the middle stands a banquet table with all kinds of rare foods and wines. Dürrenmatt pokes fun at his neighbors to the east by making the duke of Austria the clown of this scene. The duke's appetite is insatiable, and while the peace treaty is collapsing, he never notices. He calls in turn for ox, pheasant, pork, wine, more ox, salad, soup, and more wine before realizing that everyone has left the table to fight. In the ensuing battle the Bastard, Sir Richard, kills the duke of Austria and returns with his head, sticking it the first place he can find: the soup tureen. When King John returns, intoxicated with the thrill of battle, he is hungry. One try at getting soup sobers him up quickly.

While Shakespeare took liberties with chronology in order to compress as many of the salient events of John's troublesome reign into the relatively short time frame of the drama, Dürrenmatt fictionalizes the king and the historical events that much more. Sharing Schiller's predilection for fictionalizing history as he dramatized it, Dürrenmatt justified his revisionist practices succinctly: "The important thing is to write useful stories for the stage, not to establish adult education classes in history on the stage. History is material for stories, but every material must be tailored, in order to make it into a story" (11:202). Notably lacking from Dürrenmatt's cast of characters is Hubert de Burgh, to whom Shakespeare's King John gives the order to kill the captured Prince Arthur. Dürrenmatt lets John place the fate of Arthur in the Bastard's hands, a fact which gives the Bastard the greater significance Dürrenmatt intends him to have in his version. Also lacking is John's son Prince Henry, the boy who became King Henry III upon his father's death and ruled for fifty-six years, longer than any other Plantagenet. While Shakespeare makes him older than his historical age of nine at his father's death, Dürrenmatt describes him as an infant. A Dürrenmattian addition is Isabelle of Angoulême, the historical King John's second wife. In reality John married Isabelle in 1200, two years before his war with Philip of France, and she eventually bore him five children. Dürrenmatt, however, does not allow John to live beyond the first child, Henry (who historically was born in 1207), having him poisoned after the birth of his infant son and heir.

Dürrenmatt's most radical change in characterization from Shakespeare's version is Blanche (Blanka von Kastilien). The naive, idealistic lady Shakespeare presents becomes for Dürrenmatt a vamp, who drags the Bastard into bed before the end of act 1 and who succeeds in sleeping with nearly all the lords of England by the end of the play. Dürrenmatt's best characterization, however, is the one that is also Shakespeare's most successful, the Bastard. Dürrenmatt saw what Shakespeare had obviously seen, that King John is a weak character: a king with less right to the throne than his brother's son Arthur—a king who betrays the only right conviction he has, his defense of the English people against the excesses of the Catholic church, by crawling back to the pope after the nobility deserts him. Shakespeare recognized the potential for characterization in Philipp Faulconbridge (later Sir Richard), illegitimate son of Richard Coeur-de-lion, who gives up land for honor, strong where the king is weak. Dürrenmatt saw in the Bastard even more potential, and turned him into his typical courageous individual: cunning, confident, logical in everything he does, and yet totally naked against the treachery of blind chance. While Shakespeare's Philipp Faulconbridge was an ideologue and a super-patriot, Dürrenmatt's Bastard "is neither an ideologue nor a moralist. For the latter, the kings are the rulers and the folk the victims of these rulers. What he demands of the kings is simply that they rule reasonably. He tries to make John reasonable" (11:203). Dürrenmatt's Bastard stands farther outside the system than does Shakespeare's. From his new modern perspective he sees no qualitative difference between John and Philipp, England and France, church and state. It is for him all one big exploitive system (John = Philipp = feudalism), and he can analyze it critically "because he does not believe in the foundations of the system" (11:203).

Shakespeare's Bastard reveals in his first soliloquy that he has a plan of action: he will remain servile while awaiting his opportunity, and he will learn to deliver "sweet poison for the age's tooth."[3] He means he will learn the art of flattery, not as much to deceive others as to avoid being deceived by it when it begins to accompany him on his rise to fortune. Dürrenmatt's Bastard is blunter about his intentions:

> Therefore will I, the Bastard, a bastard remain!
> Playing the game I choose to play
> Noble on the outside, quite the true knight,
> Though my mind knows that all is whoring
> That this noble world does for honor.
> Disguising myself I will, so as not to deceive myself,
> Remain true to myself while deceiving the world.
> I'll climb with bold heroic deeds
> The dung encrusted chicken ladder of honor. (11:21)

The Bastard has the wits and political savvy to back up his boasts. He is fearless in battle but is constantly thinking of expedient ways to avoid battle. He seems to have everything going for him, except for the one major hurdle he cannot overcome: Dürrenmatt is writing the script. The Bastard knows that the world is irrational, yet he naively believes that he can pit his own reason against it and succeed. Möbius-like, the Bastard plots foolproof solutions to save the world, or at least his own island corner of it. He is a master tactician, using ploys that worked for the ruling houses of Europe for centuries afterward. He remains faithful to reason to the bitter end, though he sees one of his logical conclusions after another thwarted by coincidence.

The Bastard understands, for example, that the fortunes of war resemble a lottery. As long as chance will decide anyway, he argues, why should thousands of soldiers die? Instead he suggests harnessing chance, letting a kind of peaceful lottery—the will of the citizens of Angers—decide who will be king of England. Since both kings agree to accept the *vox populi,* the bloodshed seems to be averted. But the citizens of Angers will not decide, and so the first mediation attempt fails. Immediately he tries again: "You princes conclude the peace without these wretched citizens. Declare John in the right and give Arthur new privileges" (11:37). Both King John and King Philipp agree and would negotiate, but for the treachery of the duke of Austria. Having declared moments earlier: "It stinks of rotten peace, I must act" (11:35), he has left the scene to lead his troops in a sneak attack on the English from the rear. The battle spells the second failure for the Bastard's diplomacy. Whereas Shakespeare lets the Bastard suggest the wanton destruction of Angers, Dürrenmatt does not dishonor his peacemaker with this vengeful idea. He gives this dubious honor to Philipp. Instead it is the Bastard who makes the suggestion which temporarily halts the hostilities and promises to bring lasting peace: the marriage of the Dauphin Louis to Blanche of Castile, King John's niece. (In Shakespeare the First Citizen of Anger suggests this.) And the Bastard even goes further. Peace will be ensured by a double wedding. King John should marry Philipp's niece Isabelle of Angoulême. Nobody is very happy with the pairings: Isabelle is, in John's words, "ugly as the plague," and furthermore she is happily engaged to the Dauphin, who does not want to give her up even for the beautiful Blanche. Blanche, in turn, loves the Bastard and feels betrayed by him. The Bastard loves Blanche too, but as a realist he knows he must sacrifice her to the common good of two nations.

Cynical though the solution may be, it is a stroke of political genius, because it will divide the land to nearly everyone's satisfaction, and it will ensure lasting peace between the intermarried families. The peace lasts about five minutes, because of the unforeseen and incredibly ill-timed intervention of Papal Legate Pandulpho which compels the parties to fight once again. It also renders meaningless the sacrifice of Blanche, reluctantly married to the "half homosexual fat rooster" (11:44) the Dauphin. The Bastard's incredible chain of catastrophes does not end here. Appealing to reason, he entreats the king not to kill the captured Prince Arthur. Such a deed would surely cause the nobility to defect to the French cause. Rather, he should imprison Arthur in the high tower, where escape is impossible. The moment John confidently announces to the nobility that Arthur is still alive, soldiers carry in the body of the prince, who has died from a fall trying to escape. Now it looks like John has not only killed Arthur but brazenly lied about it. Of course, the same fate befalls Arthur in Shakespeare's play, but there the Bastard had nothing to do with it.

The fifth act is almost all Dürrenmatt's invention. It begins with a masterful tongue-in-cheek scene in which John, at the Bastard's urging, seeks out Cardinal Pandulpho to make peace with the pope. The cardinal, forced to winter in an unheated cell at Swinstead Abbey, is constantly cold. He entreats the king to climb under the covers with him, so that literally, not just figuratively, the state climbs into bed with the church.[4] The poisoning of John, committed in Shakespeare's play by a nameless monk, is given a plausible historical motivation (though still purely fictional) by Dürrenmatt. In doing so, Dürrenmatt brings King John's most important historical significance—an element surprisingly ignored by Shakespeare—into the drama: the Magna Charta. Fearing that John will revoke the charter after he regains the support of the nobility, Pandulpho orders Lord Pembroke in the name of the church to poison the king. It was the Bastard who first suggested the Magna Charta to John and convinced him of its political benefits. Yet John would never have been poisoned if he had not had an heir. This he now has, because Angoulême has just born him a son. Dying, King John banishes the Bastard from his sight with the words:

You have poisoned me with reason!
It was your advice to take Angoulême.
Now this cold board with which I slept
Becomes the roof of my coffin. Cursed be the hour
In which I scratched you out of the warm cow manure
Into the light of day. You brought me nothing but sorrow.
Improving the world, you only made it a more damned place. (11:111–12)

The consummate Dürrenmattian hero, the Bastard meets the world head-on with logic, but proves himself to be no match for an illogical universe.

Throughout the play Dürrenmatt has been gradually moving away from his source, until at the end Shakespeare's optimistic, patriotic message is turned into one of cynicism and resignation. So great was Dürrenmatt's distaste for patriotism that wherever Shakespeare's characters spoke a word about love of country or glorifying war, Dürrenmatt struck it.[5] Thus, while Shakespeare's Bastard concludes: "Nought shall make us rue, / If England to itself do rest but true" (V.vii.116–18), his Dürrenmattian counterpart turns his back on the whole foul system. ("What do I care about England?—About history?" [11:113]) He does not abandon reason, rather he turns it inward and applies it to his own situation. Like Augias before him, he will tend his garden. He will return to the farm, sleep with milkmaids and barmaids, and populate England with bastards like himself. As for the present, the patched-up status quo will survive—come what may.[6] The reactionary words of John's murderer Pembroke bring down the curtain:

> You Lords, bury the King anywhere
> Like anyone else. On to the affairs of state.
> To cart this land along by age-old rules,
> Down well-worn paths, undisturbed by fools. (11:113)

Play Strindberg

In between the two forays into Shakespeare, Dürrenmatt wrote and staged the most successful of his adaptations: *Play Strindberg: Dance of Death after August Strindberg.* Already the title, a reference to Jacques Loussier's jazz trio *Play Bach,* a classical parody, warns us of what is coming.[7] The subtitle of James Kirkup's translation, *The Dance of Death Choreographed by Friedrich Dürrenmatt,* more accurately describes the author's artistic independence from his source. This adaptation is really Dürrenmatt's play with Strindberg's characters. Just as he did with *King John* and to an extent with *Titus Andronicus,*

135

Dürrenmatt opens with text very closely patterned after the original and moves in the course of the play farther and farther away from the source. The attraction of Strindberg's play for Dürrenmatt lay in its portrayal of marriage as hell, of the impossibility of communication between the sexes set against a background of total isolation in which the partners must fight because they cannot run. The embittered spousal gladiators, vegetating at an island quarantine station and connected with civilization only by a telegraph machine, wage a protracted struggle to the death. The round tower room in which Edgar and Alice have reached their twenty-fifth anniversary serves as a visual representation of the devil's circle of hate and dependence in which they are hopelessly trapped. The torment of a loveless marriage is not a new theme to Dürrenmatt: it occurs most notably in *Mississippi* and *The Visit,* and to a lesser extent in *Romulus* and *König Johann.* Such disastrous loveless marriages result from one or both partners seeking social or political advantage, and achieving thereby the opposite of their goals.

Strindberg's *Dödsdansen (Dance of Death)* offered just such a matrimonial miscalculation. Alice, an aspiring though mediocre actress, gave up her career to marry the older, physically unattractive officer Edgar in the belief that it would afford her upward social mobility. Edgar, in turn, had hoped his career would be enhanced by having an attractive wife. Edgar's career has gone nowhere in twenty-five years, as he cannot even gain promotion to major. Embittered, he has made an enemy of everyone else on the island, and in his frustration he wields power over the only person he can, Alice. Yet much of this power is only in his mind, as Alice has learned to fight back in covert ways. The only person who remains true to him is his daughter Judith, who lives in the city on the mainland. However when Edgar tries to manipulate her, too, by forcing her to marry the colonel, Judith demonstrates just how much like her father she has become. Her decisive and devastating betrayal of Edgar brings about his fatal stroke.

Dürrenmatt's "comedy on a marital tragedy" reduces Strindberg's cast to three persons: Edgar, Alice, and Alice's cousin Kurt. Eliminated are Edgar and Alice's daughter Judith, Kurt's son Allan, the lieutenant (Allan's rival for the affections of Judith), the servant Jenny, and the "old woman," a grotesque death figure who appears only once. Strindberg's play is in two parts, with the first taking place in Edgar and Alice's tower; the second, by contrast, in Kurt's elegant "oval drawing room in white and gold." Dürrenmatt reduces this to twelve "rounds" in the tower, each beginning and ending with a gong. The rounds become successively shorter, so that the end of round four is the midpoint of the play. By staging the adaptation as a boxing match, Dürrenmatt shows the struggle between the partners as "at once ritualistic and senseless."[8] Likewise casting his audience into the role of spectators, he "relies on and encourages the audience's willingness to intellectualize the contents of a play, to avoid any emotional entanglement or even identification with the events on stage."[9] Of Strindberg's three plot lines—the marital war between Alice and the captain, the captain's methodical manipulation and ruination of Kurt, and the love story between Allan and Judith—Dürrenmatt eliminates the last two and concentrates on the war of the sexes. Minimal, too, is the staging: a round, windowless room with black velvet curtains on the side. On the stage stand a few necessary pieces of furniture. "In the wings to left and right two property benches with the necessary props, which the actors fetch themselves. Above the acting area hangs a circular frame carrying spots."[10]

Dürrenmatt wrote concerning this adaptation that it removed from Strindberg's play the rhetorical elements and forced the actors to be effective through their stage presence. In his own program notes, he wrote: "From Strindberg I took the story and the dramatic idea. By eliminating the literary side of Strindberg, his dramatic vision becomes more sharply focussed and more modern, related to Beckett, Ionesco, or my own *Meteor*. Strindberg's dialogue was used as the starting point of an anti-Strindberg dialogue—out of an actors' play I made a play for acting" (PS 7). Certainly one of the starkest contrasts between the original and the adaptation is the latter's rhetorical reduction to an expressionistic minimum. A contrastive example demonstrates Dürrenmatt's paucity of words. Here Strindberg's text:

ALICE: Have you ever known anyone who was really happy?
THE CAPTAIN: I'm trying to think. . . . No. . . . Yes—the Ekmarks.
ALICE: You don't mean it? But the wife was operated on last year.
THE CAPTAIN: Oh, yes, I forgot. —Well, then I can't think of anyone. . . . Yes, the von Kraffts!
ALICE: Yes, there is a family which for fifty years lived a truly bucolic life.[11]

Alice continues for several more lines describing how a distant von Krafft relative committed a crime and the whole family was shunned. The pretensions of high society that can so easily victimize an innocent family are exposed, and Edgar and Alice can find in this story some consolation and justification for their own self-imposed exile from that society. Dürrenmatt, on the other hand, is interested in nothing beyond the immediate twelve-round combat between Edgar and Alice, and his text has the brevity of punch and counterpunch:

ALICE: Have you ever seen a happy marriage?
EDGAR: The Ekmarks.
ALICE: She's in the madhouse.
EDGAR: The Von Kraffts.
ALICE: He's bankrupt.
EDGAR: Then I've never seen a happy marriage.
(Pause) (PS 18)

The parenthetical pauses are an effective device for controlling the rhythm of the dialogue. Liberally positioned, especially in the first four rounds, the pauses accentuate the superficiality of the staccato mini-dialogues. Edgar and Alice have nothing to say to each other that they have not said many times before. Each sequence of lines is a self-contained unit, and the units do not flow logically from one to the next across the pauses. A second function the pauses serve is to approximate the rhythm of a boxing match: brief seconds of relaxation and recovery between flurries of punches.[12]

As a result of the change from tragedy to comedy and of the terseness of the dialogue, Dürrenmatt's characters lose their three-dimensionality in the adaptation and appear like "mechanical dolls imitating human beings."[13] Strindberg gives his captain a past which, while not justifying his present antisocial behavior, helps to explain it. That he is capable of occasional tenderness and that he is terribly weak and insecure keeps the audience on the verge of sympathizing with him throughout much of part 1. Dürrenmatt's Edgar, by contrast, is not complex. He is merely a self-righteous bully, a *miles gloriosus* without the political savvy and occasional charm which aids Strindberg's captain in being truly diabolical. Absent any mitigating past, any glimpse of the warmth or false charm that allows Strindberg's Edgar to keep his victims off balance and control their lives, Dürrenmatt's character is merely a curmudgeon who ultimately outsmarts himself. All the seizures and blackouts Strindberg's character suffers, culminating in the final stroke, are real and taken seriously. Dürrenmatt adds his own dimension to the plot by having Edgar feign a blackout in order to set a trap for Alice and Kurt. Edgar then foolishly brags about his ruse. The predictable result is that the next real seizure is not believed and no medical help is sought. Thus, it is a very Dürrenmattian worst possible turn that brings his captain down. However, Dürrenmatt has still more irony in store for Edgar. The adaptation is, after all, a comedy, and to that purpose he changes the ending. Edgar does not die from the stroke, but meets a fate worse than death. Left lame and mute but fully conscious, he is condemned to be completely at the mercy of Alice, who remains faithfully at his side to humiliate and torment him in perpetuity. Then comes the final irony: news of Edgar's long-anticipated promotion arrives after his stroke.

Major differences are also evident in the characterization of Alice. Love and hate compete on nearly equal terms for the soul of Strindberg's Alice. Her emotional ambivalence intensifies her victimization by rendering her unable to break out of the relationship or to assert herself within it. There is a dark side to her character that inhibits the audience's sympathy with her. Barely more likable than her husband in the first scene, Alice reacts to her victimization by dominating and browbeating those whom she can, her servants. This character flaw has a secondary cause as well, namely, Alice's need to cling to two fictions: that she comes from a well-to-do family, and that she was a famous actress before she married Edgar. Dürrenmatt's staccato, expressionistic dialogue allows for much less depth of characterization here as well. He compensates by adding a two-page dialogue of his own invention, the "photo album scene," in which Alice reveals much about herself in a few words. The album is a repository of disparate photos that chronicle the couple's miserable life together. Discussing the photos, which the audience does not see, in rapid succession, Alice ties several loose ends together that would otherwise take several scenes or at least separately motivated dialogues to develop. The first two seemingly innocent snapshots belie Alice's previous contentions: "If we hadn't got married, I'd still be on the stage," and "I was a famous actress" (PS 18). The photo album dialogue begins:

ALICE: Me as Peritta.
KURT: Who's that?
ALICE: A playmate of Medea's
KURT: Very nice.
ALICE: Me as Eucharis.
KURT: Who's that?
ALICE: One of Sappho's handmaidens. (PS 34)

As we must deduce from these lines, Alice has had a couple minor roles—in *Sappho* and the *Golden Fleece* trilogy by Grillparzer. If she ever had any more, they are not highlighted in her album. Alice's hatred for Edgar becomes apparent to Kurt for the first time in this scene. The shock effect that produces comedy lies in the juxtaposition of the vitriolic beside otherwise innocuous comments about the pictures, as in this example:

KURT: . . . Your husband as a young second lieutenant.
ALICE: If he were to drop dead, I'd bust a gut laughing. As a full lieutenant. (PS 35)

A picture of two children elicits the following revealing line from Alice: "Twins. He eggs on Judith against me, and I egg on Olaf against him. The island as seen from the south" (PS 35). A snapshot of Kurt and his wife in the album reminds Alice that she had been in love with Kurt once, and she chides him for not marrying her. Kurt replies that it was Alice who had abandoned him, running off "with all your flags flying to your military man of letters to improve your position in society" (PS 36). The final picture of the family on the beach elicits the lament: "If only the ocean would just rise right up and wash us all away" (PS 36). It is a short scene, but it gives maximum insight with a minimum of words.

Dürrenmatt blunts the edges of Alice's character, in contrast to Strindberg. Her highs are not as high, her lows not as low. She does not spit in Edgar's face, as does her Swedish counterpart, but neither does she throw herself at him screaming "I would care for you, Edgar—I would love you" (DD 72). Instead she insults him, taunts him with his own trite phrases, seduces Kurt, and recites vitriolic lines with such incongruous dispassion that the result can only be comedy.

It is in the characterization of Kurt that Dürrenmatt breaks most radically with his source. Strindberg's Kurt is the incorruptible good man who stumbles into an evil he can immediately sense, but against which he has no weapons. Kurt tries to exorcise the evil in the only way he knows, with Christian charity. Strindberg's Kurt is a close kin of some of Dürrenmatt's early long-suffering fools-in-Christ: Knipperdolinck, the blind duke, and most especially Count Bodo. Such Dürrenmattian protagonists, however, belong to the past. Out of the tragic, saintly individual devoured by evil in a marital hell, Dürrenmatt evolves a descendant of Frank the Fifth—an international gangster larger than the system and therefore essential to the system. Dürrenmatt's Kurt, like the industrialists in *The Judge and His Hangman,* functions above the law. Therefore he can legitimately scoff at Edgar's accusation that he had embezzled fifty thousand dollars in the United States. Nor does Alice's threat to call the prosecutor elicit more than amusement: "Im sorry, Alice, I'm not a petty crook, I'm a big businessman. I didn't embezzle a paltry fifty thousand dollars, that was Eriksen. I made millions of dollars. The Director of Public Prosecutions cannot lay a finger on businessmen of my calibre" (PS 74).

Kurt's millions and his subsequent position above the law has afforded him the luxury to "slum it" on the island with Alice and Edgar for three days in the role of a detached observer. The petty, hateful intrigues of his cousin and her husband have been a cathartic experience and a respite from the large-scale intrigues of his world of high finance. To his great comfort Kurt has discovered that the microcosm is as corrupt and uninhabitable as the macrocosm: "it is only the dimensions that are different" (PS 75). The revelation of Kurt's wealth and power begs that we view him in light of another Dürrenmatt antagonist: Claire Zachanassian. Like Claire, he has returned to pay a "visit" on a man with whom he has a score to settle. Edgar had broken up Kurt's marriage years before, though we never find out how. How Kurt responds to what he finds on the island, however, sets him far apart from Claire. He does not demand blood revenge; he does not have to. His revenge consists of merely observing the couple that has created its own marital hell, secretly grateful to the man who unwittingly saved him from such a hell. All the emotional involvement that characterized Strindberg's Kurt is absent. Whereas *The Visit* ends with Claire handing the mayor the check, Kurt concludes *Play Strindberg* by taking back the check that Edgar had tried to extort from him. The ill-gotten wealth Kurt enjoys, with which he only tantalizes Edgar and Alice, is his revenge, and his victory.

Unable to adapt Strindberg, as he originally intended, without falsifying him, Dürrenmatt has succeeded in doing the honorable thing. From Strindberg's naturalistic dialogue he has created an expressionistic "anti-Strindberg dialogue" and from the plot of a bourgeois marital tragedy he has constructed a "comedy about bourgeois marital tragedies" (PS 8). It is exclusively Dürrenmatt's play— little of Strindberg remains beyond the names of the characters. It plays out not in Strindberg's universe, but in Dürrenmatt's, a universe where the tragic lurks below the surface but manifests itself as comedy, individual striving is futile, irony and tour de force are commonplace, and where extreme corruption masked as respectability is above the law.

Play Strindberg was a theatrical success. Together with *König Johann* it is the fruit of the nine-month Basel collaboration with Werner Düggelin— two excellent plays which owe their success to Dürrenmatt's opportunity to work closely with his own actors ensemble in revising the script, most of which took place during rehearsals.[14] They would be his last successes. Each subsequent failure would alienate Dürrenmatt that much more from the audiences and critics, until he made his ultimate decision to quit the theater and concentrate on prose.

Titus Andronicus: Eine Komödie nach Shakespeare
(Titus Andronicus: A Comedy in the Manner of Shakespeare).

Given Dürrenmatt's fascination with the grotesque and his delight in bloody spectacle, the choice of a second Shakespearean play to adapt should come as no surprise. And given his belief in the inefficacy of tragedy in a world governed by coincidence, it seems only natural that German theatergoers should have been treated two years later to *Titus Andronicus: Eine Komödie nach Shakespeare*. While the reception of *König Johann* in Basel was not unfavorable, the Düsseldorf premiere of *Andronicus* created a scandal. A reviewer for the *Frankfurter Allgemeine Zeitung* labeled the play a "grusical"[15] from the German word *gruseln,* meaning "to make one's flesh crawl." Disgruntled theatergoers booed the absent author,[16] and not many more people were left in the theater by play's end than there were live bodies on the stage.

If Elizabethan audiences thrived on gory violence, clearly the Düsseldorf audience in 1970 did not, especially when it perceived the violence to be gratuitous. Furthermore, Dürrenmatt employed the new style with which he had been experimenting since the Strindberg adaptation the previous year. A paucity of words and a choppy, staccato rhythm characterized large sections of the adaptation. This style of dialogue shortened the play and hastened the action along from one brutal deed to another before the audience had a chance to catch its breath.[17] Furthermore it effectively prevented the audience from empathizing with the characters. The pathos of Titus's outcry "When will this fearful slumber have an end?"[18] and Shakespeare's long, sympathy-arousing monologues are gone. More typical for the adaptation is Titus's reaction to Livinia's rape and mutilation:

> The hand is gone
> the heart is hardened
> the world stinks like an outhouse.
> The little hands gone
> the little tongue gone
> the world is full of mouse shit.
> The little womb open
> two rogues astride
> the world runs an evil course. (11:159)

Dürrenmatt's audience is not supposed to have the luxury of empathizing with the victims. It is simply to be subjected to the runaway horror of a world gone mad.

There is comedy in the adaptation as well, but less than one might expect from a play subtitled a comedy. It is primarily centered around the scene in which the Andronici and a group of invalids from the city (Dürrenmatt's invention) are shooting arrows into the air with pleas for justice to the Gods. The subsequent scene in Saturninus's throne room, also Dürrenmatt's invention, is the play's best piece of visual comedy. As the lights come up, Saturninus is sitting on his throne in full armor. Beside and behind him the wall is shot full of arrows from Titus and his cohorts, and more come whizzing past his head during the scene. Regal to the end, Saturninus stubbornly refuses to move. The scene is peppered with humorous dialogue and situational comedy, and only two people are taken out and hanged in the course of it. In this play, that amounts to a retardation of the action.

The most interesting characterization in a play generally lacking in that commodity is Aaron. Shakespeare's Aaron is a one-dimensional character, his black skin emblematic to the Elizabethan audience of his black heart, until that moment in the fourth act when he defends his infant son from Tamora's sons who want to kill it. Otherwise Aaron remains the absolute unrepentant villain, who can say in the end:

If one good deed in all my life I did,
I do repent it from my very soul. (V.iii.189–90)

Dürrenmatt, on the other hand, presents us with quite a different Aaron, in keeping with the spirit of modern times. He makes a human being out of him, rather than a devil, and motivates his actions by giving him a past. In the first place, he is no longer a Moor, as in Shakespeare, but rather a "noble savage" from an African tribe. The author had a definite purpose in mind when he radically altered Shakespeare's archvillain into a pitiable victim of circumstance. Dürrenmatt has always been a champion of the underdog. In 1969 he was virtually the only well-known Swiss intellectual who supported the rebellious students against the establishment. In *Sätze aus Amerika (Sentences from America)*, the published diary of a trip he and his wife took to the United States in the fall of 1969, he wrote very critically about the racial situation, coming down heavily on the side of oppressed blacks. His character Aaron is his most definitive literary statement on the subject.

Already in his first appearance, Aaron assumes the role of commentator on the ills of Roman "civilized" society from the perspective of the noble savage. As he is led in chains to hear Titus condemn Tamora's son Alarbus to death in expiation of Titus's own son's death in battle, Aaron gasps:

We slaughter whom we catch, so we may eat.
We eat him out of hunger, meat is meat.
But slaughter here is seen as holy rite
Accompanied by banquet, roasted swine
And chickens, eggs, asparagus, sweet wine,
And bawdy humor, belching—(11:122)

Titus quiets him by shouting: "Silence barbarian!" But who is the barbarian? In contrast to the cannibal tribe that spawned this captive, Rome's civilization is unmasked as a sham. Aaron's sensibilities are shocked at what he sees and can barely comprehend.

Shakespeare's Aaron is first introduced in the second act. There he boasts of his sexual prowess and his past and future conquests of Tamora, empress of the Goths, in whose bed he plans to rise to power and wealth. But where did he come from? He is only revealed as the empress's slave, brought to Rome with her after the defeat of the Goths. Dürrenmatt fills in the gaps. His Aaron justifies his future actions out of social necessity. In his soliloquy he reveals that he was captured in Egypt by a Byzantine general. First he was sodomized by the general and then he became the plaything of the general's wife. Passed, in his words, from lap to lap, he climbed into ever higher social circles until he landed in the bed of the empress of Byzantium: a fat, gaudily attired old hag. When the Goths threatened Byzantium, Aaron was sent to sleep with Tamora and thus rescue the empire. It only seems natural to him now that he has every right to climb atop Tamora to the top of the Roman world. Dürrenmatt's Aaron does not lust after evil for evil's sake. He does what he does in the service of Tamora. Dürrenmatt takes Aaron's most insidious deed and gives it to an anonymous hangman: namely, deceiving Titus into cutting off his hand and sending it to the emperor. Because Aaron is more victim than villain, Dürrenmatt spares him the final humiliation of public starvation that he suffers in Shakespeare's version. Aaron escapes, and the last we hear from him is when he rescues his newborn son. His fiery words echo the black power rhetoric of the sixties.[19] It is Dürrenmatt at his most politically polemical, his most socially engaged:

DEMETRIUS: My mother is destroyed.
AARON: No, indebted.
And to whom? to the nigger, to the one whom you despise,
Because you value white, but not the color black.
I am as smooth as ebony, but your faces
Are like arses covered with pimples;

144

And if God is beautiful, he is black like me.
The Devil surely white with golden hair. (11:167)

Devotees of treachery, revenge, bloody murder, and gourmet cooking have long relished the banquet scene in *Titus Andronicus*. Dürrenmatt chose the source well for his bloodiest drama ever. In condensed form, Shakespeare's play ends the following way: Titus stabs Livinia so that she will no longer have to live in shame. Then he reveals to Tamora that her two sons who raped and mutilated Livinia are baked into the pastry she has been eating. For good measure he then stabs Tamora. Saturninus avenges Tamora by stabbing Titus, and is stabbed in turn by Titus's son Lucius, who has just returned with an army of Goths to overthrow Saturninus and avenge his father. Lucius, by virtue of being the only one of the principals left standing, is proclaimed emperor, and the audience is left with the feeling that Rome might have a future after all. Perhaps disappointed at not being the first to write such an ending, Dürrenmatt gave those spectators who were still in the theater by that time one more bludgeoning for their money. Alarich, chieftain of the Goths and Dürrenmatt's own addition to the "grusical," turns to his victorious ally Lucius, stabs him, and recites the final lines to the audience:

> Kill whatever lives! Build mountains from the bodies,
> Pillage, plunder Rome, burn it to ashes!
> Once it was great, now it is rubble.
> Once it ruled, now we rule, and after us
> Others will have their turns. We are threatened by the Huns,
> They by the Turks, and these by the Mongols,
> All of them greedy to rule the world
> Which was ours for a brief cosmic second.
> What good is justice? What good revenge?
> They are only names for an evil machination.
> This sphere, the earth will roll away into the void
> And die as senselessly as we all die:
> What was, what is and what shall be must rot away! (11:197)

Alarich's dark prophecy echoes more harshly the warning of that other Germanic chieftain from two decades earlier, Odoaker.[20] This time, however, there is no longer the hope of even a brief respite of peace and stability. Nihilism seemed to be tugging harder at Dürrenmatt than it had at any time since his early prose, where it had been youthful experimentation. It is already present to a great degree in *The Meteor* and in the *King John* adaptation. In the meantime Dürrenmatt had suffered a career setback with the failed Basel theater cooperative and a near-fatal heart attack. It is in this light that his first completely original play in four years, *Portrait of a Planet,* staged only a month before *Titus Andronicus,* must be seen.

CHAPTER 12

Four That Failed: The Late Plays

Porträt eines Planeten (Portrait of a Planet)

An eighty-nine-year-old painter recounts his career: he began painting people and their artifacts, then moved on to landscapes. Later he abandoned perspective in favor of color compositions. "Finally I painted only circles and triangles, without filling them with color, until I left the canvas empty. Painting seemed most honest that way" (12:165). When the canvas became extraneous he sold empty frames, which the galleries bought for insane prices. But when the frames also became superfluous, nobody cared for his art any more. On the grounds of the asylum he continues to paint pure nothingness, proud that he has fulfilled the artistic task which he set for himself. Through Abel's monologue from *Portrait of a Planet,* Dürrenmatt may well be having an ironic laugh at his own expense. Certainly he has not progressed so far with his dramatic art, but the urge to minimize every aspect of a play—the cast, the dialogue, the set, the props—was reaching extreme proportions.

The author explains his radical approach in the afterword to the play:

The older I get the more I hate the literary aspect of theater, the rhetorical, beautiful sentences and beautiful statements. I dispense more and more with dramatic devices, through which the actors are forced to portray people on stage who become exhibitionists through their words. Dramaturgically I try to show things more simply, to become more economical, to leave more out, only to hint at things. The tension between the sentences is more important to me than the sentences themselves. (12:197)

The elimination of all stage sets is a logical consequence. The actors carry only the props they absolutely need. "It is certainly clear to me that with *Portrait of a Planet* I have advanced to the frontier of the theater's capabilities. It is impossible to say whether this undertaking was successful or not" (12:198).

The underlying idea (*Einfall*) is that the sun quite unexpectedly becomes an exploding supernova like a huge cosmic flashbulb, recording in the instant before it swallows the earth one final portrait of life on the planet. In practice the supposedly simultaneous but geographically diffuse events must be shown consecutively. Thus the portrait more closely resembles pictures at an exhibition or, from a more modern perspective, a series of home video vignettes that follow each other without segue. Eight characters with Old Testament names— Adam, Kain, Abel, Henoch (Enoch), Eva, Ada, Zilla, and Naema—carry twenty scenes, which are framed by a prologue and epilogue. The frame is set somewhere in the ether, amid the expanse of the Milky Way, which hangs over the scene like the Andromeda Galaxy in *Angel*. In the frame, the four male actors play detached, disinterested gods who find eternity boring. Much more remote than the *deus absconditus* who made Kurrubi, these gods do not even know whether the distant supernova they chance to observe has planets, or why it is even exploding when it seemed to be stable. "I don't understand suns" (12:99) the fourth god muses. He also confesses to knowing nothing about living things. In the prologue we learn the essential fact that the sun is about to explode. Possessing knowledge denied to the characters, the audience has a different perspective from which to watch these "banal, horrifying, ordinary, extraordinary, absurd, monotonous, grotesque, unhappy, but also happy scenes" (12:196).

The word "ironic" also belongs on this list. The worst possible turn functions in the first and longest of the twenty scenes. In order to eliminate cannibalism on a tropical island, a delegation from an international organization imports swine and cattle by the thousands from the mainland. The islanders discover they like the taste of animal meat. However the draconian measure causes a famine on the mainland in which many more people die than would have fallen victim to the cannibals. Nevertheless, the delegation defends its actions as humanitarian progress. During the celebration, word reaches the mainland of a shipwreck on the island. The savages have reverted to their recent ways and eaten the crew.

The senselessness of the Vietnam War is the subject of several vignettes, although the name Vietnam is never mentioned. In a cynical scene the ambassadors of two superpowers come out of failed peace negotiations and congratulate themselves for exercising caution at a moment when an agreement was within reach. Both powers need the war for economic and political reasons. It is their proxy war, because a direct one is too costly.

This discussion takes place with the body of Adam, a war casualty, lying center stage. The ambassadors step over his body without noticing. Adam rises immediately to play the black lover of a white woman in a chilling, if predictable, scene. The lovers feel safe in the secluded park at night, for she has told only her brother, he only his sister about the affair. Betrayed by the ones they trust, the couple narrowly escapes death at the hands of bigots who grope after them with knives in the darkness. They know their love is hopeless. "We are together for the last time," she says, "and cannot even see each other." "The darkness is too great" (12:136), he replies, indicating the darkness is as much spiritual as physical.

There is a long monologue by an aging former concentration camp guard, who reminisces about how the prisoners used to plant beautiful gardens for him. "I love flowers, and because I've loved flowers my whole life, I've always been a good person" (12:167). There is the obligatory drug scene, in which the actors and actresses snort cocaine, fix heroin, and drop acid, all in pantomime, while reciting endless variations on a surrealistic sentence. In the moon shot scene, the first male and female astronaut pair on the moon cannot restart their spaceship because of a malfunction. In love but deprived of any physical contact because of their space suits, they suffocate slowly while reciting *Romeo and Juliet* and Shakespearean sonnets to each other. Back at Mission Control, the only concern is whether the disaster will cause Congress to cut funds for the Mars mission.

Melodramatic and devoid of humor is the scene where the father tries to persuade his sixteen-year-old daughter to leave the commune, where she has already had an illegitimate child. To her shocked father she shouts:

> Listen closely you doddering old man: You have your world and we have ours. We are sick and tired of living in the world you made, according to the rules you invented, frustrated by your morals and tabus. You are paid by a state that kills. We spit on this state. Invisible blood clings to your clothes, ours are just dirty. You preach love, we live by love; that is the whole difference. For two thousand years you have had your chance, and now we have our chance. Understand? (12:159)

This scene, in which Dürrenmatt stands clearly on the side of the teenagers, is unique in the play in that it suggests a solution, shocking and radical as that solution might seem to the Western establishment: peace and love.[1]

Wherever humanity might find salvation, it will once again and this time most emphatically not come from above. After the physical cosmos has unexpectedly turned on them, the eight characters die with a futile psalm on their lips "in the greatest desperation, in the senseless hope that God might yet reverse their fates" (12:182). But the cosmos in *Portrait* is a cosmos devoid of all transcendence, the four "gods" are anti-gods, with the sole purpose of demythologizing the cosmos.[2] Dürrenmatt's universe contains only empty space and matter governed by coincidence, which equates with reality, for what we call reality is but one of an infinite number of possibilities, each in its own right improbable: "Reality is that improbability that occurs" (12:194). One of these improbable possibilities was the earth. The Judeo-Christian principle of humans as the image of their creator is nowhere in Dürrenmatt's opus more cynically treated, for in *Portrait,* humanity proves to be an all-too-exact mirror of its creator: the chaos. So human society is revealed as being truly a microcosm of the universe—a comparison which does not particularly flatter either side.

The situations are sometimes clever, but more often predictable if not downright trite: "half boring, formalistic experiment, half naive, moralizing sermon."[3] The dialogue is full of the cliches exemplified by the teenager's monologue. The impression is of an author who has lost his originality, but it is an erroneous impression. If the critics believed this was the case, and apparently many did, they missed the point. It is the audience who knows the earth is doomed. The actors who are caught up in its death agonies do not. The portrait of the planet is a candid shot, not a posed one. The camera does not lie. It is not the author who has lost his creativity, it is humanity. We have become a cliche, Dürrenmatt was trying to say. There is no originality left, no courage to be creative. "The world in which we live is neither healthy nor serious, rather it is mired in pernicious banality" (12:198). What the supernova records in its last snapshot of our planet is pathetic.

The situation is grave, but not hopeless. In an unimaginably expansive universe, Dürrenmatt postulates, there are countless supernovas. Therefore, while it is not probable, it is possible that one could destroy our planet. However, it is infinitely more probable that humanity will destroy it first, if it forgets what Adam says at the midpoint of the play: "The earth is a chance" (146). In light of a cosmic conflagration all that happens in the twenty scenes is meaningless, the portrait an insignificant snapshot in the voluminous scrapbook of the universe. But Dürrenmatt was just kidding about the supernova. He was not kidding about the portrait.

The undertaking was not successful. Although the Düsseldorf and the Zürich audiences were cordial, the critics savaged *Portrait.*[4] Rightly or wrongly, *Portrait* also suffers by comparison to a play to which it bears superficial similarity. Thornton Wilder's *The Skin of Our Teeth* was intensely popular in Germany. It is an optimistic play, a testimony to humanity's indomitable spirit. While not claiming inspiration from Wilder, Dürrenmatt certainly saw in this play a point of departure for his pessimistic message. There is enough similarity to *The Skin of Our Teeth* to remind the audience what Dürrenmatt is doing. Three of Wilder's main characters are the biblical Adam, Eve, and Cain, who have taken new names. Hanging over both plays is the sense of impending disaster—they have the approaching storm in common—and Zilla's hateful speech to her father at the commune bears striking similarity to the tirade of the rebellious son Henry Antrobus. However, the Antrobus family—that is, humanity—pits its energy and will against the ice age, great flood, and world war, and emerges invigorated and confident. Dürrenmatt's humanity fails miserably even before the unalterable natural disaster that sweeps it away. Human resiliency renders Wilder's play circular, unending. Dürrenmatt's ending is final. As he so often does, Dürrenmatt has taken a literary model and inverted it into its negative. He was not borrowing from Wilder, he was answering him. However, similarity invites comparison, and in this case it does not come out in Dürrenmatt's favor.

Nevertheless it was a bold experiment. The success of *Play Strindberg* had been reason to hope that the public was receptive to the new direction in which he was taking his theater. But the Strindberg adaptation represented a false trail with regard to its popularity. It had an engaging plot, a familiar premise since *Dödsdansen* was a known quantity to European audiences, and the boxing ring worked most effectively as a staging technique. Although he had reduced Strindberg's tower set, with its naturalistic foreground and romantic background, to the lighted black circle with only the necessary furniture, the audience did not have to use its imagination. The physical and spiritual poverty of Alice and Edgar was better expressed through the understatement. With *Portrait,* however, Dürrenmatt crossed the line from minimal sets to a bare stage.

Part of the problem was timing. The decade of the sixties had been the heyday of German documentary theater. Heinar Kipphardt, Peter Weiss, and Rolf Hochhut were among the popular producers of this most political and often controversial type of theater, which recreated or simulated real events of recent history in order to engage the audience critically. Nuclear proliferation, the Vietnam War, racial hatred, and the counterculture were popular issues for documentary plays. Dürrenmatt gives his audience all this plus the space race, drug abuse, and an unrepentant death camp guard for its money. Everything that is wrong with society passes in rapid review. Missing is the detail: names, places, dates, press accounts, interviews, and depth of critical analysis—all the trappings which gave documentary theater its connection to real life and claim to authenticity. The play seems to go to extraordinary lengths not to reveal place names, even where they are obvious beyond doubt, such as Vietnam or the White House. The only place named, "Temple University in Philadelphia," is an inside joke: Temple had given Dürrenmatt his first honorary doctorate the previous year. Where documentary theater is deep and specific, Dürrenmatt was skimming the surface, illuminating problem after problem momentarily before racing to the next one. The style resembles more that of cabaret, the medium for which Dürrenmatt had written in his youth. However, cabaret exists from humor. The vignettes in *Portrait* are much too somber to allow a cabaret-style interpretation. So the play remains mired between two expectations: too serious for cabaret, too superficial for documentary theater. There are no individual fates to inspire our sympathy. Humanity becomes an abstract quantity that overtaxes our capacity to identify.[5] Where *Portrait* is most effective is in fulfilling the mission stated in its subtitle: "Training Play for Actors." A high degree of skill and experience is demanded in order to make the numerous role and scene changes believable on a bare stage with few props, but that skill does not translate into critical acclaim for the play.

Der Mitmacher (The Collaborator)

Der Mitmacher can rightly be described as *Frank der Fünfte* absent all its charm and any semblance of humor. Never did a Dürrenmatt play less deserve the subtitle "comedy." While his earlier gangsters cavorted at Chez Guillaume, sang in the boardroom, and mostly killed their victims in the cellar out of view of the audience, only gloom pervades the world of *Der Mitmacher.* Doc's laboratory, a damp, dimly lit room five stories belowground, is the one and only set. There Doc works for the syndicate, dissolving the corpses of its victims into their liquid components to be flushed into the sewer system. Boss's gangsters bring him the bodies in steamer trunks. Doc, an ingenious scientist, works for little money. He has placed his greatest invention, the "necrodialysator," at the service of the syndicate, and lives from the satisfaction and a meager salary. However, when Cop blackmails Boss and takes over control of the syndicate, he cuts Doc in for twenty percent. In this way he fans Boss's jealousy and creates more chaos among the gangsters. Doc's love interest is Ann, who turns out to be the secret mistress of Boss. Predictably, Boss has Ann killed. Cop dies too, when his ploy to bankrupt the syndicate is discovered. Nearly everyone of consequence in the play dies, except Doc. He is doomed to live on in the rat-infested cellar, working for nothing as the slave of the syndicate.

After a performance of *Der Mitmacher* a knowledgeable, experienced Dürrenmatt audience would have to ask itself: Haven't we seen that before? How many different ways can Dürrenmatt show us society's corruption? And is he doing anything more than beating the same rhythm on the same drum? The play contains themes from *Romulus, The Judge and His Hangman,* and particularly *Frank der Fünfte,* but also from *The Visit, The Physicists,* and more recently *Play Strindberg. Der Mitmacher* is the most radical example so far of Dürrenmatt's conservation of thematic matter. While it is common for themes to recur, often from one play or novel to the next, this play seems to be a single collection vessel for all the author's previous variations on corruption.

Cop plays the role of corrupt policeman, using evidence he has gathered against Boss to infiltrate and then take over the murder syndicate. His purpose is to ruin it from within, just as Romulus only played at being emperor in order to bring Rome down. Romulus's modest success in facilitating a few years of peace shrinks in the case of Cop to "a short world-second," during which he manages to stop the wheels of the syndicate before falling victim to it himself. With the monologue in which Cop reveals his identity and his connection to Boss, we are back in the Bärlach novels. Trying to stop a jewelry store heist, a young policeman (Cop) had stepped in front of a bullet from a young hoodlum (Boss). Cop's struggle with Boss over the last twenty years sounds like an abbreviated version of Bärlach-Gastmann. "From this confrontation on we both rose quickly to the top of our professions. He advanced to king of the underworld, and I to chief of police." Boss maintained an advantage that Cop could never quite overcome, regardless of how he infiltrated his organization, paid informants, or gathered proof. "His connections, his popularity, his patriotism, his money made him unassailable. He donated two million to the war invalids fund alone." Yet the description of this lifelong vendetta lacks the passion, the urgency and allegorical grandeur, of Bärlach's struggle with Gastmann.

Cop's monologue is cold, dispassionate, and factual, punctuated with the vocabulary of the street and of organized crime. Also, it comes at a point when the outcome of the struggle is already decided. It is a victory for neither individual, certainly not for Cop. At the end of the monologue Cop admits defeat. More than defeated, he admits to being the "only guilty one, for the simple reason that in a world where justice can be stolen, I alone sought justice, as though it were not a matter for everyone, but rather for an individual" (14:77). Another *mutiger Mensch* tells his story of how he tripped over point number 18 to *The Physicists*. By now we certainly know the routine. Until this play, though, we have at least been allowed to empathize somewhat with such characters. This is no longer the case with Cop, who has remained an enigma. During his monologue Cop undergoes three rapid transformations: he describes a tragic past which helps explain his present criminal behavior; then he reveals himself as a crusader for justice who has only been masquerading as a corrupt law officer; and finally he confesses to being a defeated fool for believing he could take on injustice alone. Such series of peripeties have frequently served Dürrenmatt well as a dramatic technique. So many revelations in a four-minute monologue, however, from a character we hardly know, does not engage us in any meaningful way. Precisely the peripeties with the most dramatic potential are wasted in a monologue that renders the subsequent scene with Doc undramatic and anticlimactic.

Most noticeably we are back in the world of *Frank*. Lives are a commodity; buy low, sell high. Ann dies, not because it is her bad luck to have affairs with Boss and Doc at the same time, but because she is a convenient tool with which Boss can intimidate Doc out of his share in the profits. The murder of Frieda Fürst in *Frank* at least creates the momentary crisis of inclination versus duty for Egli. Boss experiences no such conflict when he smothers Ann with a pillow. He is not angry with her for sleeping with Doc. It is only business, nothing personal. Ann, for her part, does not arouse our sympathy. She has moved in with Boss knowing full well who he is. She has accepted obviously stolen gifts from him. Later she drags Doc into bed, either to get revenge on Boss for something or because she is ashamed of herself for not having resisted him. She herself is not sure, but she insists that she wants to become "respectable," through her affair with Doc. Ann never answers Doc's question whether she is a high-priced whore or simply an adventuress, and the staccato dialogue in the style of *Play Strindberg* does not permit any probing of her psyche. However, her stated desire to become legitimate is far from convincing in light of her actions. The only interest her death engenders is the anticipation of how Doc will react. A gangster's moll meets her predictable violent end, and we yawn. Ann's character suffers, as do Doc's, Cop's, and Bill's, from the unresolved conflict between form and content in the play. The situations themselves are often very realistic and would invite the audience's active concern, but for the terse, dispassionate dialogues that dehumanize the characters and render the interpersonal relationships unbelievable.[6]

Joining Ann as a corpse in cold storage awaiting "necrodialysis" at play's end are Doc's brother Jack, Doc's son Bill, and later Boss himself—all three victims of Cop's ploy to bring the syndicate down. Reprising a technique from *Mississippi* (there used successfully), Dürrenmatt resurrects Jack and Bill to give long speeches that fill in background to the plot. Ultimately Cop dies too, at the hand of syndicate thugs who have seen through his ruse, but not before his final confrontation with Doc. This scene contains the best piece of prose in the play: Cop's monologue of the "great corruption." Using the technique employed brilliantly in *Angel* to make Akki's excessively long monologues poetic, Cop recites his successive revelations of the extent of the corruption in society in the form of a *maqamat*. Cop's tale is reminiscent of Alfred Ill's pilgrimage in search of justice to the police chief, the mayor, and the pastor, but also of Ottilie Frank's disillusioning lecture from the president. From the prosecutor to the mayor to the governor to the Supreme Court justice, nobody wants to hear Cop's pleas for help. Each one merely demands his percentage of the syndicate profits. Boss, who seemed at the beginning of the play to be the archcriminal of the land is revealed to be merely an expendable minor player.

The wheel of corruption turns. Collaborators rise on it, fall from it, and are crushed by it. Its lure is nearly irresistible, and for those few who can resist it the same bitter fate ultimately awaits. Cynicism is pervasive. Corruption begets corruption in a cycle as hopeless as that proclaimed by Alarich at the conclusion of the *Titus Andronicus* adaptation. In *Frank* Dürrenmatt had wanted to capture the milieu of *Titus Andronicus;* in *Der Mitmacher* he succeeded. The sordid plot hastens to its conclusion with a similar orgy of disgust. Flies begin to swarm and the rats come out. Cop punctuates his speeches by throwing bottles at the rats, that have been attracted by the stench of the corpses piling up in the adjacent room. Gloom hangs over the world of *Der Mitmacher,* from which there is only one escape. It is the conclusion to which Böckmann came in *Frank:* whoever would be free, must die. Cop realizes this too as he muses on his own futile one-man crusade against corruption that had cost many lives and given the syndicate only a second's pause. Dürrenmatt referred to Cop as an ironic hero, not a tragic one: "what differentiates him from the tragic hero is the senselessness of his end. He does not serve universality with his death, cannot serve it, because there is no positive universality and because the tragic hero cannot do without this positivity, which gives meaning to his actions" (14:195).[7] All that remains of his revolt is its personal, existential significance, and he delivers his defiant "nevertheless" as the gangsters lead him off to kill him: "Whoever dies, no longer collaborates."

As one small part of his long afterword to the play, Dürrenmatt discusses the nature of collaboration. Some people collaborate because they believe in the cause, "but the truly negative collaborator in his most dubious form is the intellectual who nevertheless collaborates" (14:107). This requires a short-circuiting of the conscience, which in Doc's case, he says, was brought about by extreme despair. Instead of venting his frustration through a desperate act or escaping into insanity, Doc reached his nadir in resignation. It is this indifference that fertilizes the ground for his morally negative collaboration. "Out of stagnant waters the collaborators are touched as though by an incidental breeze, unnoticed at first and yet irresistibly driven toward the rapids" (14:121). As a nihilist out of indifference, Doc invites comparisons to Gastmann. However, he is lacking in precisely those characteristics that make Gastmann intriguing. His nihilism has not given Doc the freedom Gastmann enjoys, rather it has enslaved him. He is a follower, not a leader, and if Gastmann is larger than life, Doc is definitely smaller than life. Too indifferent or intimidated, or both, to realize his indispensability to the syndicate, he takes no initiative and simply lets his fate come over him. Doc's answer to each successive life-threatening dilemma is to deny it.[8] As a psychological character study Doc may be fascinating; as a dramatis persona in the title role he is simply uninteresting.

Frank had already failed. Repackaged and set five stories under the city—stripped of its songs and its humor while recognizable bits and pieces of the author's lifework passed in review—it fared even worse. The hundreds of pages of defense, explanation, interpretation, and accompanying narratives which Dürrenmatt gave it after the fact in the lengthy afterword, entitled *Der Mitmacher: Ein Komplex,* did little to help. He had his second consecutive failure.

Die Frist (The Grace Period)

For his *Friedrich Dürrenmatt Lesebuch* (Reader), published by Arche in 1978, the author chose not one of the canon plays—*The Visit, The Physicists,* or *The Meteor*—for inclusion, but rather *Die Frist.* He did so "in the opinion that it betrays more about him than a successful play would. The discovered offers less fascination than the undiscovered. It is far more interesting to find out why a play failed, than to understand why a play was successful" (15:148). That Dürrenmatt expected this play to fail is evident from the fact that he avoided the premiere.

Already in the stage directions—fully six pages long—Dürrenmatt was on the defensive. Sensing that the critics would search for historical reality in the pseudo-documentary about the prolonged death of a dictator, and anticipating that they would find the play wanting when measured against their expectations, he begins the directions by citing no less an authority than Aristotle. It was Aristotle's opinion that "it is not the task of the dramatist to tell what really happened, as do the historians, but rather what could have happened" (15:11). Dürrenmatt has been at pains in the past to describe reality as a series of unlikely events which nevertheless occur. Once again he patiently defends his stage as a place where everything is real; reality on the other hand is the locus of the improbable. "More and more desperately does the stage attempt to keep pace with today's reality. Whatever unrealities the theater invents, reality outstrips it" (15:11–12). The following comedy, Dürrenmatt insists, is synthetic, not analytical—that is, assembled from impressions thrust upon him by the improbable reality of the present day: "the slow death of a dictator surrounded by thirty doctors, an American secretary of state's attempts to play power politics in the style of Metternich, the lonely struggle of a scientist honored with the Nobel Peace Prize against an intolerant imperial power ..." (15:12). Dürrenmatt believes strongly that he has created a theater reality that "even if it wanted to, would never succeed in falling out of reality into a void" (15:13). He attempts to meet head-on those critics who insist on their right to analyze reality their own way, which is not the author's, and "to look for and then to miss in my

156

theater reality things which I have not put into it" (15:13). There follows more vitriol, now aimed at the "stylists" as he calls them, directors and actors who alienate his plays through improper staging and delivery of lines—"That talk about my abbreviated dialogues or that I don't put (real) people onto the stage, only reveals the inability to read me and to play me." His theater demands actors and directors, not stylists. Unfortunately it is the latter who have ruined the theater for him, so that more and more he is beginning to write for "the theater of my imagination" (15:14).

Finally, with all this off his chest, Dürrenmatt begins to describe how the stage should look when the curtain rises. So what do we find there? For one thing, we find some of the repetition and recombination of old themes, which we have come to expect: the false priest motif from *Frank,* the repetition of a staged event because of a camera failure from *The Visit,* the operation without anesthetic from *The Quarry.* We find a play infused with flashes of Dürrenmatt's wit, so lacking in the previous play—running gags which are refreshingly under control, which do not play themselves out or become tiresome. We also find—and here we can agree with Dürrenmatt's assessment in the introduction—a plot which, while not historical, is plausible. The *generalissimo* is dying, and the prime minister ("His Excellency"), a political pragmatist, foresees the chaos into which the country will be plunged within days, if not hours. The jackals are gathering: the party of the *generalissimo,* the monarchy, the Catholic church, the opposition—all are jockeying for power. Especially dangerous are the chief of the *generalissimo*'s secret police, Möller, and the duchess of Saltovenia, who has ambitions to get her daughter, Princess Silvia, the last remaining Stauffer, to the throne and restore the monarchy. Goldbaum, a concentration camp survivor and spokesman for the political opposition, has been a thorn in the government's side because of his human rights campaigns. His status as a national treasure, however—he has two Nobel Prizes to his credit—has functioned as his insurance policy against elimination by the secret police. In this regard, Goldbaum bears a strong resemblance to Andrei Sakharov, a fact which lends the play one of its few historical reference points. Goldbaum, who has seen how power corrupts, has no desire for political office. The fact that he is a physician, however, places him in the ironic position of having to try to prolong the dictator's life by extraordinary means. Eventually a team of thirty doctors and fifty nurses is staffing a state-of-the-art intensive care unit. For what reason are they prolonging the *generalissimo*'s agony? The prime minister, with the backing of the cardinal, requires a grace period in order to neutralize the factions and bring stability to the governmental transition. The prime minister's power plays and machinations during this grace period form the main thread of the plot, while from the next room, offstage, the dying dictator's groans resound.

Having grounded his plot in a recent historical event, Dürrenmatt ignores the reality of that event in order to explore the alternate possibilities inherent in it. As the Anabaptist revolt had given rise to two versions of the same ahistorical *comédie humaine,* the death of Franco has occasioned another carnival of society, in which Dürrenmatt is propelled from scene to scene by the many associations the plot suggests. "What fascinated me," he wrote in the program notes, "was the association between certain aspects of modern medicine and a concentration camp: the tortures to which the human being is subjected by the former, in order to allow him to die as late as possible, appeared to me to be similar, in a diabolical way, to the methods of certain concentration camp doctors, who had undertaken tests on people intended to explore the limits of their mortality" (15:141). The connection suggested between the intensive care unit and a concentration camp led to the idea of having a holocaust survivor employ the same methods on a fascist dictator. Goldbaum, a literary reincarnation of Gulliver, survived an operation without anesthetic. Now he, in turn, must operate the same way, because in the dictator's condition anesthetic would be fatal.

Other plot lines are driven similarly by Dürrenmatt's associations. A recent fascination with the image of Atlas staggering under the weight of the world— a picture Dürrenmatt had found himself sketching again and again—manifests itself in the fate of the dictator: "a dying Atlas, who is no longer capable of carrying the world. He had carried it the old way, trampling people, wading through blood, and now a new Atlas sets about taking the world on his shoulders. But the world the new Atlas wants to carry must be a different one: he undertakes the liquidation of the old world" (15:143). The new Atlas is the prime minister. In setting about to neutralize the various warring factions, His Excellency faces what proves to be an insurmountable obstacle. He wants to make a new beginning for society, "but he has become untrustworthy through his past, . . . this untrustworthiness brings about his downfall" (15:143–44). The prime minister is yet another variation of Dürrenmatt's familiar loner out to reform society despite the skeletons in his own closet.

The prime minister is a mathematician and understands the world logically. He has done meticulous research on all his enemies' pasts, and he can reliably predict their reactions. One by one he neutralizes the factions with a combination of diplomatic skill, ruthless tactics, and perfect timing. Two key players are hiding Nazi pasts. Dr. Arkanoff, alias Johannes Himmelreich, had been a death camp doctor and had, coincidentally, operated on Goldbaum. Möller, the chief of secret police, had been the camp's commander. The prime minister uses both men to his ends, then jettisons them at the right time: Arkanoff helps keep the *generalissimo* alive, while the threat of exposure drives Möller to suicide at the exact moment when a heart is needed for a transplant. His Excellency neutralizes the monarchy by marrying Princess Silvia to her secret lover, a commoner. The church makes itself ludicrous through the daily, televised last rites which it performs on the dictator for weeks. The prime minister fans the hostility between the archbishop and the cardinal by engaging an actor to impersonate both of them in turn during the last rites broadcasts.

A series of ironic, unforeseeable worst possible turns works against this precise mathematician to foil his calculations. The first of these is Goldbaum. The prime minister knows about Arkanoff and Möller's Nazi pasts, but cannot admit it without unleashing a scandal on himself. Goldbaum is his secret weapon to bring both men down. He waits in vain, however. Goldbaum does not expose them, because he has no idea of their identity. He does not recognize his torturers, and thus the prime minister's strategy has been based on a false premise. The second unforeseen element is the farmer Toto, who enters the prime minister's office unnoticed twice, once to warn him against executing his son Ponzo, and again near the end of the play to assassinate him at the moment when he is at the pinnacle of his power. According to Möller, Toto had died by firing squad himself two years earlier; however, Möller is hardly a reliable source. Toto's identity, Dürrenmatt claims, is ultimately not important. He may be a hired assassin or a ghost. In any case he is an emissary from the past, the prime minister's corrupt and violent past, come in the form of nemesis to exact payment for a crime from long ago. The final irony concerns the prime minister's successor. In order to keep an eye on, and effectively neutralize, the opposition, the prime minister has acquiesced to their secret demand to make Goldbaum his assistant. With His Excellency's death Goldbaum, the unpragmatic, apolitical humanist, totally unfit to function in the cutthroat political arena, must now become the new prime minister.

In keeping with Dürrenmatt's dictum that it is more interesting to find out why a play failed than why it succeeded, it remains to examine why a play with so much dramatic potential was not critically acclaimed. Dürrenmatt is most successful when he writes a tight play around a single theme: for example, *The Visit, The Physicists,* and *The Meteor,* as well as the successful Strindberg adaptation. With *Die Frist,* however, this disciplined thematic control gets lost. It appears that Dürrenmatt has one association too many for an already crowded plot: the creations he called "The Immortals" (*die Unsterblichen*), nine grotesque, ancient women in black. They range in age from one hundred fifty down to just over one hundred. Fat, bald-headed, and murderous, the Immortals are the female ancestors of the *generalissimo.* Led by the matriarch, Rosagrande, they spew venom against all men. Their hatred of the *generalissimo,* the only surviving male member of the clan, is so strong that it seems to be keeping them alive artificially. Their presence on stage at the beginning of the play before the dialogue even begins, and the fact that they speak the final long chorus and over twelve percent of the dialogue of the entire play, emphasize their importance to the author. Their choral function implies that they view the stage reality from a higher perspective. The audience is obviously to take them seriously, but why?

Turning to Dürrenmatt's explanation, we find that he intended the Immortals as political victims of the male-dominated world; women ironically cursed to populate a world by which they have been victimized. So they are not simply grotesque comic relief; however, the message of their final fifty-line-long chorus is pure nihilism in the thin disguise of radical feminism. The death of the *generalissimo* is merely a metaphor for the death of all that is male, including God:

> Evil, stubborn, lecherous, old,
> Boasting to be the father of us all,
> Smeared with blood and icy-cold. (15:130)

In the name of all women they claim the time has come to close their wombs and cast all of creation back into nothingness:

> Now back into the void sinks all
> That men created, that men thought,
> An unfruitful earthen ball
> Redeemed from sperm and battles fought (15:131)

and conclude with a *Faust* parody in which they declare the ultimate feminine goal to be "eternity and sterility."

Just as in *Titus Andronicus* the lure of nihilism has been too great for Dürrenmatt to resist. The blasphemous, hyper-feministic, nihilistic diatribe at the end destroys the message, for the Immortals are not convincing as feminists or as victims of men. Nor do they choose their own victims according to gender. They gore the archbishop, who has tried to get them to pray for the *generalissimo,* but they also trample two governesses to death and nearly kill Princess Silvia, who wanders into their quarters by mistake. Several of the Immortals are hundred-year-old virgins, whose problem seems to be sexual frustration. One cries repeatedly: "I want a man between my legs!" Two have been feeble-minded since birth, and babble only nonsense syllables. As grotesque figures they provide a type of comic relief at several points throughout the play. As mouthpieces for the oppressed female gender, however, they are severely lacking in credentials. Their venomous diatribe does not develop logically out of the plot. Its final position and the vehemence with which it is spoken beg its acceptance as the play's true moral. Yet despite lengthy reflection, we are hard-pressed to make the connection between the apotheosis of misandry we have just heard and the previous two hours of plot, in which not just the males, but also the females—the duchess of Saltovenia and the duchess of Valdopolo—are power-hungry and ruthless.

If we think away the final chorus and just look at the plot, we see an intriguing cloak- and-dagger tale in which a courageous but morally flawed reformer sets out with a mathematician's precision to better the world, only to discover that: "History is something approximate, a blasphemous farce, directed by negligence, coincidence and forgetfulness" (15:122). There is nothing new under the sun, and certainly not much that is new under Dürrenmatt's byline. The record is stuck on the "21 Points to *The Physicists.*" That having been said, however, this uncompromising satire on the human condition is far and away the best of the failed plays. Like *Der Mitmacher* it repackages numerous old themes; unlike *Der Mitmacher* it engages the audience by means of three-dimensional characters, motivated dialogue, and skillfully employed humor. Grotesque and to an extent surreal, it nevertheless presents a believable, predictably cynical but eerily accurate satire on medical technology outstripping morality, the excesses of the mass media, the corruptibility of religious institutions, the machinations of power politics, and, for good measure, the "romantic ideal world" of Goethe's *Faust.*[9] It is a play that deserved a better fate and which, when revisited objectively by future generations, will likely be granted a more prominent place in the Dürrenmatt canon.

Achterloo

Dürrenmatt's second insane asylum comedy would prove to be his farewell to the theater. While *Achterloo* never attained critical success—by this time the critics were lying in wait for the author—audiences were laughing in Zürich. This fact represented a degree of vindication for the author who had experienced his greatest successes and his most resounding failures in Zürich. *Achterloo* was to be neither. It was certainly his most ambitious theatrical experiment ever, and it had deeply personal significance for him. He dedicated the 1983 version, now known as *Achterloo I* because of later revisions, to Lotti, who had passed away before it went into production. In the audience at Zürich was his future second wife, Charlotte Kerr. While Lotti had only been able to read the manuscript, Charlotte would encourage and help him to write three further versions.

In no other play does Dürrenmatt experiment with levels of reality as in *Achterloo*. Superficial similarities to Peter Weiss's successful *Marat/Sade* drama from two decades earlier vanish almost immediately as Dürrenmatt's carnival of history begins to unfold. Unlike his previous carnivals, in which characters arising out of the particular historical situation turn into fictional players of Dürrenmatt's imaginative revisions of history, *Achterloo* draws its character constellation from hundreds of years of history, with literary creations added for good measure. One important criticism of the first version, Charlotte Kerr's criticism, was that too much was being asked of the audience. The fact that a very recent historical event was being played out could easily get lost amid the farce. Charlotte herself claimed not to have understood many of the historical allusions. The audience was laughing in the wrong places, because it did not see the reality behind the humor.[10] The telling revelation that the play was role therapy for inmates of a mental hospital did not come until the end of the play. In the final version from 1988, performed in Schwetzingen and filmed for German television, Dürrenmatt laid his cards on the table up front—which is not to say that he made the audience's task any easier.

. The play is performed by delusional inmates who believe they are famous persons from history. Some change their delusional identities in the course of the play, and argue among themselves about who they really are. The following is a sampling of the confusion facing the audience. Dürrenmatt's narrator is a wealthy heir to a pork-producing firm, who suffers from the delusion that he is Georg Büchner. Büchner is writing the play which the inmates are performing, literally as he goes along. However, the characters outstrip him, and they are performing the second act before he has completed the text of the first. Napoleon, Büchner's main character, is played by a delusional professor who believes he is General Jaruzelski. One of Büchner's own fictional characters, Woyzeck, is one of the roles assumed by an inmate who is also playing the role of Jan Hus. Büchner, in addition to writing and narrating the play, assumes the role of Benjamin Franklin. A tailor, who calls himself Sigmund Freud, plays the roles of Napoleon's nephew Plon-Plon and Karl Marx. However, there are two Karl Marxes in the play, representing Marxist theory versus practice. The second Marx is played by an insane false-teeth maker, Jean-Pierre Leuli, who claims to be Professor Hans Löffel, director of the Asylum Achterloo, but who also claims to be C. G. Jung. Leuli is also playing the role of Louis Napoleon. The real-life daughter of a Nazi concentration camp guard, who believes she is the biblical Judith, assumes the role of Jeanne d'Arc for most of the play within the play, but reverts to being Judith at the end and murders Napoleon, who has transformed himself into Holofernes. Other characters played as single roles or parts of double roles are: General Cambronne, Pope John XXIII, Cardinal Richelieu, Robespierre, Joseph Fouché, Emperor Sigismund, and several medieval popes.

Dürrenmatt maintains four levels of reality throughout the play. First are the inmates of the asylum, some of whom are identified by their real names. At the second level are the delusional identities of the inmates: Carl Jung, Sigmund Freud, Georg Büchner, and Professor Hans Löffel, among others. At the third level is the array of historical characters the inmates are playing for role therapy. Finally, there is the historical drama being acted out through "Büchner's" script: the events in Warsaw, Poland, on December 12 and 13, 1981. Between levels three and four lies a challenge for the audience, because in the eclectic cast of historical and literary figures from several centuries lie encoded the actual players in the real historical drama played out between Wojciech Jaruzelski and Lech Walesa with the whole world watching. Since Dürrenmatt does not name any of these actual players, it is left to the audience's recollection of the event to make the one-to-one connections.

The complicating factor is level three. Why was it necessary to alienate the constellation of characters around Jaruzelski and Walesa through the medium of cardinals, emperors, generals, and saints? Could Dürrenmatt not have let the inmates play the target characters directly as Peter Weiss had done? The answer lies in Dürrenmatt's pessimistic, cyclical view of history. Through his fictional scriptwriter Büchner, he explains:

I tried to write *Achterloo,* the comic tragedy of a revolution which did not take place, because through treason a war had to be prevented, which would have destroyed humanity, in order to save a peace which will destroy humanity, interwoven with causes which coincidentally became effects, which transformed themselves again into causes of new coincidental effects—a carpet which reaches back to the beginning of the universe. . . ." (GW 3:454)

This carpet, however, has a repeating pattern, unvaried as human nature, and the segments of the pattern are interchangeable. "Thus, in order to reproduce the constellation which brought about the events of the twelfth and thirteenth of December, 1981, I have taken patterns from other times, because every pattern of the eternal carpet equals any other" (GW 3:455).

Jaruzelski's declaration of martial law and the outlawing of the labor union Solidarity, which included the arrest of Walesa and many intellectuals and other political dissidents, met with sharp censure in the West as well as in liberal circles in Poland. Jaruzelski was declared a traitor to the cause of Polish autonomy, a political hard-liner, a lackey of Moscow. The justification of treason is a theme which appears as early as *Romulus* and as late as *Der Mitmacher* and *Die Frist*. However, for the first time Dürrenmatt abandoned fictional models in order to demonstrate the principle on a real and recent historical figure. Dealing with this serious historical event through the alienated medium of an insane asylum farce is the closest he ever came to documentary theater. For once, historical reality was being interpreted, and Dürrenmatt left no question about his interpretation of this event. Jaruzelski's treason, like Romulus's, was real but was justified. Soviet troops were poised to march in. Reagan was so vocal in his support of Solidarity that it was feared he would move if the Soviets did. The martial law which prevented a war between the superpowers or, at the very least, the Soviet occupation of Poland, was the lesser evil. "Someone must play the traitor," Napoleon/Jaruzelski asserts, "and I will play him" (GW 3:452).

Napoleon represents Jaruzelski in Dürrenmatt's last carnival of history. Bohemian church reformer Jan Hus becomes Walesa. Richelieu is intended to represent Jósef Cardinal Glemp, while Robespierre, the visitor whose presence arouses so much concern, most likely represents Marshal Viktor Kulikov, the Warsaw Pact commander, whose shuttle diplomacy made him the most frequent Soviet visitor in Poland during the weeks preceding martial law. Karl Marx (doubled in the 1988 version) represents more the Soviet Union in general than Leonid Brezhnev in particular. It is Marx who will march in, Napoleon believes, unless Hus is arrested. Likewise Benjamin Franklin as U.S. foreign minister represents the United States government, rather than simply Alexander Haig. Joseph Fouché equals Stanislav Kania, first secretary of the Polish Communist Party until replaced by Jaruzelski.

Beyond these identifiable correlations between Dürrenmatt's fictional roles and their historical counterparts stretches a gray area of possible correlations, noncorrelations, and outright red herrings. Because, as we have come to expect, Dürrenmatt has not stuck closely to the script of the historical events, not all the characters in Büchner's (Dürrenmatt's) play have real-life counterparts—which is not to say that they do not have significance. Several characters begin to speak their introductory monologues, only to be shouted down by the playwright and director Büchner: their roles have been struck. These may be seen to represent the many who never got the opportunity, for good or ill, to play a role in the historical event by virtue of their prior removal from their posts. Somewhat vaguer is the role of Jeanne d'Arc. On St. Catherine's orders, she lures enemies of the Communist party into bed so that Woyzeck can slit their throats. In light of her attempts to incite Karl Marx by murdering Robespierre, Jeanne appears to stand for the hard-liners in the regime who would have welcomed a bloodbath in order to make an end of the labor union's insurrection. Woyzeck is Napoleon's assassin. A barber by profession, his straight razor is quite active in the elimination of Napoleon's political foes. At Napoleon's order he slits Fouché's throat while shaving him, thus enabling Napoleon to become first secretary of the party. (Woyzeck has already done the same to five party chiefs.) He is also supposed to kill Napoleon, but he does not have the courage: "A respectable person holds his life dear, and a person who holds life dear, has no courage. Whoever has courage is a low-life" (GW 3:414). As Büchner's abused and manipulated common man he is a logical intertextual import into this play about an abusive and manipulative social order. However, if Woyzeck is to be seen as representing the Polish people in 1981—and Napoleon calls him this several times—then the image of a simpleton who unquestioningly does the regime's bidding and who lacks the courage to do what is right is disturbing. In light of the general strikes and courageous pockets of resistance throughout Poland that held out as long as possible, this image hardly squares with reality.

Most misleading, if we are to take Woyzeck as a representative of the people, is his role as Napoleon's executioner. It is Woyzeck who murders Fouché, thus permitting Napoleon to take over his position as first secretary. In reality the removal of Kania was performed by the Central Committee of the Polish United Worker's Party, because he was perceived to be too conciliatory toward Solidarity. The date of the removal was not December 12, the date in the comedy, but the preceding October. In changing the date of Kania's removal, Dürrenmatt is exercising the dramatic license that enables him to show as much history as possible in the shortest stage time. That he substitutes Kania's death for his political demise is simply a clever use of metaphor. However, that he has the common people perform the deed rather than the ruling elite amounts to an unsettling distortion of the historical facts.

The ultimate problem with Dürrenmatt's last play, and in particular its final version, is that it is simply too esoteric to be understandable to any but a small elite of historically savvy theatergoers. What do the average theatergoers really understand of Cardinal Richelieu's role in history, let alone that of the unnamed Cardinal Glemp whom they are supposed to recognize in him? The parallel between Josef Fouché, himself a footnote of the French Revolution, and his unnamed Polish alter ego Stanislav Kania, revolves around both characters' fluctuating loyalties during a time of revolutionary instability, and may be well chosen, but who in the audience has the background to immediately comprehend it? Who, in fact, could even be expected to recognize Kania in the character—assuming they knew Jaruzelski's predecessor as first secretary at all—after Dürrenmatt so alters the date and the nature of his deposition? Even the comedy's running gag is reduced to an in-joke for history buffs. Cambronne cannot remember his "famous word," and he runs through several scenes trying to recall it. General Pierre de Cambronne commanded the Imperial Guard in the Battle of Waterloo and, requested by the British to surrender the Guard, replied "*Merde!*" Whoever is not privy to this fact cannot appreciate the situational comedy of Cambronne's appearances, such as Richelieu's reply to Cambronne's lament: "I have forgotten my word." "I know it," the cardinal says. "It is appropriate for the condition of the Church. Go now" (GW 3:433).

Achterloo stands as a monument to a brilliant idea that remained hopelessly mired in its own brilliance. The criticism which Charlotte Kerr levelled against the first version has not been remedied by the fourth. The audience at a performance of *Achterloo* can laugh at what it thinks it understands, be intrigued by what it does not, and take delight in discovering a hidden connection or two, but it will almost surely not understand the play.

CHAPTER 13

The Prose of the 1970s and 1980s

Der Sturz (The Fall)

On the heels of *Sätze aus Amerika,* his essayistic look at life in the United States from 1970, Dürrenmatt turned his satirical attention to the Soviet Union the following year. Recent events had given the impression of an author leaning farther and farther to the left. He had attended a conference in the Soviet Union against the protests of the P.E.N. club, whose members were distressed about the treatment of Soviet writers. His division of his own Bern Literary Prize among three Swiss dissidents and his open affection for the hippie movement were raising conservative eyebrows back home. Finally, the *Sätze* seemed to be a slap in the face to the nation that had awarded Dürrenmatt his first honorary degree. He had gleefully butchered many American "sacred cows"—among them Billy Graham's mass conversions ("Piety remains ineffective in a falsely structured society"), Thanksgiving Day (a hypocritical ritual, since we slaughtered the Indians who inspired it), and TV ("In Russia the people are stupefied by the party, in the United States by television"). *Der Sturz* sent the message to Dürrenmatt's critics that he had not embraced Marxist ideology.

One observation he made in *Sätze,* in a comparative excursus on the U.S. and Soviet governments, particularly anticipates *Der Sturz.* Like the Mayan pyramids, that were built over each other so that the previous one is contained inside the new one, so too is the hierarchy of power in the Soviet Union. He identifies the layers from the top down as the party, the politburo, the bureaucracy, the army, the scientists, the intellectuals, and finally, at the lowest level but taking up by far the most volume in the pyramid, the people.

Der Sturz is a satirical look at the machinations of power in a totalitarian Communist state, specifically in the outer layer of the pyramid, where power is so costly and so fragile. In a general sense it is an exposé of all power collectives—Eastern as well as Western, economic as well as political—and in this regard it is closely related to *Frank der Fünfte.* The setting is a regular monthly meeting of the party's secretariat, a body composed of the chief ministers in each branch of the bureaucracy and charged with giving the party its direction. As he did in his other narrative about hierarchy in society, *Once a Greek ...,* Dürrenmatt makes liberal use of hyperbole. His Soviet Political Secretariat has no more legitimate claim to represent the top level of Soviet government than does Petit-Paysan's skyscraper to be a replica of a multinational corporation headquarters. Satire thrives on hyperbole, and in both cases it is the truth behind the exaggeration which Dürrenmatt wishes the reader to contemplate. The upper levels of management in a capitalist society are encapsulated in a fairy-tale world, far from the realities of their workers. This same encapsulation exists at the top of the Communist pyramid, where the elite live in villas, buy in special stores, lunch on caviar and champagne. Yet the top is a lonely, unstable, highly dangerous environment.

Each of the fifteen members of the secretariat is designated by a letter of the alphabet corresponding to a position in the power hierarchy. In addition each has a nickname, given by the party chief, *A,* and a ministerial designation. While the narrator maintains his critical stance outside the narrative, he also lets the reader glimpse the events from ground level—that is, through the eyes of a particular character, the postal minister, *N.* However, since *N* enjoys no higher perspective than any of the others in the room—rather, as a system insider he shares their paranoia—his commentary remains subjective and not immune to erroneous conclusions.[1] *N* is the first to enter the conference room, and from the first words of the narrative on, the overwhelming paranoia of the ministers is apparent through *N*'s reflections. He, like all the others except the party boss, *A,* only feels safe in the conference room. Although the postal ministry is theoretically one of the least dangerous positions to hold, both of *N*'s immediate predecessors in the office have vanished without a trace—and although *N* has a good relationship with the chief of the secret police, *C,* he does not dare to ask about them.

Immediately obvious is the absence of the atomic energy minister, *O.* He is the object of much discussion and private reflection as the ministers enter the conference room alone or by twos. No one doubts that *O* has been arrested, and that his arrest must signal the onset of a purge. It becomes a mind game for *N* and the others to deduce who was in on the arrest—to intuit from each other's furtive glances, from the warmth or superficiality of the greeting each gives, which ones may be threatened by the impending purge. Small alliances have formed within the committee, although the overriding paranoia precludes the formation of friendships. Thus, these fragile alliances, created for protection, dissolve and re-form as members rise and fall on the scale of power as represented by the seating order. *N* alternately feels panic and relief as small, in reality meaningless, indicators point toward and then away from other members of his clique. That he has done nothing to warrant elimination is clear to him; however, guilt by association is the Damocles sword hanging over all the ministers from foreign minister *B* down to the chief of the youth organization, *P.* The master manipulator of this paranoia is party boss *A.* A Stalin-like dictator, *A* is a loner from the steppes who lives in a bunker in the woods and has a secret love of American films, bourgeois art, and sentimental folk songs. Otherwise he rules by terror, arresting and executing "traitors" from the highest government ranks on a regular basis. Through *A,* Dürrenmatt exposes the flaw inherent in this type of power collective that exists solely for its own sake and that is out of touch with the party it purports to serve. *A*'s absolute control over the secretariat depends upon keeping the members divided against each other. Universal paranoia has been his foolproof weapon until now. Nobody trusts anybody else, even among the so-called alliances. Within a very short time, however, *A*'s house of cards collapses. What foils him is a combination of his own hubris, which renders him careless at several crucial moments, and the predictable worst possible turn.

A announces that he is dissolving the secretariat in order to "democratize" the government. In the future a popularly elected parliament will set the agenda for the party. Despite the lofty rhetoric with which he proclaims his plan, his ulterior motive is transparent. This rump-parliament composed of inexperienced delegates will be easier to manipulate even than the secretariat, where at least career politicians sit. *A* is taking a giant step toward absolute dictatorship, and he is increasing the danger to the individual ministers by removing their one element of cohesion, however weak. A desperate challenge to *A*'s authority by a perpetually drunken minister and two untimely interruptions of the meeting by a colonel bringing emergency messages delay the proceedings long enough for *A* to make the mistakes that lead to his demise. First, he orders the colonel not to return under any circumstances. When *A* calls a five-minute recess to allow the ministers to deal with their family emergencies, the ministers sense a trap and refuse to leave the room. *A* humiliates them with charges of cowardice, threatening them and accusing them of treason. Ultimately *A* completely loses his composure and insults the one man on whose good graces he is dependent, chief of secret police *C.* He accuses *C* of acting on his own to arrest *O,* and he calls the colonel to come in and arrest *C.* Instead, however, the confused colonel obeys *A*'s previous order not to enter the room again under any circumstances. *A* is finished. He has become suddenly vulnerable, and therefore no longer a threat: "For the first time for *N* the political machinery at whose levers *A* sat . . . became transparent." The use of fear had been *A*'s brutal forte, but with time he had become careless. "He forgot that he had surrounded himself with power mongers, for whom party ideology was merely a means toward a career. He forgot that he had isolated himself, for fear does not only separate. Fear also bonds together, a law which had now become *A*'s nemesis. He had suddenly become as helpless as an amateur, opposed by professionals at the game of power" (23:56).

One final fact makes it now imperative that the ministers eliminate *A*. He had drawn up a list of those ministers to be liquidated in the event the secretariat opposed its dissolution. *C* makes the list public, and for half the power collective it now becomes an actual matter of life and death. *A* is ceremoniously strangled, his body removed, and the party secretary, *D*, declares himself the new chief. As he sets about to change the seating order, atomic energy minister *O* enters the room. He had written the wrong meeting day on his calendar. The certainty of his arrest had heightened the paranoia, which had triggered the events which led to *A*'s fall. It had all been one great *Panne*. The worst possible turn struck *A* at the height of his apparent invincibility. *A* suffers the same fate as Gastmann: "executed for a crime he did not commit."[2] However, all of the credit cannot go to chance. Dürrenmatt analyzes each of *A*'s miscalculations through the eyes of *N*, the silent observer/commentator who, as the only non-participant in the discussions, can concentrate his attention on observation and reflection.

Dürrenmatt gives no indication that the ministers will take this costly lesson to heart. On the contrary, only the power hierarchy changes—not the game—as *D* takes the reins of power. Even *N*, to whom knowledge of the true nature of power came as a brief epiphany, obediently takes his new seat ahead of *D*'s archenemy *G*, and becomes the seventh most powerful man in the state. Like that arch-capitalist institution the Frank Family Bank, Dürrenmatt's fictional Political Secretariat is a power collective that is greater than the sum of its members' egos. Its energy is directed inward toward self-preservation. Thus it becomes an organism that preys on anything threatening its survival, even if that entity is its most powerful member. Inwardly chaotic, its self-preservation becomes over time essential for the stability of the state. It was as foolish for *A* to attempt to eliminate the secretariat as it was for Ottilie Frank to try to liquidate the bank. Both believed themselves to be sole owners of a commodity of which they were in reality only proprietors—an error that brings them both into close proximity with the physicist Möbius.

A's violent fall represents one model of reality—a fictional world within which the real world can be found. History has already given the Soviet Union a Stalin—a tyrant much like *A*, who nevertheless demonstrated that power, once attained, need not be gambled away recklessly. Any reading of *Der Sturz* that leads to the comforting conclusion that corrupt power is doomed, is a misinterpretation. That was Brecht's read on history, not Dürrenmatt's. Smart powermongers may hold on for a long time; less astute tyrants like *A* will fall quicker. Power and the mechanisms of power, however, are timeless. That is Dürrenmatt's pragmatic, pessimistic conclusion.

Stoffe (Subject Matter)

In 1981 Dürrenmatt published the first of two volumes entitled *Stoffe,* which translates as "Subject Matter." The three narratives published for the first time in volume 1—*The Winter War in Tibet, Lunar Eclipse* (already discussed in the context of *The Visit*), and *The Rebel*—are not among Dürrenmatt's lasting contributions to literature. Their significance is rather as points of departure for his examination of his own creative processes. This volume is the first half of a two-volume autobiography, the second volume of which he would deliver nine years later. However, the term "autobiography" already gives a false impression of *Stoffe,* for as he writes in the introduction, he considers an accurate portrayal of the events of his life impossible: "Death approaches, life evaporates. As it evaporates, one wants to give it form; by giving it form, one falsifies it" (GW 6:11). Furthermore, he considers his life as too privileged, measured against the fates of millions, to be worthy of narration. When he nevertheless writes about himself, it is not to give the history of his life, but rather the history of his subject matter—in particular that which he has never published. "By outlining these especially, I am groping my way back in the development of my thought processes as though following an animal's track, and that which I scare up from the brush is my life" (GW 6:11).

Dürrenmatt's childhood impressions of Konolfingen, his observations on the war from the privileged safety of Swiss neutrality, adolescent experiences in the labyrinthine city of Bern, near-fatal illness, university years, encounters with philosophers and artists, a memorable summer in a mountain village—all aid the creative process, not as factual elements, but as building blocks of fictions. By this exercise of tracing his literary subject matter back to its sources, Dürrenmatt wants to demonstrate that all literature is essentially autobiographical. It is the writer's task to elevate these personal experiences to the status of universal metaphor.[3] The concluding sentences to the first segment of *Stoffe I–III* explain the conservation and recombination of thematic materials that has been so apparent throughout Dürrenmatt's work: "A subject [*Stoff*] we once encounter, never releases us again. We remain within its gravitational field" (GW 6:190).

The first of the three stories is the first-person narrative of a mercenary soldier who, after the destruction of most of the world in a nuclear war, continues to fight in an obscure war carried on in a labyrinth of tunnels under the mountains of Tibet. He advances to commander of an army, few members of which he ever sees. In a sense the war is a free-for-all, for in these dark and dangerous tunnels everyone must be considered the enemy. Ultimately alone, insane, and nearly completely prosthetic, the mercenary continues to roll along in his wheelchair firing at everything that moves with his artificial machine-gun arm, and carving his memoirs into the tunnel walls with his other limb: a prosthetic parody of a Swiss Army knife. Finally, alone and near death, the mercenary solves the riddle of the Winter War. Revelation comes to him in the form of Plato's cave allegory. The shadows on the wall are the enemy, although they are cast by prisoners like himself carrying machine guns. Bullets fired at the shadows ricochet off the walls and kill those who make the shadows. "The fire that throws the shadows must have originated in prehistoric times. Every animal fears fire with good reason. Fire is something hostile, and the human being's enemy is his shadow" (GW 6:175). The Winter War was a human necessity, because the "authority" that governed the world after the nuclear holocaust had removed the one thing human beings cannot live without: the enemy. "Man is only conceivable as a beast of prey" (GW 6:175). But who is the enemy?

Central to *The Winter War in Tibet,* along with the cave allegory, is the image of the labyrinth. Immediately preceding the narrative, and following descriptions of his youthful encounters with the labyrinths of literature and of his imagination, Dürrenmatt placed an essay entitled "Dramaturgy of the Labyrinth." The labyrinth is a symbol of the mysterious world into which the author was born, like the Minotaur awakening to consciousness in Daedalus's maze. It is also a prison without gates, that anyone is free to enter, in which anyone may get lost.[4] "In so far as I . . . sketched out a labyrinth, I identified unconsciously with the Minotaur. I made the primal protest. I protested against my birth because the world into which I was born was now my labyrinth; the expression of a puzzling mythic world that I did not understand, which pronounces the innocent guilty, and whose authority is unknown." Also, he wrote, he identified with the victims of the Minotaur, and finally with Daedalus, architect of the maze: "because every attempt to get a grip on the world in which one lives, to shape it, represents the attempt to create an alternative world, one in which the world that one would like to form becomes itself as entangled as the Minotaur in the labyrinth."[5] It was during the work on *Winter War,* however, that he got the insight he needed to truly understand his own symbol. His self-identification with the Minotaur, he wrote, had been misguided, as had his proud identification with Daedalus: "Anyone who seeks to depict the labyrinth must also enter it willingly. He must become Theseus." He begins to search for the

Minotaur, wondering whether he even exists. Not finding him, he wonders why there is a labyrinth at all. "Perhaps," he concludes, "because Theseus is himself the Minotaur and every attempt to overcome this world through human thought— and even if it is only with the writer's symbol—is a struggle that one carries on with oneself. I am my enemy; you are yours."[6]

"The goal of man is to be his own enemy," the mercenary in *Winter War* concludes. "The human being and his shadow are one" (GW 6:176). The mercenary dies in a last shootout against his shadow, proclaiming: "I am the master of the world" (GW 6:176). He is, of course, a fool. The mercenary has stumbled upon the same insight that simultaneously crystallized in his creator's mind during the act of creating him. However, there is a considerable difference between the message of the essay and the ending of the narrative—between the writer's internal struggle to come to terms with the world on the one hand, and the nihilistic glorification of *homo homini lupus* ("Man is a wolf to man," the motto under which the Winter War is fought) on the other. The mercenary, caught up in a meaningless war in which he is the last combatant, represents the dangerous extreme to which a misunderstanding of the human need of an enemy and the fact that each individual is his own worst enemy can lead. An insight that could have saved him destroyed him instead.

The Rebel, the third narrative in volume 1 of *Stoffe*, after *Lunar Eclipse*, was conceived during Dürrenmatt's year at the University of Zürich, 1942–43, but not written until 1981. A young man, whose father vanished into a foreign land before his birth and whose mother pays little attention to him, sets off at age twenty to seek his father. He finds his one clue in the attic, a grammar book of an unknown exotic language. By chance he finds the country, a rural society suffering under the tyranny of a dictator no one has ever seen, but who supposedly had arrived twenty years before and assumed power during a time of anarchy. A rebellion has been fermenting for some time. The "secret parliament" waits only on the prophesied rebel, an outsider conversant in their language, who will lead them against the tyrant. The young man is assumed to be this messiah—the people line the streets as he rides into the capital on a donkey— and reluctantly he accepts the role under the urging of the religious leader. All the circumstantial evidence leads to the conclusion that the reclusive dictator is his father, and a priest warns him that the old religious leader and the dictator are one and the same. The arrest of the rebel, ordered by the captain of the palace guard as a diversionary tactic, signals the beginning of the revolt. Suddenly all conspiratorial unity collapses. The secret parliament becomes indecisive, doctrinaire infighting paralyzing its resolve. The revolution is postponed, then forgotten. Imprisoned in his cell with mirrors on all four walls and on the floor and ceiling, the young man gradually goes insane, talking to his mirror images as though they were an army with which he will overthrow the tyrant.

At its inception *The Rebel* was to have been a novel. The Zürich year marked the first breath of freedom for the author, and Dürrenmatt fancied himself quite the young rebel. It was a time of little formal study but much intellectual growth, and Dürrenmatt felt no obligation to keep his parents informed of the bohemian lifestyle he had adopted: "I assumed up front they would not understand me. Unjustifiably so. But a rebel needs this precondition for rebellion" (GW 6:313). Dürrenmatt credits the artist Walter Jonas with the inspiration for the ending of *The Rebel,* by suggesting the question of how a play with only one actor would be constructed. Dürrenmatt's solution: "I saw a man in a hall of mirrors as a prison" (GW 6:313). Undeniably, the most obvious literary presence in *The Rebel* is Kafka, in the pervasive paranoia and mysterious, inaccessible bureaucracy, as well as in the estranged, ultimately deadly father-son relationship. However, in contrast to Kafka, Dürrenmatt does not indulge in uncompromising literary father-bashing. Whereas Kafka regularly portrayed his father as an omnipotent tyrant, Dürrenmatt combines the tyrant father and the kindly religious leader into a character with a dual personality, emphasizing the ambivalence of his feelings in later years toward his father the pastor.

The second volume of *Stoffe,* with the title *Turmbau,* written between 1987 and 1989 and published in 1990, begins with more insight into the creative process: a discussion of how imagination complicates memory. "Whether something was possible is sometimes more important in memory than what really happened. Not only ideology falsifies history, imagination does so even more. If memory is the foundation, possibility is the playground of imagination. Its desire to vent its energy overcomes the burden of being exact" (TB 11). However, it is in the future that imagination is most at home. There it represents pure possibility unencumbered by memory. The first chapter, "Encounters," deals with the one inevitability with which the imagination cannot deal: death. Three personal encounters—the death of a family dog, of his artist friend Varlin, and finally of his wife Lotti—are described reverently, but dispassionately. If death is unimaginable, the feelings it engenders in the survivors are beyond the boundary of the expressible. "What remained was crystallized memory: a woman and a man who once loved each other and now belonged to the past. But I have long since drifted into the indescribable. Feelings cannot be described, death is only representable externally" (TB 18).

For the remainder of *Turmbau* the narration bounces around in desultory fashion through the author's life, interspersing experiences, philosophical reflection, and unpublished short stories in the manner of the first volume—

whereby the experiences and reflections greatly overshadow the narratives. Only two of the six chapters actually contain short stories: "Das Haus" and "Vinter"—lightweight, late-published early prose narratives that belong thematically to the nihilistic tales of the forties and early fifties. More intriguing are the insights provided by descriptions of the youthful author's aborted dramatic attempt to build the Tower of Babel, and his collaboration with Max Frisch on the concept for an (unwritten) sequel to *Biedermann und die Brandstifter* (The Firebugs).

In the chapter entitled "The Bridge" Dürrenmatt takes the reader through a fascinating treatise on logical and illogical belief, as thirteen different versions of the twenty-two-year-old student F. D. tries to cross (or not to cross) the Kirchenfeldbrücke in Bern. He comes to the conclusion which he has demonstrated so often in dramas and narratives through his worst possible turn: "Reality represents an improbability that has occurred." Political systems are the subject of the expository essay "Automobile and Railroad States," a satire on the excesses of capitalism and communism reminiscent of the "Wolf Game" and "Good-Shepherd Game" from the "Monster Lecture on Justice and the Law." Swiss patriotism comes under scrutiny in the essay entitled "The Overfed Cross." Disguised as a fictional soccer team, "F.C. Helvetia 1291," Switzerland is portrayed historically as a once proud team playing an international schedule, but now reduced to the status of a club team that only practices for the day when someone might challenge them to a game. It is a scenario for a critical look at Swiss nationalism, universal conscription, and "intellectual national defense."

However, Dürrenmatt reserves his most scathing criticism in *Turmbau* for Christianity. With all respect for the person of Christ—Dürrenmatt calls him "perhaps the first religious atheist . . . who no longer sought God in metaphysical speculation but rather in himself" (TB 195)—Dürrenmatt deplores what has happened since in Christ's name. He blames Paul for taking the human being and positing him as "literally God's son, crucified and resurrected to save mankind that had become guilty through original sin" (TB 195). Paul launched thereby a wave of metaphysical speculation resulting in two thousand years of theological dogma that includes the trinity (which has become a quaternity through the Catholic reverence of the Virgin Mary), the physical assumption of Mary into heaven, the sacrament of the Eucharist with transubstantiation, the infallibility of the pope, and, of course, the devil and hell. Particularly offensive to him is the supposition that only those who can accept all this can attain eternal life: "so that the millions of Jews who died in the hell of the extermination camps without exception have to go to Hell afterward, while their Christian hangmen, in case they should later do penance and receive the last rites, are

175

automatically enrolled in the host of the redeemed" (TB 200). Dürrenmatt concludes that nobody really believes the Christian dogma any more. "It is a story, developed out of the dialectic of theology and as such fantasy, which explains every one of its contradictions as a mystery that the human mind is insufficient to comprehend, and that to believe it represents a grace, without which the human being would be lost" (TB 201). Only the fear of hell, he states, causes the masses to give lip service to the creed. He considers the question of God's existence irrelevant. God is a "sympathetic word," a subjective statement that cannot be transformed into objective knowledge, cannot be incorporated into structural thought.

The second and final volume of *Stoffe* ends with an essay that Charlotte Kerr considered his best piece of prose ever. "Das Hirn" (The Brain) replaces the hypothetical point of matter, out of which the big bang created the universe, with a human brain. A complete tabula rasa with no external stimuli, the brain has sixteen billion years to discover its identity and evolve to its modern complexity. In this time the brain first comes to consciousness of numbers, then of time; constructs mathematics and logic; conceives of life, first as single cells, then as complex organisms; and imagines the entire evolutionary process by trial and error, ultimately conceiving of the primates, and *homo erectus* in particular. The brain imagines human history—pagan rituals, the first murder, the matriarchy followed by the patriarchy, dynasties and wars—not only as history unfolded but also other courses it could have taken, until it arrives at the twentieth century and conceives of the author who is at the same time conceiving of it. The brain thinks in due course of everything real as well as everything possible, whether those possibilities have become reality or not. Finally Dürrenmatt takes the reader on a tour of the death camps at Auschwitz and Birkenau. They were not conceived by the fictional brain, nor by any other. "It is unthinkable, and what is unthinkable cannot be possible, because it has no sense. It is as though the place had invented itself. It simply exists, senseless and inconceivable as reality and without reason"(TB 266).

Minotaurus

The "Dramaturgy of the Labyrinth" reemerged in 1985 with a short narrative composed in poetic prose entitled *Minotaurus: A Ballad,* which Dürrenmatt also illustrated. Already in the essay he had emphasized the Minotaur's innocence, his unjust imprisonment as metaphor for the individual born into an incomprehensible, labyrinthine world. The creature was not at fault for the transgression of his mother, Pasiphae, who, with the consent of her husband Minos, had Daedalus sew her into the skin of a cow so that she could mate with the *bos primigenius,* the great bull King Minos had rustled from the herd of the god Poseidon. The misshapen offspring with the head (and brain) of a bull and the body of a man created a dilemma for Minos. Wishing to be just but merciful toward his fundamentally innocent but potentially violent stepson (Dürrenmatt's reasoning), Minos commissioned Daedalus to construct a maze so intricate around the creature that escape would be impossible. Athens owed tribute to Crete every nine years, which Minos demanded in the form of seven maidens and seven young men to be driven into the maze and sacrificed to the Minotaur. Theseus, son of the Athenian King Aegeus, heroically volunteered to join the other sacrificial victims. Once in Crete, Theseus won the love of Minos's daughter Ariadne, who gave him the sword with which to kill her half-brother the Minotaur and the ball of thread with which to find his way back out of the labyrinth.

Dürrenmatt begins his "ballad" with the Minotaur awakening in the maze for the first time. He compresses the events from this point until the Minotaur's death into a twenty-four-hour period, and takes several other liberties with the myth. Primarily he embellishes, filling in details from his own imagination. What makes this uniquely Dürrenmatt's myth, however, is his radical altering of the perspective. Whereas the traditional myth makes an evil creature of the Minotaur and a hero of Theseus, Dürrenmatt reverses the roles. Incapable of rational thought, the instinctual creature is still half human. That a moral sensorium is lacking is not the beast's fault. He could just as easily have been born with a human head on an animal's body, similar to a centaur. Individuation becomes the man-beast's first challenge. Separation of the self from the other might have been problematic—there is only one Minotaur in the whole world and he is alone in the maze—had Dürrenmatt not borrowed an innovation from his own *Rebel* narrative. The walls of the labyrinth are covered with mirrors. Owing to this presumed kindness on the part of Daedalus, the Minotaur dimly comprehends that he has countless companions on both sides of him as he grazes down the corridors. A feeling akin to happiness wells up in the creature as he perceives that all the other creatures respond to his every move with the same move. He waves, they wave back; he smiles, they smile back. Feeling like a god, if he only knew what a god is, the Minotaur begins to dance with his companions.

Then he notices a creature who does not move when he moves. Naked with long hair she stands very still, and her mirror images stand very still. For the first time the creature feels another body against his. That he rapes her occurs out of pure animal instinct; that he kills her is an accident. What does the Minotaur know of his own strength? What does he understand of death? He falls asleep, and when he awakens, the birds have already consumed the girl's corpse. He forgets her. Then more of the creatures that are different than the Minotaurs appear. They begin to dance, the Minotaur dances with them, until one of them thrusts a sharp object into the creature's chest. For the first time the Minotaur feels rage. He does not understand why, but he senses darkly the animosity of the others. On his rampage he gores all the different creatures with his horns. Turning his attention to the other Minotaurs, the creature makes a discovery that brings him closer into the sphere of the human: the existence of the enemy. As he gazes at his mirror images with the intention of attacking them, he notices that they also want to attack him. One by one, as he butts his head into them (and they are charging at him) they shatter and disappear, until suddenly one Minotaur stands there who does not act like the others. He is warm, not cold and smooth, and he moves independently of the others. A joyful dance ensues: "the dance of brotherhood, the dance of friendship, the dance of security, the dance of love, the dance of nearness, the dance of warmth" (GW 5:446). And as the Minotaur embraces his other, Theseus thrusts the dagger deep into his back, pulls the bull's head off, and retreats following a red thread. "Then, before the sun came, came the birds" (GW 5:447).

This is Dürrenmatt's saddest and at the same time most moving narrative. At the very moment when the beast is on the verge of becoming human in the noblest sense of the word—the lost "I" has discovered the "thou,"[7] and emotions that had only been possible in the creature's dreams have emerged to bless his waking state—the Minotaur falls victim to the worst that human nature has to offer: betrayal. Like the mercenary soldier in his tunnel labyrinth, the Minotaur, not even realizing that he is in a maze or what one is, meets his mortal enemy in his own mirror image. This, like the mirrored walls, is Dürrenmatt's own addition. In the ancient myth there is no mention of betrayal. Rather, one may assume, Theseus fought the Minotaur head on: the Minotaur aided by his size and fierceness, Theseus by the sword from Ariadne. There Theseus was brave and heroic, here only cunning and deceitful.[8] By reversing the perspective and letting the reader see, hear, and feel the narrative through the senses of the "monster," Dürrenmatt has turned the monster into a victim, the hero into a villain, and an ancient myth into a myth for modern times.

Justiz (*The Execution of Justice*)

In the same year in which *Minotaurus* appeared, Dürrenmatt's publisher with Diogenes Press, Daniel Keel, urged him to retrieve an old manuscript from the drawer and publish it as a fragment. The work in question was a novel entitled *Justiz*, begun in 1957 and interrupted when the author went to work on *Frank der Fünfte*. Instead of publishing a fragment, Dürrenmatt rewrote the novel in the form of a narrative set in the 1950s with a modern frame. There are two words for "justice" in the German language. The first of these, *Gerechtigkeit*, is the abstract concept of justice. The second word, *Justiz*, means the practical application of *Gerechtigkeit*. It is the human apparatus for the administration of justice. The tension between these two concepts—the wide gulf between the ideal and reality, between theory and practice—forms the basis of the novel.

Dürrenmatt's first nonchronological novel is characterized by a postmodern playfulness. The inebriated first-person narrator of the novel's first and second parts repeatedly confuses present with past and narrates past events out of sequence, only to apologize and attempt to correct the confusion. In part 3 the narrative perspective changes to that of the author Dürrenmatt, but he narrates from no higher perspective initially than does his drunken chronicler. The confusion caused by the anachronisms is one type of labyrinth the reader must negotiate. A second is the search for truth. Through this maze the author leads the reader down corridors of conjecture, into walls of contradiction, down new corridors, each fraught with blind alleys. This is not detective fiction, at least not in the conventional sense of the word. After Dürrenmatt's "Requiem to the Criminal Novel" there can be no such encore. This is rather a novel about the elusive nature of truth. That *Justiz*, the human apparatus of executing justice, is such a fallible and so easily corrupted instrument, is shown to be a logical consequence of the daunting labyrinth surrounding and shielding the truth from all but the most dedicated and crafty Theseus.

The plot is complicated, but at its core is a miscarriage of justice. Dr. h.c. Isaak Kohler enters a crowded restaurant, walks up to the table where an acquaintance, Professor Winter, is dining, pulls out a revolver and kills Winter with one shot. He then walks calmly out past the shocked witnesses, gets into his limousine, picks up a lady, and goes to a concert as if nothing had happened. Kohler neither denies the crime nor offers a motive. However, after his conviction he hires a struggling young attorney, Spät, to construct a scenario in which someone else could have committed the crime. It is to be a simple parlor game to entertain Kohler, for which the rich prisoner can pay handsomely—or so Spät rationalizes his role. After all, the restaurant was full of witnesses. But Spät, with the help of his underworld connections, does his detective work too well. The testimony of the witnesses is contradictory in key points, the murder weapon has never been found, and a business rival of Kohler, former Swiss national pistol champion Dr. Benno, had been sitting at an adjacent table when the murder occurred. The scandal caused by the investigation ruins Benno's reputation, and he hangs himself. His suicide is taken as a confession of guilt and Kohler is granted a new trial and acquitted.

Spät waits for Kohler to return from a long trip. He plans to kill him when he steps off the plane, then kill himself. That act, he believes will restore justice. Perpetually drunk, Spät passes the time by writing his version of the events before and after Winter's murder. The constellation of characters in Spät's manuscript stretches from the enormously wealthy but grotesquely deformed dwarf Monika Steiermann (an industrial magnate), the beautiful seductress Daphne Müller who poses as Monika Steiermann for public relations purposes, Kohler's daughter Hélène (ostensibly involved in her father's crime, but how?), the overzealous public prosecutor Jämmerlin, and the high-powered but unscrupulous lawyer Stüssi-Leupin, down to the pimp "Lucky" and his whores, whom Spät is later reduced to representing. Whereas Dürrenmatt usually prefers to structure his political and criminal intrigues on the model of the chess game, *The Execution of Justice* employs the metaphor of billiards. Spät first meets Kohler while watching a billiard game between Dr. Benno and Professor Winter. "*A la bande.* That's how you have to beat Benno,"[9] Kohler tells Spät. When Spät confesses that he knows nothing about it, Kohler laughs: "You'll understand it someday all the same" (EJ 9). Later, when Kohler summons Spät to the prison and offers him the case, Spät asks: "And why have you turned to me, of all people?" Kohler answers: "Because you don't know anything about billiards" (EJ 51–52).

Spät narrates the first five-sixths of the novel, but the "truth" he is able to ascertain in this time, from which he deduces the absolute necessity to kill Kohler, amounts to only a fragment of reality. He perceives the tip of an iceberg and mistakes it for a mountain of evidence. Stüssi-Leupin, the lawyer who wins the appellate case for Kohler, suggests that Kohler and Dr. Benno were business rivals. Kohler was managing Monika Steiermann's affairs. He needed to eliminate Benno, and he did so effectively by murdering Winter and implicating Benno. In other words, he had played a carom shot, taking out Benno *a la bande*. There is an element of truth to this theory, but Spät refuses to follow up on it. He is too committed to his own conception of Kohler as a Gastmann figure—a nihilistic monster who treats justice as a game. His obsession with Hélène's complicity in her father's crime stifles the opportunity he once had (they used to be lovers) to acquire her considerable insights into the real motive for murder.

Spät is a pathetic character, but he is hardly one who should arouse much of the reader's sympathy. Like virtually all of Dürrenmatt's protagonists of drama or prose, Spät is a comic rather than a tragic figure. His name means "late" and is in itself a commentary on his relationship to the truth, which he always ascertains too late to do him any good. On the one hand, he wants to get out from behind his mentor's shadow and rise to the top rung of the legal profession. On the other hand, he has far too many scruples to challenge a ruthless lawyer like Stüssi-Leupin. With the Kohler case he has the opportunity either to make his breakthrough into the big time, albeit at the expense of justice, or to prove himself to be a principled man of mettle and at least escape with his self-esteem intact. Tempted by the bright lights but paralyzed by scruples, Spät lays the foundation for Kohler's acquittal, then steps aside at the very last minute, enabling Stüssi-Leupin to claim all the professional glory. Disillusioned, he becomes a pro bono defender, finds one too many loopholes for one too many prostitutes, and is disbarred.

Part 3 begins with a false sense that the "Editor's Afterword" will shed little light on the elusive facts of the case, for the manuscript breaks off as Spät is leaving for the airport to kill Kohler and himself. However, as in *The Pledge,* Dürrenmatt has reserved the epilogue as the actual locus of discovery. Here as there, this discovery comes about years later through coincidence. The author finally reads the manuscript by chance—his habit is never to read unsolicited manuscripts—and only considers it further because of a fascinating old man he had met recently at a soiree in Munich. Kohler, now nearly one hundred years old, tells a story that everyone present, except his daughter, takes for a genial fiction. He speaks of a man, "whose influence in the firm he had to eliminate," and who "was in the habit of dining at this hour in a very well-known restaurant" (EJ 190). Kohler describes how he committed the murder, then got back into his Rolls Royce with a sleeping British government minister, in whose pocket he hid the revolver. "He could only note that he had acted in the best interest of the corporation, which went bankrupt all the same" (EJ 192).

Later the author stumbles, again by coincidence, upon an alcoholic lawyer in a small village who tells his story to anyone who will buy him a drink. He, the lawyer, claims to have argued in court and gotten a man acquitted of murder whom he later found to be guilty. He tells a fantastic tale about killing the murderer, then defending himself before the same judges who had acquitted the guilty man, and who now had to acquit him. Spät's self-aggrandizing story does not square with the manuscript, or with the fact that Kohler is alive and well. It does, however, render Spät an even more unreliable narrator than originally thought and casts further doubt on the reliability of the manuscript itself, which was also written under the influence of alcohol.

Now the narrator/author takes up the search for the truth. Unlike the writer from *The Judge and His Hangman,* Dürrenmatt no longer lays claim to what Martin Burkard calls the "Daedalus perspective." Instead he posits himself in the fiction as a type of Theseus and gropes through the maze after the elusive truth.[10] He sends Spät's manuscript to Hélène Kohler, and she invites him to visit her. Her narrative is the true moment of discovery in the novel. Hélène must be regarded as a reliable narrator because, unlike her father or Spät, she has nothing to gain by embellishing the events, and because she too is seeking the truth and doubts that she has all the facts. Concerning the motivation for murder, Hélène describes being raped by Professor Winter and Dr. Benno at the estate of Monika Steiermann. Her father had warned her not to accept Monika's dinner invitation, but the rebellious daughter had gone anyway. The feeling that she had walked into a trap came too late. The gang rape, in which even Daphne Müller participated, had been arranged in order that the misshapen dwarf Monika, incapable herself of having sex, could enjoy vicarious stimulation by watching. Hélène related how she went to her father and demanded that he avenge her. Kohler placed four billiard balls on the table and played them into the pocket: Winter, Benno, Daphne, Monika. Each would die in turn. Leave the rest to him. And in fact each had died, in exactly that order—Daphne and Monika having been found murdered in seemingly unrelated cases.

Apparently it had not been business after all, but revenge for his daughter's rape that had prompted Kohler—an extreme but understandable response. In light of Hélène's narrative, Kohler suddenly emerges as a purveyor of a type of previously uncomprehended divine justice. But Hélène has still one nagging doubt. Did her father not know that she would reject his advice to decline Monika's invitation? Could he not, in fact, count on his rebellious daughter to do the opposite of what he said? In that case, might he not have set her up, knowing Monika's penchant for staging gang rapes for her own voyeuristic amusement? Is it not possible that he let her go in order to provide himself the perfect justification for doing what he wanted to do all along, eliminating his business rivals—all of them, including Monika Steiermann? Dürrenmatt leaves this final question, of whether Hélène herself had been the cue ball in her father's game, ultimately open. No further information sources can fill in the gaps, as Kohler, now over a hundred, has lapsed into the delusion that Dr. Benno actually killed Professor Winter. As the author leaves, he passes Kohler. "The old man was still playing billiards in his study. *A la bande*" (EJ 213).

Der Auftrag (The Assignment)

In 1986, amid the flurry of prose output that characterized his career in the mid-1980s, Dürrenmatt published a novella in twenty-four chapters, each chapter one sentence long.

While it has been suggested that Dürrenmatt patterned the novella after Bach's "Well-Tempered Piano," giving it "a kind of fugal phrasing that brooks no periodic interruptions,"[11] there is no apparent correlation between the plot and the external structure. Especially in German, where sentences tend to be longer than in English as a matter of course, and where comma splicing is commonplace, the chapter-long sentences pose no hindrance to comprehension.

Unique to *The Assignment* is the type of protagonist. She is a strong, courageous, and resourceful woman who is neither monstrous, mad, promiscuous, nor out for revenge. There is a good, logical reason for this. The heroine of the novella, identified only as F., is a journalist famous for her film portraits. Dürrenmatt was married to such a woman. Charlotte Kerr begins her book on her life with Dürrenmatt by stating: "Die Frau im roten Mantel bin ich"[12] (I am the woman in the red coat)—this in reference to the red fur coat that F. finds in the bazaar and wears throughout the second half of the story. Kerr's book also provides confirmation of the source of the novella. When she first met Dürrenmatt, she had just acquired the film rights to *Der Fall Franza* (*The Franza Case*), Ingeborg Bachmann's fragmentary novel. Franza is driven to a nervous breakdown by her husband, a famous Viennese psychiatrist, who uses her as a case study. Rescued by her brother, an archaeologist, she accompanies him into the Egyptian desert. Here she is determined to come into her own again. However, instead of providing psychic healing, the desert experience confronts her repeatedly with shocking examples, past and present, of the exploitation of women by men. Her emotional rape in Vienna is ironically paralleled at the foot of the Great Pyramid of Giza by her physical rape. She dies the next day as the result of a brain hemorrhage, caused when she banged her head in impotent rage against the pyramid. Charlotte Kerr gave up the film rights to *The Franza Case* and filmed the Dürrenmatt documentary instead. It appears—or we may speculate—that Dürrenmatt did more than simply write a story of mystery and political intrigue. In a romantic gesture he made his new wife the protagonist in an adaptation of the story she had planned to film. She herself had planned to change the ending to allow her heroine to survive the confrontation.[13] Dürrenmatt could do no less, now that Charlotte was in the starring role.

The Assignment is not merely a repackaging of *The Franza Case* with an altered ending. Rather, it is a mystery story, a suspenseful tale of personal courage and self-discovery against a backdrop of international corruption, that stands among Dürrenmatt's best narrative accomplishments. However, while the term "adaptation" hardly does justice to the originality of *The Assignment,* Bachmann's fragmentary novel is clearly his point of departure. From the single character Franza, Dürrenmatt fashions three individuals, each of whom embodies an aspect of Franza's life and fate. Tina Lambert, the woman originally thought to be dead, corresponds to the Franza of Bachmann's first chapter. She has fled from her husband, the psychiatrist Otto von Lambert, who had been treating her for a mental disorder and had written a detailed dossier on her case that she happened to read. However, it is a second Franza—Tina's physical double, the Danish journalist Jytte Sörensen—who goes into the desert. She is investigating a news story with international implications, and the dangerous trail leads her deep into the wilderness of Morocco. This second Franza becomes the victim of male aggression. Jytte's raped and mutilated body is later found at the foot of the Al Hakim ruin.

All of this is in the prehistory. The novella begins with Otto von Lambert commissioning the filmmaker F.—it should now be apparent why Dürrenmatt chose this initial—to find Tina's killer. The body found in Morocco has been misidentified as Tina. Otto, torn by remorse over his role in driving his wife away, has had the body buried without looking at it—an error which goes undiscovered until halfway through the novella. The labyrinth we have come to expect in the prose of the eighties is here, as in *The Execution of Justice,* a labyrinthine search for truth. This time, however, Dürrenmatt has hidden a pair of real live monsters in the maze, as grotesque as Monika Steiermann but more deadly. F. hesitates, but then accepts the assignment that will take her into the African desert to reconstruct a murder. F.'s journey is likewise a journey of self-discovery. Preceding the novella and in a sense hanging over it is an existentialistic passage from Kierkegaard's *Either/Or,* a passage Bachmann could equally well have applied to Franza's mental state:

What will come? What will the future bring? I do not know. I have no presentiment. When a spider plunges from a fixed point to its consequences, it always sees before it an empty space where it can never set foot, no matter how it wriggles. It is that way with me: before me always an empty space; what drives me forward is a consequence that lies behind me. This life is perverse and frightful, it is unbearable.[14]

F. finds the Kierkegaard quote written in Danish, crumpled up in a waste can, in her room at the Hotel Marshall Lyautey. It comes as a warning from the grave, written by Jytte Sörensen as she was about to set out into the desert. F., at a crossroads in her quest, must now make the decision to quit or continue. In her recent past lies a mysterious incident in an abandoned artist's studio back home—an apparent portrait of Tina that seemed to be a portrait of F., and the fleeting glimpse of the shadow leaving the studio behind her. Had she stayed in Switzerland to pursue that strand of the mystery, an innocent prisoner would not be dead, the victim of an execution staged by the government to make F. think the murderer had confessed. The chief of police had ordered her out of the country, after confiscating her film. Then came the discovery of the red fur coat at the bazaar in the shop of the blind mute, planted for F. to find—the coat of the murdered woman. A warning perhaps? Finally, there was the midnight visit by the chief of *secret* police, rival of the police chief for control of the government. F. should stay, he suggested, alone without her camera team, and solve the mystery. He would ensure her safe passage into the desert.

The Hotel Marshall Lyautey stands at the edge of the desert, the boundary between civilization and the complete unknown, between relative safety and certain danger. It is a mysterious place where incomprehensible things happen: thunder and lightning on the horizon at night, although no storm ever approaches; the frantic visit of the photographer Björn Olsen, who cannot believe that F. does not speak Danish; and the maid who treats F. like a ghost. The decision to cut the lifeline and push out into the unknown is complicated one more time by the revelation that the dead woman is really the Danish journalist. Tina Lambert has been found hiding in the artist's studio and is safely in the arms of her husband again. Jytte Sörensen had travelled to Morocco with Tina's passport and red coat. But what secret did she stumble onto that got her killed? The fusing of the three Franzas into one is complete. First Jytte had taken over Tina's identity, and now F. was experiencing a similar metamorphosis: "She felt herself transformed into this other woman, the Danish journalist Jytte Sörensen, and perhaps that had to do, mainly, with the Kierkegaard quote, for she too felt as helpless as a spider falling into empty space" (A 77). Armed with less information than Jytte had possessed—that is, dangling by a thinner thread over the abyss—F. lets go, and until the moment of her rescue is in helpless free-fall.

Dürrenmatt makes a personal appearance in the early chapters as the "Logician D." It is his most intrusive interjection of himself into a narrative since the character of the writer in *The Judge and His Hangman*. Here as there, he speaks with the authorial voice and anticipates later revelations in the story. Tina seems to have fled her husband upon discovery of how closely he was scrutinizing her. But D. wonders if not being observed does not engender a deeper crisis in the human soul. Being observed implies importance, not being observed implies insignificance. Scientific discoveries of the immensity of the universe have rendered the concept of "a god as world regent and father who keeps an eye on everyone" (A 19) inconceivable. Humanity compensates for this unbearable cosmic isolation and insignificance, D. reasons, by creating the necessity (the cold war and the arms race) and the means (technology) for continuous reciprocal observation.

It is in the second half of the novella that Dürrenmatt's more recognizable themes emerge: pervasive corruption in society, the excesses of technology, and a theme particularly prominent in the late prose, sexual violence against women. The corruption of the government and the police force that F. and her team encounter in this North African state is only a microcosm of that which F. discovers on her odyssey into the desert. The photographer Polypheme, whom she meets at the start of her journey by the wreckage of Björn Olsen's VW Bus, becomes her guide to this corruption. She cannot know at this point that it was Polypheme who killed Olsen, and that he plans to have her killed as well. Polypheme for his part is open and forthcoming with information, because he has no intention of allowing her to pass it on. He reveals that a proxy war has been underway for several years deep in the desert. Fought between the country she had entered and a neighboring country over a meaningless stretch of wilderness, the war represents a financial windfall for the two countries involved, for it has become a testing ground for the weapons of the major nations of the world. Arms manufacturers test weapons here before selling them on the world market. All this is carried out under strict security although—and at this point the reader must suspend disbelief—every nation involved has surveillance equipment trained on the battles. Why, then, should the chief of secret police allow, even encourage, F. to make the discovery, assuming that she will expose the proxy war? That is precisely what the chief of secret police wants: a scandal, international moral outrage, and the overthrow of the government.

Polypheme's tale of his own rise through the ranks of international corruption bears initial similarity to Cop's career in *Der Mitmacher.* Polypheme, too, began as a victim of a crime and became a fighter against the criminal element in society, using photography to catch criminals, until his camera began accidentally exposing corruption in the power structure. Pursued by both the criminals and the authorities, he had taken refuge in the military, where his services were at first appreciated. However, he soon began exposing corruption there as well. He had no choice but to drop out of society entirely and survive in the international underground, where he rose to the top of his profession though skill and ruthlessness at playing adversaries against each other. His labyrinthine underground observation bunker, which becomes F.'s prison, is a surreal high-tech world with monitors recording every aspect of the desert war. But the technology which made Polypheme possible is about to make him obsolete. Everything is now done from the sky with spy satellites. Computers are monitoring the satellites, and bigger computers the smaller ones. People are no longer observing each other, machines are observing machines. More than Polypheme's existence, his raison d'etre is threatened, and he has retreated into morbid fantasy. He subscribes to a theology in which God is the pure observer, "unsullied by his creation," and he rationalizes his own actions through this God. Echoing the Logician D., Polypheme believes that all past events are by definition memory and thus falsified. Only the camera can capture "the space and time within which experience took place" (A 107). Fascinated with two things, death and video documentary, Polypheme arranges murders in order to immortalize the moment on film. He exploded Björn Olsen's bus and had Jytte murdered for that reason. It was not Jytte's bad fortune to stumble upon the proxy war, a story worth risking her life for. It was instead her incredibly bad luck (Dürrenmattian luck) to encounter on her odyssey Polypheme—half man, half machine; with the omnipresent video camera like a huge cyclopean eye—and his companion monster in the maze, Achilles.

The former professor of classics, whom Polypheme calls Achilles, is himself a victim of the world's inhumanity. As a helicopter pilot in Vietnam, he had saved Polypheme's life but had had part of his brain blown away in the process. This humanitarian-turned-monster now rapes and murders the women Polypheme captures. Possessing the body of a man but the mind of a wild beast, Achilles is a modern Minotaur. Like his classical counterpart, whose abnormality was a result of an act of betrayal by his mother, Achilles subhuman state results from a betrayal by his own government. The enemy had been tipped off to the secret mission he was flying, so that the helicopter's defense system could be tested in combat. Achilles' brutal acts are purely instinctual, as rational thought is no longer possible. This modern Minotaur, who raped and murdered Jytte and would have done the same to F. but for the deus ex machina appearance of the chief of secret police, his soldiers, and an army of cameramen, is the human being at the instinctive level, stripped of the veneer of humanity. By calling rape and murder "the only desire it was still capable of feeling" (A 116), Dürrenmatt posits these actions as the deepest-seated instincts in the human psyche—or, one could argue, specifically in the male psyche. Violence against women has been a pervasive theme particularly in the late prose, but not only there. The half-witted Albert Schrott from *The Pledge* is a much earlier example of a pedophile/sex murderer who acts instinctively. However, Dürrenmatt's exemplum reaches beyond gender issues. The frightening implications of this demythologized Minotaur Achilles must not be overlooked. The beast lurks beneath the surface layers of civilization; *Homo homini lupus* is as much biological as cultural fact. And it does not take an artillery shell or an accident of birth to peel back these layers and expose the beast: it can be ideology, religious ecstasy, or the hypnotic spell of evil. The holocaust was a collective descent into bestiality.

It has taken all these years, but Dürrenmatt's courageous individual has finally switched gender. Resembling Bärlach in many ways, this female version of the knight without fear or reproach rides out alone against her own monsters. Like Bärlach with Emmenberger, she is unable to slay them without the help of a deus ex machina, but just as Bärlach's ordeal was one of self-discovery, so is F.'s. The three female characters who seem to be mirror images of each other, products of the triplication of Ingeborg Bachmann's protagonist, experience three very different but possible endings to the story. Tina Lambert returns to her psychiatrist husband, reconciles with him, and has his child. Jytte's quest, like Franza's, ends in the desert—she is a victim of the timeless, deep-rooted cycle of violence by men against women that Bachmann portrayed. F. faces her fears, discovers the depth of her inner strength, and returns to join Dürrenmatt's select circle of courageous individuals. It is a group with whom she has more in common than courage and good intentions. She has had no more success than any of the earlier ones in effecting significant change. There are two fewer monsters in the world, but the chief of secret police, who rescued her, is arrested and executed for treason, the proxy war continues, and the news agencies refuse, without comment, to carry F.'s story.

Durcheinandertal

Like much of Dürrenmatt's opus, *Durcheinandertal* was conceived many years before it was written down. While visiting filmmaker Lazar Wechsler in the spa hotel in Vulpera (Unterengadin)—it was 1957 and Dürrenmatt was working on the film script for *It Happened in Broad Daylight*—he had the idea for a novel. He imagined a gangster syndicate owning such a spa hotel and installing gangsters to wait tables, work as lift boys, and so on. The gangsters exploit their positions to gather information on the customers and use this information to determine when and where they can break in. Then, in winter, the hotel is used to hide syndicate members from the law. But boredom sets in quickly in the winter months, and the gangsters begin to terrorize the town. The police do nothing; they have all been bribed. Finally the townspeople take matters into their own hands and burn the spa hotel to the ground, gangsters and all (TB 40–41).

More than thirty years later this plot resurfaced to form the core of *Durcheinandertal*. While the word translates as "Valley of Confusion," it is best to leave the title in German, because it is the fictional proper name of a valley and because of the subtle linguistic connection to "Neanderthal," a term with more sociological than geographical implications for the novel. The Unterengadin, the valley of the Inn river in the far eastern corner of Canton Graubunden, may have served Dürrenmatt as his physical model for the valley in the novel, but he is hardly committing satire specifically on the people of this region. "Durcheinandertal" is a Swiss version of "Schilda," the German fools' paradise where everyone does everything the hard way—or is it Wieland's dispersed Abderites who have settled in this valley? It is a place where, for example, a division of the Swiss Army must be called in to shoot a dog. The dog escapes, but the army manages to cause an international incident by blowing away part of a mountainside in a neighboring country in the attempt. Dürrenmatt's scattershot satire hits as diverse institutions as rural Swiss society, the police, the army, politicians, lawyers, academics, religion, the bureaucracy of state, and mini-neighbor Liechtenstein.

After the brutal *Winter War,* the bittersweet *Minotaurus,* and the two narratives of murder and intrigue *Justice* and *The Assignment,* it is easy to forget that it was Dürrenmatt who wrote: "Comedy is the only thing that can still reach us." *Durcheinandertal,* his last novel, stands as a late monument to the brilliance of his satirical, grotesque wit. The novel contains three layers of reality and several individual plot strands that converge in the final conflagration scene. The least ambiguous level is the society in the village. Reminiscent of the rural setting in *Mondfinsternis,* the village is located far from civilization. The church has been unattended for so long that it is being gradually dismantled for lumber by the populace. Except for the pubs, everything else in the village exists to service the spa hotel located across the gorge on the sun-side of the valley.

The second layer of reality is that of the gangsters: Big Jimmy, Marihuana-Joe, Baby Hackmann, Holy-Brandy, Alaska-Pint—the most infamous killers from the syndicate. They murder, rape, and steal during the warm months, then winter together under the supervision of Count von Kücksen from Liechtenstein in the spa hotel. Here a plastic surgeon gives them new identities as needed. Boredom leads to the rape of the mayor's daughter Elsi by the gangster Big Jimmy. The mayor's dog Mani gives a second would-be attacker, Marihuana-Joe, a severe bite wound on his buttocks. Afraid to get Mani in trouble, the mayor (more concerned about his dog than his daughter) does not report the rape to the police, but von Kücksen, fearing a report and wanting to keep the gangsters' presence in the spa hotel a secret, claims the dog attacked his night watchman. The futile attempts of first the local police, then the cantonal police, and finally the Swiss Army to shoot Mani provide much of the novel's satire.

Tangential to this gangster milieu is the corrupt evangelist Moses Melker. Melker (his name comes from the verb "to milk" or "fleece") lives in the Emmental, and has married and murdered in turn three very rich, but grotesquely fat and ugly women. Yet poor Moses suffers under the weight of the tremendous wealth he has thus amassed, and longs for the simplicity of poverty. In his "theology" the poor are already saved by virtue of their poverty; it is the rich who require the special grace of God. Thus he has become the minister to the rich. It is Melker who suggests to the syndicate boss that he buy the spa hotel and turn it into a "House of Poverty," where the rich can come in the summer to play at being poor and receive balm for the soul.

The third level is the most ambiguous. It is a fantastic reality out of time and space that weaves its way in and out of the mundane world of the other two levels. It begins on the first page of the novel with a linguistic ambiguity. "The Great Old Man" is the legendary syndicate boss, a corpulent "godfather" figure who "looked like the God of the Old Testament without a beard."[15] However, Moses Melker, who cannot conceptualize God without anthropomorphizing him, refers to God as "The Great Old Man." For Dürrenmatt's tongue-in-cheek narration the distinction "Beardless God" for the syndicate boss and "Bearded God" for the biblical God suffices. But Melker's insistence on the use of "the Great Old Man" for both creates an ongoing confusion that is at the same time comical and profound. Disorientation strikes anyone who ventures into the sphere of the Great Old Man. The reader shares this disorientation through the use of parenthetical conditional clauses: "Back in Minerva Street it occurred to the attorney why the Great Old Man (if it was the Great Old Man) had sent for him" (D 25), or: "Moses Melker . . . did not even know where he was, in which solar system, in which galaxy, in which universe, but dozing off he had a sudden urge for a cigar, and immediately he had a Havana between his lips, if it was a Havana, and if this Kingston was located on earth and not in another universe, composed of antimatter or something else" (D 117).

The confusion stretches far beyond the linguistic sphere. Is the Great Old Man a crime boss or God or both? On the one hand his methods, insofar an anyone really has insights into his methods, seem to be those of a syndicate chief with absolute power and far-reaching influence. It is rumored that he is being challenged by a new syndicate founded by Jeremiah Belial, but none of the gangsters can verify this. Mystery shrouds his dealings. His lawyers, the firm of Raphael, Raphael and Raphael, keep changing location as well as identity. His mail, millions of letters a week (prayers and supplications perhaps), always seems to find him—by truck, by helicopter, by plane—wherever he happens to be hiding out: on a deserted beach, on some tropical island, or at the south pole. He never reads nor answers them, only occasionally does he use one to light his cigar. Otherwise they float out to sea or sink to the bottom of the swimming pool unopened.

One scene in which the novel momentarily leaves the time-space continuum and enters the plane of reality of the Great Old Man is the description of his summit conference with his rival, Jeremiah Belial. South of the King Haakon

Plateau in Antarctica two helicopters land simultaneously, or perhaps it was only one helicopter meeting its reflection in the ice. Assertions about the private sphere of the Great Old Man are always equivocal. These meetings always occur at the same location, but the last time the climate had been tropical, the earth's axis at a different angle. The Great Old Man is the exact mirror image of his counterpart Jeremiah Belial, just as their secretaries, Gabriel and Sammael, are mirror images of each other, and so on down the chain of command to their lawyers—the three Raphaels drawn together into one person is the reflection of Jeremiah Belial's attorney Beelzebub. Two coffee mills appear, and as the Great Old Man begins to grind clockwise and Jeremiah Belial counterclockwise, the universe and the antimatter universe begin to spin in opposite directions, passing through each other without ever meeting. And as the others sleep, the two adversaries silently drink their coffee: God and Anti-God, but with a twist. Both are sleepy old men who can make the universe spin faster or slower, but who do so absentmindedly, with no purpose. Beside the *deus absconditus* stands the *diabolus absconditus,* both drinking coffee, staring at each other in silent boredom. Then the helicopters take off again, leaving tables, chairs, and coffee mills for the next meeting. Only the package of coffee is taken along: "Kaffee-Oetker Fr. 10.15."

Moses Melker dies in contemplation of his own theology as the east tower of the spa hotel burns around him. He has not always been what he is now, a greedy, murderous prophet to the rich. In his youth he had fantasized a God of sensuality, and in his pubescent sensuality he had felt close to the divine. Later, when he became a missionary, God took on qualities he could not comprehend: immortality, omniscience, omnipotence. Melker then sought out someone he could identify with and found him in God's son. But here too the theologians cheated him. They deified the person: "He was imagined without the whores and tax collectors with whom he felt comfortable, whose jokes he heard and at whose lewd remarks he laughed. . . . God's son became something abstract, more abstract than the father, but also something trite, a marzipan savior on a cross" (D 172). Rather than a theological abstraction, Melker needed a human being with whom he could identify, who could comprehend him in all his sinfulness. And so Melker's god became the Great Old Man with the beard. As the flames lick up around him he realizes the foolishness of any theology: "It became swindled by itself, stumbled into the trap of its concepts, thought of God as perfect and the world imperfect, a pure creation of the mind all that, with no connection to reality" (D 174). Thus he comes full circle to the God of his youth, the sensual God who created out of the sheer joy of creation and loved all his creations without judging them. Melker's final thought is the recognition that the Great Old Man was his own creation, and that if God was his creation, the world must also be his creation; further, that alongside his god there must exist as many different gods and as many differently created worlds as there are people with imaginations to construct them: each as valid or as invalid as the next. As he thinks these things he begins to laugh in the face of the fire that consumes him. This Moses like his namesake receives a revelation through the fire, but unlike the burning bush the burning spa hotel reveals not God's presence, but his absence. Like Knipperdolinck from the first drama, a God-seeker is dying. This time, however, there is no grace, no vision of redemption—only the nihilistic realization that all meaning to human existence is a construct of the human imagination. Melker's laughter, symptomatic of encroaching insanity, is the laughter of one who has solved the riddle at last and sees how simple it really was. For all Melker's moral turpitude, Dürrenmatt identifies with this character and speaks his philosophical insights through him at the novel's conclusion.[16] Melker's inner monologue, as briefly summarized above, is itself a summary of the author's thoughts in his "Argument against Christianity" from *Turmbau*. Dürrenmatt the agnostic leads the reader into the labyrinth on a whimsical search for the place where God dwells, knowing full well that this infinitely branching path ends in an enigma. His message: the irrelevance of all systematic theology.

The world of stupidity, the world of greed, the world of corruption—it all goes up in flames at the end. Fools are fools, and Dürrenmatt commits Durcheinandertal to the flames as he once did to Abdera. The villagers destroy themselves in trying to destroy the gangsters. The Nibelungen-style conflagration, with mock-heroic battle scenes through which the villagers attempt to rid themselves of the gangster plague, spreads quickly to the surrounding woods and "consumes" the inhabitants who set it as well as the gangsters. Only the Great Old Man mysteriously escapes, leaving behind his calling card, a package of Kaffee-Oetker Fr. 10.15. The other survivors are Mani the dog, Elsi, and the unborn child in her womb.

A postscript: hardly had Dürrenmatt finished writing *Durcheinandertal* when the Spa Hotel in Vulpera, where he had gotten the inspiration for the novel three decades earlier, mysteriously burned to the ground.[17]

Conclusion

In the introduction to his thorough study, Timo Tiusanen wrote of "a host of Dürrenmatts." This description is accurate. Dürrenmatt is certainly not identical with himself over time. He differs from work to work; more obvious developments can be marked by decades. There are also constants among the variables. Most significant among these constants are a strong distrust of political ideologies and organized religions, love of the grotesque, loathing of critics, Helvetian satire, and general non-conformity in the realm of theater practice, exemplified by a blurring of the traditional distinction between tragedy and comedy.

Theologically Dürrenmatt walked a curving path. His early flirtations with nihilism were merely that, a mask from behind which he tried to come to grips with his Protestant upbringing. He continued to wrestle with the problem of humanity's separation from God and the possibility of divine grace for approximately a decade, into the mid-1950s, after which began the drift into agnosticism. There is no basis anymore on which to consider the dramas and narratives of the 1960s and 1970s confessions of a true believer. Whether Dürrenmatt ever truly became the atheist that he claimed to be in 1990 is not clear from statements such as "I consider the question whether God exists senseless" (TB 201).

One label that seems to fit Dürrenmatt snugly is that of pessimist. Between the torturer God and hellish nightmares of the 1940s and the *homo homini lupus* of the 1980s stretches a portrait of a planet where chaos reigns, and the worst possible turn thwarts human endeavor. It is a corrupt world controlled by fiends through wealth or technology, in which individual heroism proves as futile as attempts by collectives to bring about change for the better, and where the best that individuals can do is to survive and find personal consolation in small, individual acts. However, there was another side to Dürrenmatt, best exemplified by a narrative from 1975.

"Connections: Essay About Israel" ends with the following parable: Around the year 760 Caliph Abbaside al-Mansur arrests the Koran scholar Abu Chanifa after a theological argument with him. Out of a strange sense of justice he also arrests a rabbi, Anan ben David, and imprisons the two men together in a dungeon. There they languish for decades, forgotten by the caliph. Out of initial animosity grows with time a kind of friendship between the two, and they begin to bridge their religious differences: "When the Jew speaks a passage from the Torah, the Arab speaks a sura from the Koran that fits the passage from the Torah. In a mysterious way the two books seem to complement each other; even if according to their texts no agreement exists, they nevertheless agree" (18:73–74).

The caliph's successor orders the release of the two holy men, but due to a whim of an old jailer, only Anan ben David is released. For over a millennium he wanders Ahasverus-like through the Middle East and Europe, even surviving the Holocaust, before returning, by chance, to Baghdad. A series of coincidences leads him into the vicinity of the dungeon and down through a shaft deep into the cell where Abu Chanifa still sits in the darkness. Through all the centuries he has remained alive, fed by the rats that he had once fed in better times, waiting for Allah to speak to him. The two men have long since forgotten each other, but each is aware of being in the place where God had spoken to him long ago. The dungeon is sacred ground and each will defend it against the other with his life. "The battle is murderous, merciless, each defends with his freedom the freedom of his God to designate a place for those who believe in Him" (23:85). Their strength spent, the opponents bend forward to see each other's faces in the dim light:

But gradually the hatred in their nearly blind, stony eyes melts. They stare at each other as they have stared at their God, at Jahweh and Allah, and for the first time their lips, silent for so long, for a millennium, form the first word: not a passage from the Koran, not a word from the Pentateuch, only the word 'Thou.' Anan ben David recognizes Abu Chanifa and Abu Chanifa recognizes Anan ben David. Jahweh was Abu Chanifa and Allah was Anan ben David. Their struggle for freedom was senseless. (23:86)

Less theological and more humanistic than it initially appears, this is a rare moment of grace—a fairy-tale considering political probability—but not unique. The colonists on Venus from the early radio play achieve the same kind of cooperation under extreme conditions that the two holy men achieve in their dungeon, and Archilochos in *Once a Greek...* learns the lesson about unconditional love that alone makes possible the hope that there is meaning behind all the horror. On balance, however, Dürrenmatt must be seen as a pessimist, for the apocalyptic visions far outnumber the occasional beautiful dreams. Unlike Brecht he did not believe we can change the human condition by changing the economic conditions, but he was also too savvy a satirist to hold the mirror up to human folly in vain. Dürrenmatt did not believe that humanity had a promising future on this planet, and he created scenario after scenario to demonstrate this conclusion. However, as one whose stated purpose it was to create possible worlds out of building blocks of reality and fiction, he was keenly aware of how many more possible worlds there are. Very occasionally he created one that turned out well in the end, if only for a limited time, and if only to show us that the matter is not yet settled and that we do still have a choice.

Notes

Chapter 1: Biography

1. Dürrenmatt, *Gesammelte Werke in sieben Bänden* 6:203. Hereafter cited parenthetically in the text as GW.
2. Schnauber, 5.
3. Heinz Ludwig Arnold, 16.
4. Dürrenmatt, *Turmbau: Stoffe IV–IX*, 21–22. Hereafter cited parenthetically in the text as TB.
5. Karter, 32.
6. Karter, 33.
7. Karter, 38.
8. Heinz Ludwig Arnold, 33.
9. Tiusanen, 266.
10. Bänziger, "Dürrenmatt-Chronologie," 19.
11. Dürrenmatt, *Werkausgabe* 14:98. Hereafter cited parenthetically in the text by volume and page number.
12. Kerr, 17.
13. Dürrenmatt, *Gedankenfuge*, 141.

Chapter 2: Earliest Prose and Dramatic Works

1. Three of the early narratives, "Die Wurst," "Der Sohn," and "Der Alte" were not included in *Die Stadt.* "Der Alte," Dürrenmatt's first published work, appeared in *Der Bund* in 1945. The other two did not come out until 1978. All three are in volume 18 of the *Werkausgabe.* The order of the narratives in *Die Stadt,* different from the order in the *Werkausgabe,* is as follows: "Weihnachten," "Der Folterknecht," "Der Hund," "Das Bild des Sisyphos," "Der Theaterdirektor," "Die Falle," "Die Stadt," "Der Tunnel," "Pilatus." The order in the *Werkausgabe* reflects the order in which the narratives were written.
2. Tiusanen, 32.
3. Spycher, *Das erzählerische Werk,* 53.
4. Zimmermann, 231. See also Tiusanen, 38.
5. I have used my own translation here instead of that by Carla Colter and Alison Scott published in the *Evergreen Review.* Colter and Scott translate the final line: "Nothing. God let us fall. And now we'll come upon him."
6. Spycher, *Das erzählerische Werk,* 111–12. See also Diller, 30; Zimmermann, 235.

196

7. Diller, 30.

8. Whitton, *Reinterpretation,* 25.

9. Tiusanen, 60.

10. Goertz, 27.

11. Kierkegaard, *Fear and Trembling,* 57.

12. In *Turmbau,* Dürrenmatt devotes several pages to a discussion of Barth's theology, ending with the statement: "Barth educated me to become an atheist," 208. For other discussions of Barth's connection with *It is Written,* see Descher, 227–34. See also Tiusanen, 53–55.

13. Barth, 39.

14. Armin Arnold, *Friedrich Dürrenmatt,* 20. See also Pestalozzi, 388; Eifler, 48.

15. Bänziger, *Frisch und Dürrenmatt,* 147.

Chapter 3: The Turn to Comedy

1. *Four Plays by Friedrich Dürrenmatt,* 67. Subsequent quotes cited parenthetically in the text by FP and page number.

2. Dürrenmatt, Anm. 1 to *Romulus der Große, Werkausgabe* 2:120.

3. Whitton, *Theatre,* 54.

4. Bänziger, *Friedrich Dürrenmatt,* 154.

5. The 1958 translation by Gerhard Nellhaus of this pivotal essay, which can be found in *Four Plays by Friedrich Dürrenmatt,* does not convey the German intention accurately in several key passages. In this chapter and for the remainder of this study, all quotes from "Problems of the Theater" are taken from Susan H. Ray's adaptation in *Friedrich Dürrenmatt: Plays and Essays.* Hereafter cited parenthetically in the text by P&E and page number.

6. Wagener, 205.

7. Tiusanen, 83.

8. Profitlich writes of the value system which allows power politicians like Theoderich to be considered "great," while rulers who make possible unheroic, peaceful periods in history are given short shrift. "Geschichte als Komödie," 256–57.

9. Daviau, "Dürrenmatt's *Romulus der Große,*" 108.

Chapter 4: Three Detective Stories

1. Dürrenmatt, *The Quarry,* 93. Subsequently cited in the text by Q and page number.

2. Knopf, 52.

3. Tschimmel, 175.

4. Waldmann, 34–37; see also: Tschimmel, 176; Knapp, *Friedrich Dürrenmatt,* 41.

5. Dürrenmatt, *The Pledge,* 12. Subsequently cited in text by TP and page number.

6. Chapter designations from the German original are missing in the translation, which is rendered as one long, unbroken narrative.

7. Felix Müller, 547.

8. Dürrenmatt, *The Judge and His Hangman,* in *Plays and Essays,* 208. Subsequently cited in the text by P&E and page number.

9. Gontrum, 90.

10. The plot summary of the film version is condensed from a lengthier version by Peter Spycher, *Friedrich Dürrenmatt,* 281–88.

11. Armin Arnold, "Dürrenmatt als Erzäüler," 94. See also Armin Arnold, "On the Sources of Friedrich Dürrenmatt's Detective Novels," 201.

12. Burkard, 227–28.

13. Spycher, *Friedrich Dürrenmatt,* 279.

14. Daviau, "The Role of *Zufall,*" 291.

15. Profitlich, *Komödienbegriff,* 71.

16. Tschimmel, 188.

17. Tiusanen 171–72.

18. Usmiani, "Friedrich Dürrenmatt Escape Artist," 38. See also Felix Müller, 557.

Chapter 5: Two Plays about Ideologies and God's Remoteness

1. Michaels, 60–61; see also Phelps, 159.

2. Tiusanen, 95; Michaels, 62. See also Grimm, "Nach zwanzig Jahren," 218; Marahrens, 97.

3. Dürrenmatt, *The Marriage of Mr. Mississippi,* in *Four Plays,* 123. Subsequently cited in the text by FP and page number.

4. Friedrich Dürrenmatt, "Bekenntnisse eines Plagiators," *Die Tat* 9.8. 1952. Reprinted in *Werkausgabe* 3:211 ff.

5. Marahrens, 111.

6. Whitton, *Theatre,* 71. See also Grimm, 224; Michaels, 62.

7. Grimm, 230. See also Donald, 202.

8. Whitton, *Theatre,* 72.

9. Heinz Ludwig Arnold, 64–65.

10. Dürrenmatt, *An Angel Comes to Babylon,* in *Four Plays,* 203. Subsequently cited in the text by FP and page number.

11. Tiusanen, 111.

12. Whitton discusses the influence of Nestroy on this play, *Theatre,* 80–81. See also Jauslin, 82.

13. Translator William McElwee has sometimes had to resort to extreme paraphrasing in order to achieve the internal rhyme in Akki's *maqamat.* As this sentence is missing in McElwee's version, the translation of it is mine.

Chapter 6: The Radio Plays

1. All quotes from the radio plays are from *Gesammelte Hörspiele* (Zürich: Die Arche, 1960). Subsequently cited in the text by GH and page number.

2. Armin Arnold, *Friedrich Dürrenmatt,* 62.

3. Brock-Sulzer, 227.

4. Kenneth Whitton supposes a name connection between Baldur von Moeve and the Nazi youth leader Baldur von Schirach. *Reinterpretation,* 64. Another likely association, I believe, is with the Germanic God Baldur (or Balder), who, according to myth, could only be released from the underworld if everyone wept for him.

5. Brock-Sulzer, 216.

6. Profitlich, *Komödienbegriff,* 68.

7. Whitton, *Reinterpretation,* 73.

8. Dürrenmatt, *Episode on an Autumn Evening,* 26.

Chapter 7: Consolation from Dürrenmatt

1. The translators have omitted the title "Ending for Lending Libraries" entirely and translated the second ending as a continuation of the first.

2. Armin Arnold, *Friedrich Dürrenmatt,* 59.

3. Dürrenmatt, *Once a Greek . . .,* 18. Subsequently cited parenthetically in the text by OG and page number.

4. Spycher, *Friedrich Dürrenmatt,* 400, n. 25.

5. Spycher, *Friedrich Dürrenmatt,* 208. Spycher points out several more such visual clues in the course of his thorough chapter on this novel.

6. The bishop does not bring God into the equation until the following day at the wedding ceremony, when talking in generalities about God provides him welcome relief from the embarrassing specifics about Chloë.

7. Fringeli, *Nachdenken,* pages unnumbered. Translation mine.

8. Fringeli, same unnumbered page as previous note.

9. Barth, 321–25.

Chapter 8: The Corruption of Justice

1. Dürrenmatt, *The Visit,* 39. Subsequently cited parenthetically in the text by V and page number.

2. For some reason Patrick Bowles chose to translate Claire's "Eine Milliarde für Güllen . . ." as "a million for Güllen." The proper amount should have been a billion (British milliard).

3. Tiusanen, 224.

4. Jenny, *Dürrenmatt: A Study of his Plays,* 74.

5. Dürrenmatt, *Werkausgabe* 5:141.

6. Hortenbach, 150.

7. Rolf Müller, 81–90. Müller discusses the objectification (*Verdinglichung*) of human beings in the comedy at considerable length.

8. Sandford, 342.

9. Fickert, "Dürrenmatt's *The Visit* and *Job,*" 389. Kenneth Whitton, however, finds the connection of the name to the French pronoun "doubtful." *Theatre,* 122.

10. Hortenbach cites many more parallels in her thorough article than those listed in this paragraph.

11. Daviau and Dunkle, 315.

12. Innes, 117.
13. Dufresne, 46–47.
14. Kierkegaard, *Fear and Trembling,* 64.
15. Niggl, 81.
16. Whitton, *Theatre,* 119.
17. Dürrenmatt, "Problems of the Theater," 255.
18. Goertz, 76.
19. Peppard, 53.
20. Dürrenmatt, *Traps,* 43. Subsequently cited parenthetically in the text by T and page number. The radio play, which has not been translated into English, is so similar to the novella up until the ending that I have used English translations, where applicable, from the novella for the corresponding passages in the radio play. Passages taken directly from the radio play, I have translated myself. These will appear with volume and page number from the *Gesammelte Hörspiele* (GH).
21. Spycher, *Friedrich Dürrenmatt,* 235; Peppard, 105.
22. Spycher, *Friedrich Dürrenmatt,* 243.
23. Kirchberger, 8.
24. Schuster, 167. See also Tschimmel, 185.
25. Kenneth Whitton makes reference to a British performance in 1977 in a translation by James Kirkup. This translation has not been published.
26. Knopf, 100.
27. Dürrenmatt, *Frank der Fünfte,* 34. Hereafter cited parenthetically in text by FF and page number. I have chosen to cite the 1960 version instead of the revised 1980 version, because of the considerable changes made in the latter, especially in the ending.
28. Brecht, *Collected Plays* 2:182.
29. Bienek, 126.
30. Brecht, *Collected Plays* 6:198.
31. Durzak, 106.
32. Helbling, *Frank der Fünfte,* 94.
33. Jenny, *Friedrich Dürrenmatt,* 95; Tiusanen, 258; Armin Arnold, *Friedrich Dürrenmatt,* 74.
34. Tiusanen, 262; Armin Arnold, *Friedrich Dürrenmatt,* 75.
35. Tiusanen, 262.

Chapter 9: Of Heroism, Failure, and Resignation

1. Bertolt Brecht, *Galileo,* 124. Subsequent quotes cited parenthetically in the text by page number.
2. Dürrenmatt, *The Physicists,* 80–81. Subsequently cited parenthetically in the text by P and page number.
3. Jenny, 108.
4. Quoted from the *Bhagavad Gita* by Robert Jungk, *Brighter than a Thousand Suns: A Personal History of the Atomic Scientists,* trans. James Cleugh (New York: Harcourt, Brace & World, 1958).

NOTES TO PAGES 170–137

5. Durzak, 122. See also Taylor, 22–23, 27.
6. Dürrenmatt, *The Physicists,* addendum following the text of the play, pages unnumbered.
7. Innes, 121.
8. Dürrenmatt uses the neutral German term *Weltraumfahrer* (space travellers). The specifically Soviet term "Cosmonauts" was the interpretation of translator James Kirkup.
9. Durzak, 123.
10. Niggl, 85; Armin Arnold, *Friedrich Dürrenmatt,* 80.
11. Dürrenmatt, *Werkausgabe* 25:151; *Turmbau,* 33.
12. Whitton, *Theatre,* 158.

Chapter 10: Improbable Grace

1. Dürrenmatt, *The Meteor,* 64. Subsequently cited parenthetically in the text by M and page number.
2. Hans Mayer, "Friedrich Dürrenmatt," 483.
3. Durzak, 131–32.
4. Spycher, "Friedrich Dürrenmatts *Meteor,*" 167. See also Whitton, *Theatre,* 168–69.
5. Jenny, "Lazarus der Fürchterliche," 12.
6. Keller, 46. See also Durzak, 133.
7. Knopf, 117.
8. Freund, 110–21.
9. Ketels, 99.
10. Heinz Ludwig Arnold, 60.
11. Ketels, 100.
12. Ketels, 100. See also "Sätze über das Theater," *Werkausgabe* 24:197.
13. Brock-Sulzer, 158–59.

Chapter 11: The Adaptations

1. Brock-Sulzer, 163; Tiusanen, 319. However, Dürrenmatt rejected a direct identification of Bockelson with Hitler. *Werkausgabe* 10:135.
2. Cory, 262; Tiusanen, 337.
3. Shakespeare, *The Life and Death of King John,* I.i.213. Subsequently quoted in text by act, scene, and line number.
4. Cory, 263.
5. Stamm, 43.
6. Subiotto, 145.
7. Brater, 125; Knapp, "Play Dürrenmatt," 231; See also Whitton, *Theatre,* 125; Tiusanen, 322–23.
8. Knapp, "From *lilla helvetet,*" 234.
9. Knapp, "From *lilla helvetet,*" 234.

10. Dürrenmatt, *Play Strindberg,* 11. Subsequently cited in text by PS and page number. For a discussion of the significance of the minimal staging, see Brater, 126–27.
11. Strindberg, *The Dance of Death,* 36. Subsequently cited parenthetically in the text by DD and page number.
12. Tiusanen, 325.
13. Sharp, 301.
14. Tiusanen, 323. See also Brock-Sulzer, 201.
15. Hans Schwab Felisch in *Frankfurter Allgemeine Zeitung,* December 14, 1970.
16. Whitton, 207.
17. Cohn, 37.
18. Shakespeare, *The Tragedy of Titus Andronicus,* III.i.252. Subsequently cited in the text by act, scene, and line number.
19. Tiusanen, 349.
20. Mehlin, 81.

Chapter 12: Four That Failed: The Late Plays

1. Knopf, 140.
2. Winter, 27–28.
3. Jenny, 158.
4. For a summary of the critics' comments, see Whitton, *Theatre,* 218.
5. Goertz, 99–100.
6. Usmiani, "Die späten Stücke," 148.
7. Krättli, "Wie soll man es spielen?" 75.
8. Deering, 64. Dürrenmatt once compared *The Collaborator* to "The Drama of Peter." Doc also commits a threefold denial: of his beloved, of his son, and finally of himself. Heinz Ludwig Arnold, 38.
9. Usmiani, "Die späten Stücke," 156.
10. Kerr, 17.

Chapter 13: The Prose of the 1970s and 1980s

1. Spycher, *Friedrich Dürrenmatt,* 357.
2. Tiusanen, 396–97.
3. Göbel, 17.
4. Donald, 199.
5. Dürrenmatt, "Dramaturgy of the Labyrinth," 216.
6. "Dramaturgy of the Labyrinth," 218–19.
7. See Knapp, 150. Knapp, in turn, is quoting from Dürrenmatt's interview with Carlo Bernasconi in the *Börsenblatt* from January 9, 1990.
8. Donald, 228.
9. Dürrenmatt, *The Execution of Justice,* 9. Subsequently cited parenthetically in the text by EJ and page number.
10. Burkard, 258.

11. Helbling, "I am a Camera," 178.

12. Kerr, 5.

13. Kerr, 5.

14. Dürrenmatt, *The Assignment,* unnumbered page preceding text. Subsequent references given parenthetically in text by A and page number.

15. Dürrenmatt, *Durcheinandertal,* 5. Subsequently cited parenthetically in the text by D and page number.

16. Knapp, *Friedrich Dürrenmatt,* 164.

17. Dürrenmatt, *Turmbau,* 43.

Bibliography

Works by Friedrich Dürrenmatt

Individual Works in English Translation

An Angel Comes to Babylon: A Fragmentary Comedy in Three Acts. Trans. William McElwee in *Four Plays.*

The Assignment: Or on the Observing of the Observer of the Observers. Trans. Joel Agee. New York: Random House, 1988.

"Dramaturgy of the Labyrinth." Trans. Thomas F. Barry in *Play Dürrenmatt,* ed. Moshe Lazar and Ron Gottesman, 209–19. Malibu: Undena, 1983.

Episode on an Autumn Evening. Trans. Gabriel Karminski. Chicago: Dramatic Publishing Co., n.d.

The Execution of Justice. Trans. John E. Woods. New York: Random House, 1989.

The Judge and His Hangman. Trans. Cyrus Brooks and adapted by Susan H. Ray in *Plays and Essays.*

The Marriage of Mr. Mississippi. Trans. Michael Bullock in *Four Plays.*

The Meteor. Trans. James Kirkup. New York: Grove Press, 1974.

"A Monster Lecture on Justice and the Law." Trans. John E. Woods in *Plays and Essays.*

Once a Greek . . . Trans. Richard and Clara Winston. New York: Knopf, 1965.

The Physicists. Trans. James Kirkup. New York: Grove Press, 1964.

Play Strindberg: The Dance of Death Choreographed by Friedrich Dürrenmatt. Trans. James Kirkup. New York: Grove Press, 1973.

The Pledge. Trans. Richard and Clara Winston. New York: Knopf, 1959.

"Problems of the Theater." Trans. Gerhard Nellhaus and adapted by Susan H. Ray in *Plays and Essays.*

Romulus the Great. Trans. Gerhard Nellhaus in *Four Plays.*

The Quarry. Trans. Eva H. Morreale. Greenwich: New York Graphic Society, 1962.

Traps. Trans. Richard and Clara Winston. New York: Knopf, 1960.

The Tunnel. Trans. Carla Coulter and Alison Scott in *The Evergreen Review* 5, no. 17 (1961): 32–42.

The Visit: A Tragi-Comedy. Trans. Patrick Bowles. New York: Grove Press, 1962.

Collections in English Translation

Four Plays by Friedrich Dürrenmatt. New York: Grove Press, 1965.

Friedrich Dürrenmatt: Plays and Essays. Ed. Volkmar Sander. New York: Continuum, 1982.

Works in German

Durcheinandertal: Roman. Zürich: Diogenes, 1989.
Frank der Fünfte: Oper einer Privatbank. Zürich: Verlag der Arche, 1960.
Gedankenfuge. Zürich: Diogenes, 1992.
Gesammelte Hörspiele. Zürich: Verlag der Arche, 1961.
Gesammelte Werke in sieben Bänden. Ed. Franz Josef Görtz. Zürich: Diogenes, 1988.
Komödien II und Frühe Stücke. Zürich: Verlag der Arche, 1963.
Das Mögliche ist ungeheuer: Ausgewählte Gedichte. Zürich: Diogenes, 1993.
Turmbau: Stoffe IV–IX. Zürich: Diogenes, 1990.
Werkausgabe in dreißig Bänden. Zürich: Diogenes, 1980.

Interviews with Dürrenmatt

Arnold, Heinz Ludwig. *Friedrich Dürrenmatt: Gespräch mit Heinz Ludwig Arnold.* Zürich: Arche, 1976. The most thorough published interview with Dürrenmatt. Valuable insights into the person and the theory.

Bieneck, Horst. *Werkstattgespräche mit Schriftstellern.* München: Deutscher Taschenbuch Verlag, 1965.

Fringeli, Dieter. *Nachdenken mit und über Friedrich Dürrenmatt: Ein Gespräch.* Breitenbach: Jeger Moll, 1977.

Jenny, Urs. "Lazarus der Fürchterliche: Urs Jenny im Gespräch mit Friedrich Dürrenmatt über dessen neue Komödie *Der Meteor.*" *Theater heute* 7 (1966): 10–12.

Ketels, Violet. "Friedrich Dürrenmatt at Temple University," *Journal of Modern Literature* 1 (1971) 89–108. Dürrenmatt's most philosophical interview. Particularly revealing on his political and religious views as of 1971.

Other Primary Sources Cited

Barth, Karl. *The Epistle to the Romans.* 6th ed. Trans. Edwyn C. Hoskins. London: Oxford University Press, 1933.

Brecht, Bertolt. *Collected Plays.* Ed. Ralph Manheim and John Willett. New York: Random House, 1976.

———. *Galileo.* Trans. Charles Laughton. New York: Grove Press, 1966.

Jungk, Robert. *Brighter than a Thousand Suns: A Personal History of the Atomic Scientists.* Trans. James Cleugh. New York: Harcourt, Brace & World, 1958.

Kierkegaard, Søren. *Fear and Trembling and The Sickness unto Death.* Trans. Walter Lowrie. Princeton: Princeton University Press, 1954.

Shakespeare, William. *The Life and Death of King John.* Ed. Stanley T. Williams. New Haven: Yale University Press, 1927.

———. *The Tragedy of Titus Andronicus.* Ed. A. M. Witherspoon. New Haven: Yale University Press, 1926.

Strindberg, August. *The Dance of Death.* Trans. Arvid Paulson. New York: Norton, 1976.

Critical Works

Individual Works

Allemann, Beda. "Dürrenmatt: Es steht geschrieben." In *Das deutsche Drama vom Barock bis zur Gegenwart,* ed. Benno von Wiese, 420–38. Düsseldorf: Bagel, 1964. Thorough study of the author's first play, with emphasis on the transition from the traditional view of heroism in drama to Dürrenmatt's impossibility of heroism as exemplified by Knipperdolinck's unheroic death.

Arnold, Armin. "Dürrenmatt als Erzähler." In *Interpretationen zu Friedrich Dürrenmatt,* 187–203.

———. *Friedrich Dürrenmatt.* New York: Unger, 1972. Concise, often too concise, treatment of Dürrenmatt through the 1960s (*Traps* in one page, *The Visit* in four). Good for an overview.

———. "On the Sources of Friedrich Dürrenmatt's Detective Novels." In *Play Dürrenmatt,* 189–202. Disputes the often-made claim that Dürrenmatt patterned his Commissioner Bärlach after Glauser's Wachtmeister Studer. Makes a case instead for Simenon's Inspector Maigret.

Bänziger, Hans. "Die Gerichte und das Gericht: Alfredo Traps in einer ländlichen Villa." In *Friedrich Dürrenmatt: Studien,* 218–32.

———. "Dürrenmatt-Chronologie," in *Interpretationen zu Friedrich Dürrenmatt,* 7–22. An expanded timeline, critical as well as biographical.

———. *Frisch und Dürrenmatt.* Bern: Francke, 1971. Less a comparative study than the title would suggest. Two separate, insightful studies which come together in the conclusion.

Bloch, Peter Andre, ed. *Gegenwartsliteratur: Mittel und Bedingungen ihrer Produktion.* Bern, 1975.

Brandner, Véronique. *Der andere Dürrenmatt: Auf der Brücke zwischen zwei Welten.* Bern: Lang, 1993. A psychological, primarily Jungian interpretation of Dürrenmatt's prose.

Brater, Enoch. "*Play Strindberg* and the Theater of Adaptation." In *Play Dürrenmatt,* 125–37.

Brock-Sulzer, Elizabeth. *Friedrich Dürrenmatt: Stationen seines Werkes.* Zürich: Arche, 1970. One of the very first books on Dürrenmatt (which reached its third edition by 1970) by a critic close to Dürrenmatt (a rarity indeed). Liberal inclusion of Dürrenmatt's drawings.

Buri, Fritz. "Der Einfall der Gnade in Dürrenmatts dramatischem Werk." In *Der unbequeme Dürrenmatt,* 35–69. Treats God's grace as the primary theme in works of the fifties.

Burkard, Martin. *Dürrenmatt und das Absurde: Gestalt und Wandlung des Labyrinthischen in seinem Werk.* Bern: Lang, 1991. Published doctoral dissertation on the labyrinth theme in the early prose, *Winter War, Minotaurus,* and the criminal novels. Particularly interesting interpretation of *Justiz,* on which little has been written.

Cohn, Ruby. *Modern Shakespeare Offshoots*. Princeton: Princeton University Press, 1976.

Cory, Mark E. "Shakespeare and Dürrenmatt: From Tragedy to Tragicomedy." *Comparative Literature* 32 (1980): 253–73. Cory takes an unorthodox view in that he sees in the collapse of the old order at the end of both adaptations a hint of optimism and renewal.

Daviau, Donald. "Dürrenmatt's *Romulus der Große:* A Traitor for our Time?" *Germanic Review* 54 (1979): 104–9. Disputes Dürrenmatt's claim for Romulus's actions as patriotic and justified. They are plain and simple treason. The problem of Romulus's guilt remains unsolved.

———. "The Role of *Zufall* in the Writings of Friedrich Dürrenmatt." *The Germanic Review* 44 (1972): 281–93. Coincidence is seen as providential in that it can work to save humanity from falling prey to materialism. Claims for Dürrenmatt a "fundamental Christian view of the world."

Daviau, Donald, and Harvey Dunkle. "Friedrich Dürrenmatt's *Der Besuch der alten Dame:* A Parable of Western Society in Transition." *Modern Language Quarterly* 35 (1974): 302–16.

Deering, Claudia. "Friedrich Dürrenmatt's *Der Mitmacher:* Old Themes and a New Cynicism." *Colloquia Germanica* 10 (1976–77): 55–72. Stresses the impression that Dürrenmatt is a moral pessimist and a cynic. There is no longer the hope formerly inherent in coincidence. Chance of the earlier works has been replaced by fate.

Descher, Margareta N. "Dürrenmatt's *Die Wiedertäufer:* What the Author has Learned." *The German Quarterly* 44 (1971): 227–34. Comparison of the two Anabaptist plays. Dürrenmatt replaced the concept of God in the former with "reality" in the latter.

Dick, Ernst. "Dürrenmatts Dramaturgie des Einfalls: *Der Besuch der alten Dame* und *Der Meteor.*" In *Europäische Komödie*, ed. Herbert Mainusch, 389–435. Darmstadt: Wissenschaftliche Buchgemeinschaft, 1990.

Diller, Edward. "Friedrich Dürrenmatt's Chaos and Calvinism." *Monatshefte* 63 (1971): 28–40. A Calvinistic interpretation which stops with the works of the mid-fifties, although the article appeared in 1971.

Donald, Sydney G. "Of Mazes, Men and Minotaurs: Friedich Dürrenmatt and the Myth of the Labyrinth." *New German Studies* 14 (1986–87): 187–231. Traces the labyrinth theme from the early prose (*Die Stadt, Aus den Papieren eines Wärters*) to two narratives on the theme from the 1980s.

Dufresne, Nicole. "Violent Homecoming: Liminality, Ritual and Renewal in *The Visit.*" In *Play Dürrenmatt*, 39–53. Good scholarly piece on the ritual of scapegoating in general and as it pertains to Güllen.

Durzak, Manfred. *Dürrenmatt, Frisch, Weiss: Deutsches Drama der Gegenwart zwischen Kritik und Utopie*. Stuttgart: Reclam, 1972. An excellent comparative study, which places Dürrenmatt's works in their historical perspective. Particularly strong on parallels to Brecht and modern documentary theater.

Eifler, Margaret. "Das Geschichtsbewußtsein des Parodisten Dürrenmatt." In *Friedrich Dürrenmatt: Studien*, 44–52.

Ellestad, Everett. "Friedrich Dürrenmatt's Mausefalle." *German Quarterly* 43 (1970): 770–79.

Esslin, Martin. "*Die Frist:* Dürrenmatt's Late Masterpiece." In *Play Dürrenmatt,* 139–53. Blames the failure of the play on the production and gives it claim to masterpiece status based on the text.

Federico, Joseph. "Time, Play, and the Terror of History in Dramatic Works by Dürrenmatt." In *Play Dürrenmatt,* 19–38. A discussion of relationship between history and play (role and game playing) in *Romulus, The Physicists, The Anabaptists* and *The Grace Period.*

Fickert, Kurt. "Dürrenmatt's *The Visit* and *Job.*" *Books Abroad* 41 (1967): 389–91.

————. *To Heaven and Back: The New Morality in the Plays of Friedrich Dürrenmatt.* Lexington: University of Kentucky Press, 1972. Christian interpretation of the plays through *The Meteor.* Some valuable insights on the early plays, but fails to acknowledge Dürrenmatt's religious skepticism from the mid-fifties on.

Freund, Winfried. "Modernes Welttheater: Eine Studie zu Friedrich Dürrenmatts Komödie *Der Meteor.*" *Literatur in Wissenschaft und Unterricht* 6 (1973): 110–21. Interprets the play as secular world theater.

Gallati, Ernst. "*Herkules und der Stall des Augias:* Mythos, Parodie und Poesie." In *Interpretationen zu Friedrich Dürrenmatt,* 110–23. Important for comparison of the play's characters with counterparts in Greek mythology.

Göbel, Helmut. "Annäherung an Friedrich Dürrenmatts *Stoffe I–III.*" *Text + Kritik* 56, *Friedrich Dürrenmatt II* (1984): 8–29.

Goertz, Heinrich. *Friedrich Dürrenmatt in Selbstzeugnissen und Bilddokumenten.* Reinbek: Rowohlt, 1993. Somewhat short shrift given to the late prose, but a good overview with pictures of Dürrenmatt's art, candids of his home life, and photos from stage productions.

Gontrum, Peter B. "*Ritter, Tod und Teufel:* Protagonists and Antagonists in the Prose Works of Friedrich Dürrenmatt." *Seminar* 1 (1965): 88–98. Discusses the dialectic between the allegorical figures of justice and evil in the prose works, mainly the detective novels.

Grimm, Reinhold. "Nach zwanzig Jahren: Friedrich Dürrenmatt und sein *Ehe des Herrn Mississippi.*" *Basis: Jahrbuch für deutsche Gegenwartsliteratur* 3 (1972): 214–37. Thorough treatment of the play with parallels drawn to later plays. Grimm considers the play a typical work of the conservative fifties, an apotheosis of the status quo.

Groseclose, D. Sydney. "The Murder of Gnadenbrot Suppe: Language and levels of reality in Friedrich Dürrenmatt's *Der Blinde.*" *German Life and Letters* 28 (1974–75): 64–71.

Heidsieck, Arnold. *Das Groteske und das Absurde im modernen Drama.* Stuttgart: Kohlhammer, 1969.

Helbling, Robert E. "*Frank der Fünfte:* Eine kritische Bilanz der Gangsterbank nach über zwanzig Jahren." In *Interpretationen zu Friedrich Dürrenmatt,* 85–96. Attempts to save the reputation in retrospect of a play which failed at its premiere. Rejects the contention that *Frank* was a conscious parody of Brecht.

————. "I am a Camera: Friedrich Dürrenmatt's *Der Auftrag.*" *Seminar* 24 (1988): 178–81.

Hortenbach, Jenny C. "Biblical Echoes in Dürrenmatt's *Der Besuch der alten Dame*." *Monatshefte* 57 (1965): 145–61. Interprets *The Visit* as a serious passion play, a contention effectively refuted by later scholarship.

Innes, Christopher. *Modern German Drama: A Study in Form*. Cambridge: Cambridge University Press, 1979.

Jauslin, Christian Markus. *Friedrich Dürrenmatt: Zur Struktur seiner Dramen*. Zürich: Juris, 1964. Much wider in scope than its subtitle would indicate, this is a comprehensive treatment of the plays before 1964 with a concluding chapter on the dramatic structure.

Jenny, Urs. *Friedrich Dürrenmatt: A Study of his Plays*. Trans. Keith Hamnet and Hugh Rorrison. London: Eyre Methuen, 1978. The actual study is dominated by plot summary. However, the gem in this book is the last chapter, "Dürrenmatt on the stage," which discusses key international performances with their staging techniques and audience and critics' reception.

Jost, Dominik. "Vom Gelde: *Der Besuch der alten Dame*." In *Interpretationen zu Friedrich Dürrenmatt*, 71–84. Argues that *The Visit* is not about justice but about revenge and the corrupting power of money.

Karter, Egon. *Hommage an Friedrich den Grossen von Konolfingen: Geschichten von und mit Friedrich Dürrenmatt*. Basel: Egon Karter Verlag, 1991. A not unbiased, anecdotal, personal reminiscence by a friend and publisher of Dürrenmatt's.

Keller, Otto. "Die totalisierte Figur." *Text + Kritik* 50–51, *Friedrich Dürrenmatt I* (1976): 43–56.

Kempf, Franz R. "Brecht und Dürrenmatt als Dramatiker: Antipoden oder Dioskuren?" *Literatur für Leser* 3 (1991): 185–97. Argues that their only point of tangency is as "children of the Enlightenment." Otherwise Brecht's positive dialectic stands in opposition to Dürrenmatt's negative dialectic. Brecht the Hegelian "optimistic therapist"—Dürrenmatt the Kantian "pessimistic diagnostician."

Kerr, Charlotte. *Die Frau im roten Mantel*. München: Piper, 1992. Intimate (sometimes almost too intimate) look at her seven years as Dürrenmatt's wife. A valuable document of their collaboration and their influence on each other's career.

Kesting, Marianne. "Dürrenmatt und Frisch." In *Handbuch des deutschen Dramas*, ed. Walter Hinck. Düsseldorf: Bagel, 1980: 453–64.

Kieser, Rolf. "In eigener Sache: Friedrich Dürrenmatt und sein *Meteor*." In *Interpretationen zu Friedrich Dürrenmatt*, 124–35. Sees Dürrenmatt's personal crisis of waning energies encoded in the character of Schwitter.

Kirchberger, Lida. "*Kleider machen Leute* and Dürrenmatts *Panne*." *Monatshefte* 52 (1960): 1–8.

Knapp, Gerhard P. "Die Physiker." In *Interpretationen zu Friedrich Dürrenmatt*, 97–109. Contra-Mayer in the question of whether *The Physicists* represents a "Retraction" of *Galileo*.

Knapp, Gerhard P. *Friedrich Dürrenmatt*. Stuttgart: Metzler, 1993. Thorough study which gives the late prose works their due. Most recent monograph on Dürrenmatt. Exhaustive bibliography.

———. "From *lilla helvetet* to the Boxing Ring: Strindberg and Dürrenmatt." In *Structures of Influence: A Comparative Approach to August Strindberg*, ed. Marilyn Johns Blackwell, 226–44. Chapel Hill: University of North Carolina Press, 1981.

———. "Play Dürrenmatt: Ein Beitrag zur kritischen Dramaturgie der spätsechziger Jahre am Beispiel der Strindberg Adaptation." In *Facetten*, 225–41.

Knopf, Jan. *Friedrich Dürrenmatt*. München: Beck, 1988. Chronological arrangement rather than groupings by genre. Intentionally not hagiographic, Knopf's study looks for and finds contradictions in the author's life's work.

Koelb, Clayton. "'Der Einfall' in Dürrenmatt's Theory and Practice." *Deutsche Beiträge zur geistigen Überlieferung* 7 (1972): 240–59.

Krättli, Anton. "Der lange Tod des Generalissimus: *Die Frist* von Dürrenmatt," *Schweizer Monatshefte* 57 (1977): 606–10.

———. "Wie soll man es spielen? Mit Humor!: Friedrich Dürrenmatts Selbstkommentar *Der Mitmacher—ein Komplex*." *Text + Kritik* 56 (1977): 71–79. Claims the *Komplex*, in particular the two narratives contained in it, eclipse the play in importance as a document of the late Dürrenmatt.

Labroisse, Gerd. "Die Alibisierung des Handelns in Dürrenmatts *Der Besuch der alten Dame*." In *Facetten*, 207–23. Analyzes the alibiing strategies of the Güllner and their social-political implications for society at large.

Lehnert, Herbert. "Fiktionale Struktur und physikalsiche Realität in Dürrenmatts *Die Physiker*." In *Rice University Studies: Studies in German in Memory of Andrew Lewis*, ed. Robert L. Kahn, 115–30. Houston: Rice University, 1969.

Marahrens, Gerwin. "Friedrich Dürrenmatts *Die Ehe des Herrn Mississippi*." In *Friedrich Dürrenmatt: Studien*, 93–124. Excellent section on Dürrenmatt's onomastics in *Mississippi*. Thorough character study of the ideologues and long expose of their ideologies. Disputes previous religious interpretations.

Masurawa, Tomoko. "Behind the Law: Staging of Guilt in Kafka via Dürrenmatt." *Journal of the American Academy of Religion* 60 (1992): 35–55.

Mayer, Hans. "Dürrenmatt und Brecht: oder die Zurücknahme." In *Der unbequeme Dürrenmatt*, 97–116. Seminal essay interpreting *The Physicists* as Dürrenmatt's retraction of Brecht's *Galileo*.

———. *Dürrenmatt und Frisch: Anmerkungen*. Pfüllingen: Neske, 1963. Contains the previous entry on Dürrenmatt and Brecht as well as an important essay on *Die Panne*.

———. "Friedrich Dürrenmatt." *Zeitschrift für deutsche Philologie* 87 (1968): 482–98.

Mehlin, Urs. "Claus Bremer, Renate Voss: *Die jämmerliche Tragödie von Titus Andronicus*—Friedrich Dürrenmatt: *Titus Andronicus*—Hans Hollmann: *Titus-Titus*— Ein Vergleich." *Jahrbuch der deutschen Shakespeare-Gesellschaft, Heidelberg* (1972): 73–98.

Michaels, Jennifer E. "Vom *Romulus zum Engel*" in *Interpretationen zu Friedrich Dürrenmatt*, 54–70. A concise, readable, quotable treatment of the first three comedies, which already contain all the elements of Dürrenmatt's dramatic theory.

Morley, Michael. Dürrenmatt's Dialogue with Brecht: A Thematic Analysis of *Die Physiker*." *Modern Drama* 14 (1971): 232–42.

Müller, Felix. "Der Anhauch des Nichts und der Kampf für das Gute." *Schweizer Monatshefte* 59 (1979): 545–58. The heros of Dürrenmatt's detective novels take a middle ground between the optimists who close their eyes to reality and the pessimists who capitulate. His heros are pessimists who nevertheless act, including the absurd "humbly" in their calculations.

Müller, Rolf. *Komödie im Atomzeitalter: Gestaltung und Funktion des Komischen bei Friedrich Dürrenmatt.* Frankfurt: Lang, 1987.

Nagel, Bert. "Friedrich Dürrenmatt und Franz Kafka." *Modern Austrian Literature* 20 (1987): 37–51. Guilt in Dürrenmatt and Kafka, particularly a comparison of *Mississippi* and the *Penal Colony.*

Neumann, Gerhard. "Friedrich Dürrenmatt: Dramaturgie der Panne." In G. Neumann et al. *Dürrenmatt—Frisch—Weiss: Drei Entwürfe zum Drama der Gegenwart.* 27–59. München: Fink, 1969. Chance has replaced fate. "Everything is just theater," in which the characters play "as though" governed by fate, "as though" the world were just and not merely chaotic.

Niggl, Günter. "Tragik und Komik bei Friedrich Dürrenmatt." *Literaturwissenschaftliches Jahrbuch im Auftrag der Görres-Gesellschaft* 19 (1978): 77–93.

Oberle, Werner. "Grundsätzliches zum Werk Friedrich Dürrenmatts." In *Der unbequeme Dürrenmatt,* 9–29.

Pausch, Holger A. "Systematische Abnormität: Zur Technik der Personengestaltung im dramatischen Werk Dürrenmatts." In *Friedrich Dürrenmatt: Studien,* 191–202. Dürrenmatt, like Kafka, settles his protagonists outside accepted societal norms. Related to the Grotesque, this "Systematic Abnormality" functions as "poetic mirroring of social, economic and moral structures of society." The article concentrates on *The Visit.*

Peppard, Murray. *Friedrich Dürrenmatt.* New York: Twayne, 1969. For years one of the few monographs on Dürrenmatt in English, unfortunately ending with *The Meteor.*

Pestalozzi, Karl. "Friedrich Dürrenmatt." In *Deutsche Literatur des 20. Jahrhunderts: Strukturen und Gestalten,* ed. Otto Mann and Wolfgang Rothe, 2: 385–402. Bern: Francke, 1967.

Phelps, Leland R. "Dürrenmatt's *Die Ehe des Herrn Mississippi:* The Revision of a Play." *Modern Drama* 8 (1965): 156–60.

Profitlich, Ulrich. "*Der Besuch der alten Dame.*" In *Die deutsche Komödie: Vom Mittelalter bis zur Gegenwart,* ed. Walter Hinck, 324–41, 406–9. Düsseldorf: Bagel, 1977.

———. *Friedrich Dürrenmatt: Komödienbegriff und Komödienstruktur.* Stuttgart: Kohlhammer, 1973. Very important study of the typology of Dürrenmatt's heroes and fools.

———. "Geschichte als Komödie—Dürrenmatts *Romulus der Große.*" In *Geschichte als Schauspiel: Deutsche Geschichtsdramen: Interpretationen,* ed. Walter Hinck, 254–69. Frankfurt: Suhrkamp, 1981.

Reber, Trudis E. "Dürrenmatt und Shakespeare." In *Friedrich Dürrenmatt: Studien,* 80–89.

Roe, Ian F. "Dürrenmatt's *Die Physiker:* Die drei Leben des Galilei?" *Forum for Modern Language Studies* 27 (1991): 255–67. Roe believes Dürrenmatt's three physicists represent three different stances of Brecht's Galilei.

Sammern-Frankenegg, Fritz. "Exit Strindberg: Zur Eliminierung Strindbergs in Friedrich Dürrenmatts *Play Strindberg.*" *Studia Neophilologica* 63 (1991): 89–92.

Sandford, John E. "The Anonymous Characters in Dürrenmatt's *Der Besuch der alten Dame.*" *German Life and Letters* 24 (1970–71): 335–45. A look at the characters in *The Visit* who are named only by their professional designation or have been given a dehumanizing nickname by Claire—people with "Everyman" characteristics and those who must function as part of a "machine-like system."

Sarcevic, Susan. "Wilders *Wir sind noch einmal davongekommen* und Dürrenmatts *Porträt eines Planeten*: Eine Gegenüberstellung." *Schweizer Rundschau* 71 (1971): 330–39. Enlightening comparison of the two plays.

Schnauber, Cornelius. "Friedrich Dürrenmatt in Los Angeles." In *Play Dürrenmatt,* 1–5.

Scholdt, Günter. "Romulus der Große?" *Zeitschrift für deutsche Philologie* 97 (1978): 270–87. Comparison of the first version with later versions. Scholdt blames the contradictions in the comedy on the later changes.

Schuster, Ingrid. "Dreimal *Die Panne:* Zufall, Schicksal oder moralisches Resultat." In *Interpretationen zu Friedrich Dürrenmatt,* 160–72. Comparison of the three versions which considers the prose version as the most significant. One of the very few existing treatments of the stage play.

Sharp, Sister Corona. "Strindberg and Dürrenmatt: The Dynamics of Play." *Modern Language Quarterly* 38 (1977): 292–303.

Speidel, E. "Aristotelian and Non-Aristotelian Elements in Dürrenmatt's *Der Besuch der alten Dame.*" *German Life and Letters* 28 (1974–75): 14–24.

Spycher, Peter. *Friedrich Dürrenmatt: Das erzählerische Werk.* Frauenfeld: Huber, 1972. This is a standard work for Dürrenmatt scholarship on the prose up to *The Fall.* Spycher makes a virtue out of a vice (excessive plot summary) by skillfully interweaving it with interpretation.

———. "Friedrich Dürrenmatts *Meteor:* Analyse und Dokumentation." In *Friedrich Dürrenmatt: Studien,* 145–87. A combination interpretation–state of research on the play. Very thorough analysis of the supporting roles around Schwitter and of the religious controversy the play unleashed.

Stadtfeld, Frieder. "Friedrich Dürrenmatts Historiogramm." *Literatur in Wissenschaft und Unterricht* 5 (1972): 286–98. Intriguing theory that Dürrenmatt encoded a chronology of the fall of Western civilization into the train schedule references in "The Tunnel."

Stamm, Rudolf. "King John—König Johann: Vom Historienspiel zur politischen Moralität." *Jahrbuch der deutschen Shakespeare-Gesellschaft, Heidelberg* (1970): 30–48.

Strelka, Joseph. "The Significance of Friedrich Dürrenmatt's Play *The Collaborator.*" In *Play Dürrenmatt,* 97–105.

Subiotto, Arrigo V. "The Comedy of Politics: Dürrenmatt's *King John*. In *Affinities: Essays in German and English Literature,* ed. R. W. Last, 139–53. London: Oswald Wolff, 1971.

Taylor, Heimtraut F. "The Question of Responsibility in *The Physicists.*" in *Friedrich Dürrenmatt: A Collection of Critical Essays,* ed. Bodo Fritzen and H. F. Taylor, 19–35. Normal, Ill.: Applied Literature Press, 1979.

Tiusanen, Timo. *Dürrenmatt: A Study in Plays, Prose, Theory.* Princeton: Princeton University Press, 1977. Scholarly, readable, authoritative. One of the best studies in any language on Dürrenmatt. Especially thorough in its summary of the theater critics' reviews.

Tschimmel, Ira. "Kritik am Kriminalroman." In *Facetten,* 175–90. Contrasting of Dürrenmatt's criminal novels to "Classical" criminal novels. Through grotesque and fairy-tale elements, Dürrenmatt emphasizes the irrationality of the genre, which postulates a "rationally structured world."

Usmiani, Renate. "Die späten Stücke: *Porträt eines Planeten, Der Mitmacher, Die Frist.*" In *Interpretationen zu Friedrich Dürrenmatt,* 136–59. Examines the influence of contemporary alternative theater on Dürrenmatt's late plays. Her analysis of *Die Frist* is justifiably very complimentary. Here, she believes, Dürrenmatt has achieved a synthesis of modern and traditional theater.

———. "Friedrich Dürrenmatt as Wolfgang Schwitter: An Autobiographical Interpretation of *The Meteor.*" *Modern Drama* 11 (1968): 143–50.

———. "Friedrich Dürrenmatt Escape Artist: A Look at the Novels." *Mosaic* 3 (1972): 27–41.

———. "Masterpieces in Disguise: The Radio Plays of Friedrich Dürrenmatt." *Seminar* 7 (1971): 42–57. Makes a lofty claim that to understand Dürrenmatt, one must understand the radio plays. Perhaps not, but Usmiani demonstrates how Dürrenmatt created these works of art with total disregard for the "rules" of the genre.

Wagener, Hans. "Heldentum heute? Zum Thema Zeitkritik in Dürrenmatts *Romulus der Große.*" In *Facetten,* 191–206.

Waldmann, Günter. *Theorie und Didaktik der Trivialliteratur: Modellanalysen— Didaktikdiskussionen—literarische Wertung.* München: Fink, 1973. Waldmann assigns Dürrenmatt's detective novels to the classification "trivial literature," finding in them several characteristics of pulp fiction including fatalism(!).

Weber, Emil. "Die Welt der frühen Werke, oder vom Einfall des Schrecklichen und von der Kunst, sich recht zu ängstigen." In *Interpretationen zu Friedrich Dürrenmatt,* 23–41. A primarily religious interpretation of the early prose and the first two dramas. Dürrenmatt, for Weber, was a true believer.

White, Alfred. "History and its Adaptation: Shakespeare, Brecht, Dürrenmatt." *Modern Languages: Journal of the Modern Language Association, London* 58 (1977): 195–200.

Whitton, Kenneth. *Dürrenmatt: Reinterpretation in Retrospect.* New York: Berg, 1990. The sequel to *The Theater of F. D.* ten years later. The emphasis here is on the prose works and the essays.

————. *The Theatre of Friedrich Dürrenmatt: A Study in the Possibility of Freedom.* London: Oswald Wolff, 1980. Particular emphasis on placing Dürrenmatt in the traditions of Attic Comedy.

————. "The Zürcher Literaturstreit." *German Life and Letters* 27 (1974): 142–50.

Wieckenberg, Ernst-Peter. "Dürrenmatts Detektivromane." *Text + Kritik* 56 (1977): 30–41.

Winter, Michael. "Friedrich Dürrenmatt: Positionen einer radikalen Aufklärung," In *Facetten,* 9–39. Shows Dürrenmatt as the proponent of a new, radical Enlightenment, using examples from his earliest and late works.

Wyrsch, Peter. "Die Dürrenmatt-Story." *Schweizer Illustrierte,* March 18–April 22, 1963, no. 12, 23–26; no. 13, 23–25; no. 14, 23–25; no. 15, 23–25; no. 16, 37–39; no. 17, 37–39. Serialized article on Dürrenmatt in six installments. Source of many firsthand insights into the early years of the struggling writer.

Zimmermann, Werner. "Friedrich Dürrenmatt: Der Tunnel." In Werner Zimmermann, *Deutsche Prosadichtungen der Gegenwart.* 3:229–36. Düsseldorf: Pädagogischer Verlag Schwann, 1960.

Collections of Essays

Facetten: Studien zum 60. Geburtstag Friedrich Dürrenmatts, ed. Gerhard P. Knapp and Gerd Labroisse. Bern: Lang, 1981.

Friedrich Dürrenmatt: Studien zu seinem Werk, ed. Gerhard P. Knapp. Heidelberg: Lothar Stiehm, 1976.

Interpretationen zu Friedrich Dürrenmatt, ed. Armin Arnold. Stuttgart: Klett, 1982.

Play Dürrenmatt, ed. Moshe Lazar and Ron Gottesman. Malibu: Undena, 1983.

Der unbequeme Dürrenmatt, ed. Reinhold Grimm et al. Stuttgart: Basilius, 1962.

Index

215